British Expeditionary Force
The Final Advance

British Expeditionary Force
The Final Advance
September to November 1918

Andrew Rawson

Pen & Sword
MILITARY

AN IMPRINT OF PEN & SWORD BOOKS LTD.
YORKSHIRE – PHILADELPHIA

First published in Great Britain in 2018 by
Pen & Sword Military
An imprint of
Pen & Sword Books Ltd
Yorkshire – Philadelphia

ISBN 978 1 52672 344 4

A CIP catalogue record for this book is
available from the British Library.

Printed and bound in the UK by TJ International Ltd, Padstow, Cornwall.

Pen & Sword Books Limited incorporates the imprints of Atlas, Archaeology,
Aviation, Discovery, Family History, Fiction, History, Maritime, Military,
Military Classics, Politics, Select, Transport, True Crime, Air World,
Frontline Publishing, Leo Cooper, Remember When, Seaforth Publishing,
The Praetorian Press, Wharncliffe Local History, Wharncliffe Transport,
Wharncliffe True Crime and White Owl.

For a complete list of Pen & Sword titles please contact

PEN & SWORD BOOKS LIMITED
47 Church Street, Barnsley, South Yorkshire, S70 2AS, England
E-mail: enquiries@pen-and-sword.co.uk
Website: www.pen-and-sword.co.uk

Or
PEN AND SWORD BOOKS
1950 Lawrence Rd, Havertown, PA 19083, USA
E-mail: Uspen-and-sword@casematepublishers.com
Website: www.penandswordbooks.com

Contents

Regiments		vii
Introduction		xi
Chapter 1	Insufficient to Build an Enduring Defence	1
Chapter 2	Ceaseless, Wearing, Unspectacular Fighting	7
Chapter 3	On this Day We Buried all our Hopes for Victory	21
Chapter 4	The Most Desperately Fought Engagement of the War	31
Chapter 5	Fighting with Dash and Determination	45
Chapter 6	An Orgy of Fighting and Killing	57
Chapter 7	The Reception Accorded the Troops was Historic	73
Chapter 8	Reorganise, Push On and Get the Objective	83
Chapter 9	More Anxious to be Accepted as Prisoners than to Fight	97
Chapter 10	A Most Enthusiastic Reception	113
Chapter 11	What is the Good of Going On?	129
Chapter 12	A Magnificent Feat of Cool Resolution	147
Chapter 13	Practically a Route March	157
Chapter 14	Hammering the Hun had Broken Jerry's Heart	171
Chapter 15	Completely Used Up and Burnt to Cinders	191
Conclusions		199
Index		204

Regiments

Regiments in Alphabetical Order	Abbreviations Used
Argyll & Sutherland Highlanders Regiment	Argylls
Bedfordshire Regiment	Bedfords
Black Watch Regiment	Black Watch
Border Regiment	Borders
Buffs (East Kent) Regiment	Buffs
Cambridgeshire Regiment	Cambridgeshire
Cameron Highlanders Regiment	Camerons
Cameronians (Scottish Rifles) Regiment	Scottish Rifles
Cheshire Regiment	Cheshires
Coldstream Guards	Coldstreamers
Connaught Rangers	Connaughts
Devonshire Regiment	Devons
Dorsetshire Regiment	Dorsets
Duke of Cornwall's Light Infantry	DCLI
Duke of Wellington's (West Riding) Regiment	Duke's
Durham Light Infantry	Durhams
East Lancashire Regiment	East Lancashires
East Surrey Regiment	East Surreys
East Yorkshire Regiment	East Yorkshires
Essex Regiment	Essex
Gloucestershire Regiment	Gloucesters
Gordon Highlanders	Gordons
Green Howards (Yorkshire) Regiment	Green Howards
Grenadier Guards	Grenadiers
Hampshire Regiment	Hampshires
Herefordshire Regiment	Herefords
Hertfordshire Regiment	Hertfords
Highland Light Infantry	HLI
Honourable Artillery Company	HAC
Irish Guards	Irish Guards
King's (Liverpool) Regiment	King's

King's Own (Royal Lancaster) Regiment	King's Own
King's Own Scottish Borderers	KOSBs
King's Own (Yorkshire Light Infantry) Regiment	KOYLIs
King's (Shropshire Light Infantry) Regiment	Shropshires
King's Royal Rifle Corps	KRRC
Lancashire Fusiliers	Lancashire Fusiliers
Leicestershire Regiment	Leicesters
Leinster Regiment	Leinsters
Lincolnshire Regiment	Lincolns
London Regiment	Londoners
Loyal North Lancashire Regiment	Loyals
Manchester Regiment	Manchesters
Middlesex Regiment	Middlesex
Monmouthshire Regiment	Monmouths
Norfolk Regiment	Norfolks
Northamptonshire Regiment	Northants
North Staffordshire Regiment	North Staffords
Northumberland Fusiliers	Northumberland Fusiliers
Oxford and Buckinghamshire Light Infantry	Ox and Bucks
Princess Patricia's Canadian Light Infantry	PPCLI
Queen's (Royal West Surrey) Regiment	Queen's
Queen's Own (Royal West Kent) Regiment	Queen's Own
Rifle Brigade	Rifle Brigade
Royal Berkshire Regiment	Berkshires
Royal Dublin Fusiliers	Dublin Fusiliers
Royal Fusiliers	Royal Fusiliers
Royal Inniskilling Fusiliers	Inniskilling Fusiliers
Royal Irish Fusiliers	Irish Fusiliers
Royal Irish Regiment	Irish Regiment
Royal Irish Rifles	Irish Rifles
Royal Munster Fusiliers	Munsters
Royal Scots Regiment	Royal Scots
Royal Scots Fusiliers	Scots Fusiliers
Royal Sussex Regiment	Sussex
Royal Warwickshire Regiment	Warwicks
Royal Welsh Fusiliers	Welsh Fusiliers
Scots Guards	Scots Guards
Seaforth Highlanders	Seaforths

Sherwood Foresters (Notts and Derbyshire)	Sherwoods
Somerset Light Infantry	Somersets
South Lancashire Regiment	South Lancashires
South Staffordshire Regiment	South Staffords
South Wales Borderers	SWBs or Borderers
Suffolk Regiment	Suffolks
Welsh Guards	Welsh Guards
Welsh Regiment	Welsh
West Yorkshire Regiment	West Yorkshires
Wiltshire Regiment	Wiltshires
Worcestershire Regiment	Worcesters
York and Lancaster Regiment	York and Lancasters

Introduction

This is the final book in my ten-part series on the Western Front in the Great War. It covers the last ten weeks of the war, the final battles of the British Expeditionary Force's offensives in the autumn of 1918. It starts with the small engagements in front of the Hindenburg Line in September 1918 before moving on to three days of offensives along most of the line. Second, First, Third and Fourth Armies formed the northern wing of Maréchal Ferdinand Foch's offensive, attacking in turn between 27 and 29 September. The south wing of the attacks was made by the French and American divisions in the Argonne.

The narrative continues with the wave of attacks all along the BEF's line throughout October. Battles were fought across the River Lys, the l'Escaut Canal (Schelde Canal in Belgium), the Haute Deule Canal, the Selle stream and the Sambre Canal. Huge forests such as the Mormal, the Raismes and the Andigny had to be fought through, and the towns of Courtrai, Cambrai, Lille and Valenciennes had to be surrounded and cleared.

In between the accounts of bravery and battle there are heart-warming stories of liberation. Stories of civilians welcoming the columns of British and Empire troops with flowers, cheers and gifts. Of villagers emerging from their cellars after surviving the fight for their village, helping the advancing troops whenever they could.

The narrative of the fighting concludes with the final days of the war. It was a pursuit in bad weather along cratered roads and over broken bridges. It was a pursuit the BEF could not win because the Germans could stop and defend the best positions before retiring to fight another day.

The book concludes with a summary of the letters, meetings and intrigues which led up to the armistice. By 30 September, the German generals were aware the end was in sight, but what sort of end would it be?

The backbone of the story comes from the two relevant volumes of the Official History of the Great War. The first covers the fight for the old British trenches in front of the Hindenburg Line in the middle of September 1918. The second covers the late September offensive and the pursuit that followed. The publication of both volumes had been delayed to

1947 because of the paper shortage caused by the war. The Committee of Imperial Defence probably felt it had little to learn from the Great War after the huge advances in military tactics and hardware made by 1945.

Record-keeping during these battles was variable during this time. It was detailed during the static battles of September but tailed off during the pursuit of the final days of the war. It was as though keeping a record of the end of over four years fighting lost its significance. Brigadier General James Edmond and his assistant, Lieutenant Colonel Robin Maxwell-Hyslop, had little incentive to create a complete account. Their efforts have resulted in an unbalanced account which was detailed in places and superficial in others.

Fighting across the BEF's 150 mile front was a costly business in lives. Tried and tested tactics using tanks, artillery mortars and planes proved successful: huge numbers of men and material were captured; but there were large numbers of casualties. Accurate numbers are always difficult to pin down but the BEF suffered around 150,000 casualties between 18 September and 11 November. This was also the period when the influenza epidemic was sweeping Europe. Soldiers were particularly vulnerable because of a limited diet and extended periods exposed to cold, wet weather.

Much information was taken from the dozens of divisional and regimental histories published after the Great War. These books vary in quality. Some draw heavily from the unit war diaries, others give limited information,but all give more information than the Official History. Divisions and regiments like to explain their successes in detail while blaming others for their failures.

Many divisional and regimental histories can be studied for a small fee at the militaryarchive.co.uk. You can also view medal rolls and awards for a year for the same cost as a day in the London archives. Some information comes from the WO95 war diaries held by the National Archives at Kew. These are the primary sources for units' battle experiences but the information about the autumn battles are sometimes sketchy because of the fast moving nature of the fighting. The war diaries can be accessed through ancestry.co.uk and similar websites, again for a reasonable fee.

I have had to estimate what depth of detail to include, as with all the volumes in this series. It would be too superficial if there was too little detail but turgid if there was too much. This is not an exhaustive narrative of the BEF's attacks at the end of the war but it is a comprehensive account of the battles between mid-September and 11 November 1918.

The emphasis of the narrative is, as it has been with all the books in the series, on the experiences of the British and Empire soldiers. There is little information on the liaison between the War Cabinet, the Chief of the

Imperial General Staff, the BEF's General Headquarters and the French *Grand Quartier Général* (GQG). British planning and tactics are covered and the German reaction to them but the detail about German units rarely goes below army level.

Few details of casualties are discussed unless they were exceptionally high or unusual. Casualties ranged from light to very high in these fast moving battles. Both sides suffered and thousands of prisoners were taken. This is a time when the men were advancing several miles in a day – a complete contrast to the advances earlier in the war.

The day by day attacks by each corps and division are discussed, along with the reasoning behind the accomplishments and difficulties. Often the men who led the attacks or who stopped the counter-attacks are mentioned; so are all the men who were awarded the Victoria Cross. I have chosen quotes which reflect the men's pride in their fighting abilities and what they thought of their experiences during the final days of the war.

The well-used saying is 'a picture is worth a thousand words' and I believe the same applies to battle maps. Most books on the Great War use too few maps of too small a scale and they do little to complement the narrative. The Official Histories suffer from this problem as paper shortages reduced the maps to small inserts at the back of the books. So sixty tactical maps are included in this book to help the reader understand the campaign. Typically there is one for each corps covering each stage of the battle and 1:40,000 maps (the sort used by the artillery) have been used because the advances made in the summer of 1918 were so long. Plenty of detailed maps has been a feature of all the books in this series.

My inspiration for this ten-part series was *A Testing of Courage*, a book on the 1863 battle of Gettysburg during the American Civil War. I had consulted several books on the subject but they had left me confused. The many maps in Noah Trudeau's book prepared me for a visit to the battlefield. It has been my ambition to do the same for the Western Front and I have created over 600 maps for the series.

The symbols indicating movements are the same on all the maps. The start lines at the beginning of a phase are marked by a solid line, while the limit of the advance is marked by a line of dots. Rivers are marked by dashed lines and army and corps boundaries are marked by a line of dashes and dots. Each corps and division is marked with its number but it was impossible to chart the brigades and battalions because they changed places so quickly. It is easy enough to estimate their movements by checking the text and the maps. Events are described from left to right or from north to south unless the sequence of events dictates it is best to describe them in a different order.

I have enjoyed learning about the final battle of the Great War because there is always something new to learn about the Western Front. This book brings to an end an intense period of study covering four years and I now have a much better understanding of the experiences the soldiers of the British Empire went through between 1914 and 1918. Hopefully you will get the same from my books and they will inspire you to go on to do your own research.

I stayed at Hotel Regina on the Groote Markt in Ypres while I was looking at the Flanders battlefields. My 'oasis' while on the Somme was No 56 Bed and Breakfast in La Boisselle. David and Julie Thomson have looked after me many times during my research trips and they even drove me around the Hindenburg Line area.

My twenty-year interest in the Great War mirrors my friendship with Professor John Bourne, who has guided me through my long research and writing career. Again he has given me useful advice when I have asked for it and his wide-ranging knowledge of the BEF generals is always useful. But even after prolonged study, I still feel as if I have just scratched the surface of what happened on the Western Front between August 1914 and November 1918.

Andrew Rawson 2018

Chapter 1

Insufficient to Build an Enduring Defence

After four months of fighting off German attacks, it was the turn of the Allies to make their counter-stroke. The final German attack, Operation Peace Storm (*Friedensturm*), had started on 15 July against the French along the Chemin des Dames, driving them across the River Aisne and then back some 30 miles to the River Marne. But Généralissime Foch had held his nerve and he encouraged General Philippe Pétain to prepare a counter-offensive with the French, Italian and British troops assembling in the area.

The attack opened on 18 July, striking the flanks of the huge German salient, and it was only a matter of days before they were falling back to the Aisne. The attack ended at the beginning of August because a new combined offensive was being planned. On 8 August, masses of tanks joined the Fourth British Army and the First French Army as they advanced side by side across the Santerre plateau, south of the River Somme. They broke through the German defences across a 30-mile-wide front, advancing up to 8 miles in places on what would be described by General Erich Ludendorff as the 'black day of the German Army'.

Reinforcements were rushed to the area to contain the breakthrough and the Allied attack was called off after a few days so another could be launched further to the north. The next attack was made by Third Army on 21 August between Arras and Albert, where again the British troops advanced considerable distances. It was followed up by a renewal of operations astride the Somme which allowed Fourth Army to cross the 1916 battlefield in a matter of days.

The BEF's attack widened with fresh assaults east of Arras, which pushed the Germans all the way back to the Drocourt–Quéant Line and the River Somme. Both obstacles had been broken or bypassed by early September, sparking a German withdrawal to the old British trenches in front of the Hindenburg Line. There General Max von Boehn was hoping to stall the British so that his men could upgrade the neglected defensive positions.

There had been several developments on other parts of the line. The First French Army had advanced alongside Fourth Army as far as the Hindenburg

Line in front of St Quentin. The Third and Tenth French Armies had also pushed the Germans back from the Soissons salient and the shortening of the line had allowed General Pétain to pull Third Army into reserve. Even the Americans had had success, when their attack on 12 September had sparked a withdrawal from the St Mihiel salient, south-east of Verdun.

As the summer campaign progressed, thoughts for a combined autumn offensive had begun on 30 August, when Field Marshal Sir Haig suggested launching a three-pronged offensive to General John Pershing, the commander of the American Expeditionary Force (AEF). The northern attack would be aimed towards Cambrai and St Quentin, and it would be made by the British Expeditionary Force and the left wing of the French armies. The south attack would be made astride the River Meuse, with the right of the French armies and the AEF heading towards Mezières. The French centre would follow up by moving north between the two wings.

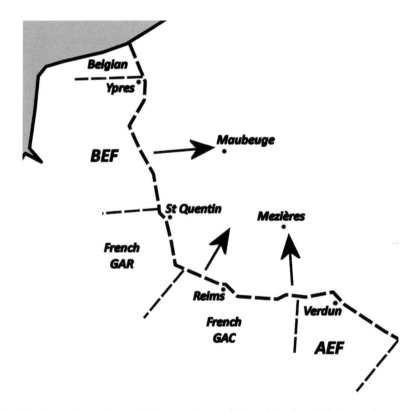

The Western Front in mid-September 1918, with the Allied armies poised to attack all along the line.

Three days later, Foch asked Haig and the Belgian army for their attack plans. Haig was able to report that the Germans were already retiring from the Lys salient and he expected them to go back further to release reserves to send south. On 4 September, Foch issued instructions to start planning for a new wave of attacks all along the front, starting on 20 September. Five days later he explained how he intended to confuse the German high command by hitting their line at different points over a series of days.

The first attack was to be made by French and American divisions on 26 September between Reims and the River Meuse. General John Pershing's First American Army would breach the Hindenburg Line between the Argonne Forest and Verdun. It would advance towards the Buzancy Line, outflanking the German line opposite Fourth French Army. General Henri Gouraud's troops would then widen the attack front to 65 miles as the French and Americans pushed north beyond the Rethel–Vouziers Line in the direction of Charleville-Mezières.

The second phase would be made by the centre of the BEF on 27 September. General Henry Horne's First Army and General Julian Byng's Third Army would advance side-by-side through the Hindenburg Line and push either side of Cambrai. They would then head east towards Maubeuge, forming the northern jaw of the pincer move against the flanks of the Soissons salient.

The third phase, on 28 September, would involve the Flanders Group of Armies, a combined command of Belgian, French and British troops gathered under the king of the Belgians. The attack would cover a 25-mile-wide sector, including General Herbert Plumer's Second Army which would cross the Ypres salient to cover the BEF's left flank.

The final strike would be made by General Henry Rawlinson's Fourth British Army and General Marie-Eugène Debeney's First French Army on 29 September. They would attack the Hindenburg Line either side of St Quentin and then push north-east, supporting the right flank of the BEF's attack. This in turn would increase the pressure on the Soissons salient, so General Charles Mangin's Tenth French Army and General Berthelot's Fifth Army could join the advance.

Maréchal Foch wrote to Field Marshal Haig, General Pétain, General Pershing and General Jean Degoutte (the French chief of staff of the Flanders army group) on 27 September. Between them they had sixty-five divisions in reserve, ready to make a second wave of attacks or pursue the enemy. He believed that four attacks at different points on four consecutive days would confuse the German high command, so they would be unable to deploy their reserves effectively.

Foch thought the German soldier had lost confidence in his generals, after the failure to break the Allied line during the spring offensives followed by the repeated defeats during the summer. He went so far as to say they were 'insufficient to build an enduring defence'. Meanwhile, he thought the Allied troops were full of confidence after the summer successes and he advised his generals to be ready to take up the pursuit if the German line collapsed. Everything was in the Allies' favour but, as far as he was concerned, command and leadership were as important for winning a battle as were tactics and weapons.

> The battle now depends on the determination of corps commanders and on the initiative and energy of divisional commanders. Once more, I repeat, the last say in battle comes not from the endurance of the troops alone, who never fail if appeal is made to them, but also from the impulse of the commanders.

The Meuse-Argonne Attack, 26 September

The artillery (most batteries were manned by French gunners) starting shelling positions along a 45-mile front across the Argonne at 11 pm on 25 September. General Henri Gouraud had assembled twenty-two infantry divisions and a cavalry corps in his Fourth French Army while General John Pershing had fifteen infantry divisions (which were double the size of a French or British division) and a cavalry division in the First US Army.

Both the Crown Prince and General Max von Gallwitz knew the attack was coming but there was little they could do about it. The French infantry went over the top at 5.25 am accompanied by 297 light and 29 heavy tanks. Five minutes later the Americans advanced in the Argonne Forest, assisted by 189 light French tanks.

Most of the objectives were taken on the first day, as the French and Americans fought their way through the German outpost line. However, the advance then slowed, particularly in the American sector where they were fighting through wooded terrain. Pershing had no option but to keep pushing on with his inexperienced troops, even fighting off counterattacks made by German reinforcements. The Americans 'were necessarily committed, generally speaking, to a direct frontal attack against strong, hostile positions fully manned by a determined enemy'. Even so, they had advanced 6 miles, taking many prisoners and heavy guns, by the time a pause was ordered on 3 October.

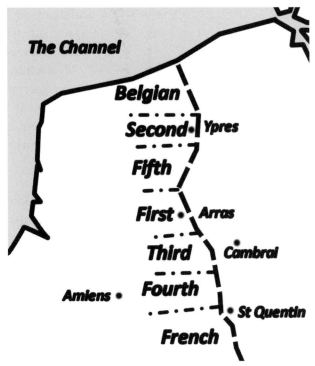

The line-up of the BEF's armies in mid–September 1918. The plan was to attack in the centre, then in the north and finally in the south, to spread the German reinforcements.

Chapter 2

Ceaseless, Wearing, Unspectacular Fighting

Third Army and Fourth Army

12 to 26 September

Third Army, 12 to 26 September

VI Corps

Guards Division, 12 September

Major General Torquhil Matheson had taken over because Major General Feilding had just returned to England. His men were busy establishing posts across the Canal du Nord. They found that the best place to cross was at Moeuvres.

52nd Division, 17 to 21 September, Moeuvres

Captain Harvie of the 1/4th KOSBs was wounded driving the Germans back from Moeuvres on 17 September but some of the 1/5th HLI were cut off. Corporal David Hunter refused to surrender and his group held out for 48 hours. He would be awarded the Victoria Cross. The 1/4th Royal Scots held onto Moeuvres during an attack on 21 September but the 1/7th Royal Scots suffered the 'worst ordeal that they ever endured' as their front line companies were overrun. Captain Robertson was wounded rallying the survivors but Captain Ballantyne helped them retake the lost trenches.

3rd Division, 18 September, Havrincourt

A counter-attack on 18 September threatened to drive the 2nd Royal Scots back in what was 'no kid glove affair'. Lieutenant Colonel Henderson sent forward reinforcements to make sure the Spoil Bank, next to the Canal du Nord, was secure.

IV Corps

62nd Division, 12 September, Havrincourt Wood

Major General Robert Whigham's division had breached the Hindenburg Line before, during the battle of Cambrai, and 'the success of the previous year was debated with fresh interest.' But there were no tanks this time and careful timing was needed to get everyone between the Canal du Nord and Havrincourt chateau moat.

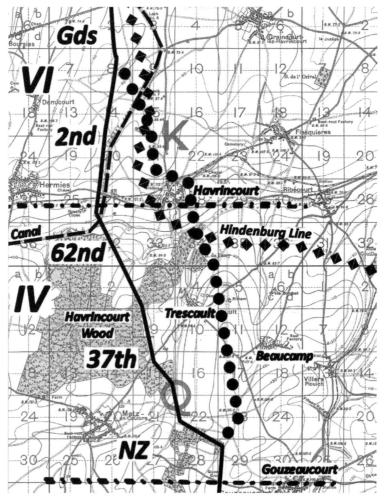

Third Army gained a foothold in the Hindenburg Line around Havrincourt on 12 September.

Sergeant Laurence Calvert silenced two machine-gun crews as Lieutenant Colonel Peter's 5th KOYLIs advanced south-west of Havrincourt and eighty men surrendered. He was awarded the Victoria Cross. Captain Crow secured the final objective while the 2/4th York and Lancasters moved up. Lieutenant Colonel Walker's 5th Duke's skirted the chateau moat, crossed the Hindenburg front line and then cleared up Havrincourt, while Lieutenant Colonel Wilson's 2/4th Duke's took 170 prisoners amongst the tree stumps that had been Havrincourt Wood. The 2/4th Hampshires then later cleared the chateau but Lieutenant Colonel Crouch's 9th Durhams (Pioneers) could only advance a short distance beyond the Hindenburg front line.

37th Division, 12 to 18 September, Trescault

The 13th KRRC and the 13th Rifle Brigade cleared Trescault on 12 September and then the 10th Royal Fusiliers were engaged in 'the most protracted bitter and evenly contested actions of this phase' two days later. Second Lieutenant Frank Young silenced a machine gun so the 1/1st Hertfords could escape from Triangle Wood late on 18 September and he 'was last seen fighting hand to hand against a considerable number of the enemy'. He was posthumously awarded the Victoria Cross.

New Zealand Division, 12 September, Gouzeaucourt Wood

Major General Andrew Russell's men advanced into Havrincourt Wood and Gouzeaucourt Wood. Lance Corporal Turner silenced two machine guns so the 4th Rifle Brigade could advance onto the Trescault Spur, alongside 1st Rifle Brigade. The 2nd Rifle Brigade 'got close down to the barrage in splendid style' and entered African Trench. One patrol was cut off after capturing a battery but Sergeant Harry Laurent made sure over one hundred prisoners were escorted back. He was awarded the Victoria Cross.

V Corps

5th Division, 18 September, Gouzeaucourt

The 2nd KOSBs' left reached African Trench in front of Gouzeaucourt but the right was pinned down, so Lieutenant Colonel Furber had to withdraw his men.

38th Division, 18 September, Gouzeaucourt

The 16th Welsh Fusiliers and 14th Welsh Fusiliers reached the outskirts of Gouzeaucourt but the 16th Welsh Fusiliers had to fall back due to enfilade fire until the 13th Welsh Fusiliers covered their left flank. The 13th Welsh came under enfilade fire but Second Lieutenant William White, of the 38th Battalion, Machine Gun Corps, silenced the enemy machine guns. He would be awarded the Victoria Cross. The 14th and 15th Welsh took the rest of the objective in front of Gouzeaucourt.

17th Division, 18 to 20 September, Gouzeaucourt and Gauche Wood

The 10th Lancashire Fusiliers, 12th Manchester and 9th Duke of Wellington's came under fire as they crossed Chapel Hill at 5.20 am in what was the 'the stiffest task of the day'. Contact planes warned the 7th East Yorkshires about enemy movements while the 10th West Yorkshires and 6th Dorsets moved closer to Gouzeaucourt. The 7th Lincolns took some 200 prisoners around

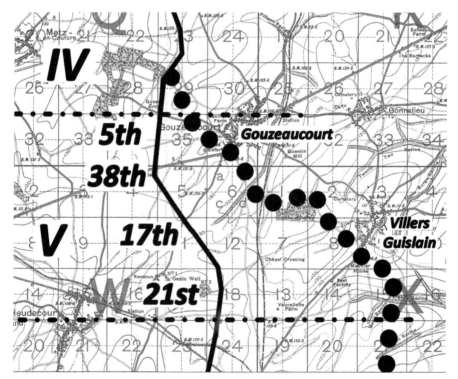

Third Army advanced towards Gouzeaucourt and Villers Guislain to cover Fourth Army's flank as it pushed through the old British trenches.

Gauche Wood while the trench mortars silenced 'an armoured machine-gun nest' made out of four derelict British tanks. The 7th Border Regiment and the 10th Sherwoods were then able to enter Gauche Wood. The 6th Dorsets and 10th West Yorkshires took Quentin Redoubt during the night but Lancashire Trench held out. Brigadier Sanders was killed by machine-gun fire while inspecting the captured position on 20 September.

21st Division, 18 September, South of Villers Guislain

The 'appalling weather' meant that the 1st Lincolns, 12/13th Northumberland Fusiliers and 2nd Lincolns were only just ready in time but 'they fell upon the enemy with great determination' around Chapel Hill. The 1st East Yorkshires, 9th KOYLIs and 1st Wiltshires increased the prisoner tally to 700 as they advanced to the next objective but the 6th Leicesters came under enfilade fire because 58th Division could not take Peizières. A counter-attack then drove the Wiltshires back, so the rest of the advance was postponed.

33rd Division, 21 to 24 September, South of Villers Guislain

Lieutenant Colonel Campbell's 2nd Argylls attacked Meath Post, while Lieutenant Colonel Norris's 4th King's advanced astride Gloucester Road early on 21 September. The 5/6th Scottish Rifles and 1st Scottish Rifles advanced along Targelle Ravine but it was soon 'choked with dead, mercilessly mown down by machine-gun fire or picked off, man by man, by snipers.' Major Scott recaptured the gully during the night and Captain Clark's company of the 5/6th Scottish Rifles held onto it until the 9th HLI arrived.

Lieutenant Colonel Campbell had to withdraw the 2nd Argylls the following day after the 1st Queen's and the 1st Scottish Rifles became pinned down in Targelle Ravine. Lieutenant Colonel Spen's 5th Scottish Rifles captured Meath Post later on while the 2nd Worcesters discovered that Limerick Post had been evacuated. Lieutenant Colonel Stoney then advanced down Pigeon Ravine early on 23 September.

Fourth Army, 12 to 26 September

Fourth Army faced the three old British trenches which had once faced the Hindenburg Line. Patrols reported that the long grass which had grown over the summer was hiding many dangers. The Germans were also sure something was afoot and their artillery soaked the assembly areas with mustard gas the night before the attack. Rawlinson planned a pre-dawn attack on 12 September and there would be no preliminary bombardment to alert the Germans between Hesbécourt and Holnon. At 5.20 am, nearly 1,500 artillery pieces opened fire along Fourth Army's front while sixteen tanks approached the old British reserve line in thick mist.

III Corps

General Georg von der Marwitz was worried III Corps would cross the St Quentin tunnel between Vendhuille and Bellicourt so extra steps had been taken to fortify the nearby villages. It would lead to 'ceaseless, wearing, unspectacular fighting'.

58th Division, 18 to 22 Septemberv, Peizières towards Vendhuille

One tank helped the 2/2nd London through Peizières while a second tank turned south, joining 12th Division's battle around Épehy. The 3rd London and 2/24th London took a long time to mop it up and the first Major General Frank Ramsey knew of the success was when the German guns started firing at Peizières. The new attack on 19 September failed, so Brigadier General Corkran organised bombers to clear the area east of Peizières. Both the 2/10th and 12th London were pinned on 22 September but Captain Scrimgeour led the 1/4th Suffolks (Pioneers) along a sunken road to outflank an enemy position. The 9th London Regiment took the rest of the trenches between Limerick Post and Catelet Copse.

12th Division, 18 to 24 September, Épehy

The 35 Brigade would make the southern pincer attack on Épehy while 36 Brigade cleared the ridge south-east of the village. Two tanks were knocked out as the 7th Norfolk and 9th Essex entered Épehy from the south-west. A third tank which had strayed from 58th Division's area then opened fire on them, so they could not take Fisher's Keep. Lieutenant Colonel Clayton's 1/1st Cambridge Regiment eventually cleared the strongpoint, so the Norfolks and Essex could advance to Prince Reserve trench. The 9th Royal Fusiliers could not capture Malassise Farm but the 7th Sussex reached the old reserve trench. The Germans eventually withdrew from Épehy, so the 5th Berkshires and 5th Northants (Pioneers) could clear the area between Tétard Wood and Chestnut Avenue.

The following morning, the 5th Northants and 1st Cambridge Regiment were struggling east of Épehy until Major Stamper brought his battery forward. Meanwhile the 6th Buffs cleared Old Wood while the 6th Queen's cleared Malassise Farm. The 6th Queen's and 6th Queen's Own made little progress on 20 September and neither did the 7th Sussex and 9th Royal Fusiliers the following morning. The 5th Berkshires would take Little Priel Farm, 'a post bristling with machine guns', later that night. The Germans recaptured the Dados Loop from the Royal Fusiliers on 24 September while the Berkshires could not make any progress along Dados Loop on the 26th.

18th Division, Ronssoy and Lempire, 18 to 21 September

Major General Richard Lee wanted to avoid crossing the low ground either side of Ronssoy and Lempire, so the engineers 'made most beautiful and realistic dummy tanks'. Unfortunately, the mist was so thick that the Germans could not see them but they did serve as 'most excellent accommodation for a divisional conference held in stormy weather' the following day.

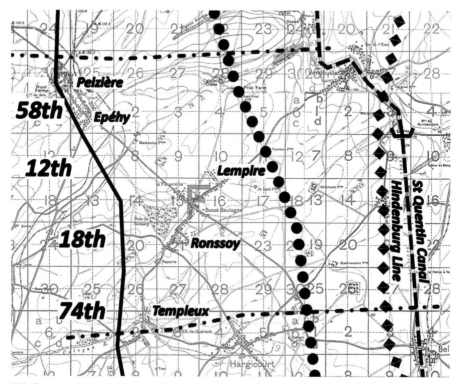

III Corps cleared the old British trenches in front of the Hindenburg Line, so Fourth Army's left was close to the St Quentin Canal.

At 5.20 am four 'real' tanks led Lieutenant Colonel Hickson's 7th Queen's Own through the two villages. Major Keep's 2nd Bedfords reinforced them when they lost the barrage while the 24th Welsh mopped up behind. Troops could cross the low ground once the ridge had been cleared and two tanks helped the 6th Northants clear the Ronssoy Wood area. Lance Corporal Allan Lewis silenced the machine-gun teams enfilading the advance but would be killed on 21 September. He was awarded the Victoria Cross posthumously. A third tank accompanied the 11th Royal Fusiliers as they crossed the Basse Boulogne valley, east of the villages.

The 8th East Surreys got drawn into the fight for Lempire and it was midday by the time they were east of the villages. Everyone then had to take cover in sunken roads and trenches until dusk before another bombardment could be arranged. The East Surreys then advanced a short distance but the 6th Northants could not take Tetard Wood. Brigadier General Wood felt it was wise to withdraw his men to the first objective when it was dark. The brigadier had captured thirty armed men single-handed armed only with a cigar and a walking stick. Most had been cowed into submission by a shower of old boots and lumps of chalk into their dugout.

The 7th Queen's and 7th Buffs continued 'nibbling', capturing X, Y and Z Copses in front of the Hindenburg Outpost Line. Major General Richard Lee's next objective was the Knoll because it 'commanded the village and canal crossing of Vendhuille, and gave a great view of the whole Hindenburg Line'.

The 10th Essex advanced to Le Tombois Farm early on 21 September but Lieutenant Colonel Frizell had to withdraw his men after five tanks had been knocked out. The 7th Queen's Own then retired from Le Sart Farm. Four tanks had supported the 6th Northants and the 2nd Bedfords but they were unable to hold on to the ground around Gillemont Farm. Three tanks (two of them supply tanks) reached Guillemont Farm on the right flank but the infantry had been driven back by 'the hottest machine-gun fire' of the war.

The following afternoon, Major Keep organised a counter-attack against Duncan Post with the 2nd Bedfords, and Lieutenants Oldfield and Pennington killed or captured 400 Germans trapped between them and the 6th Northants. The rest were hit as they fell back to Doleful Post and 'the enthusiastic excitement of the troops who took part in the literal annihilation of the enemy was unprecedented.' Major General Lee could ask for no more from his men because 'their endurance had been pushed to its utmost limit. Never were the infantry more exhausted but they stuck it out.'

74th Division, 18 to 21 September, Templeux-le-Guérard

Major General Eric Girdwood's engineers used decoy tanks of painted canvas covering wood frames to unsettle the Germans. The 24th Welsh then cleared Ronssoy while the 25th Welsh Fusiliers and the 16th Devons 'took their objective with the greatest dash'. Lance Sergeant William Waring was mortally wounded clearing a strongpoint in front of the Welsh Fusiliers; he was posthumously awarded the Victoria Cross. The 10th Shropshires joined the advance but they could not go any further because 18th Division was pinned down around Lempire on their left.

The 16th Sussex advanced towards the north half of Templeux-le-Guérard while Lieutenant Colonel Tuck's 15th Suffolks moved through the Australian area, south of the Cologne stream, taking many prisoners in the quarries beyond. The 10th Buffs and 12th Somersets then headed towards Malakoff Farm until they were stopped by their supporting barrage.

Major General Girdwood had to get his left flank in line with his right, so a second attack was arranged for 21 September. All four tanks were disabled but the 25th Welsh Fusiliers still took 150 prisoners around the Quadrilateral. Unfortunately 18th Division had not advanced to the left while the 16th Sussex and 10th Buffs were nowhere to be seen on the right. The 24th Welsh had also lost their way, allowing the Germans to infiltrate the Welsh Fusiliers' position and less than 200 escaped. Lieutenant Colonel Howell-Evan's 10th Shropshires took 200 prisoners around the Quadrilateral the following morning.

Australian Corps

The Australians were given just eight tanks for 18 September but they also deployed dummy ones 'with wooden frames covered by painted hessian. These would be taken before zero hour to high ground near the start line and would be moved a little distance by pioneers with long drag ropes to points where the Germans would see them after dawn.' Lieutenant General Sir John Monash had assembled around 200 machine guns to create an 'especially dense' barrage but Lieutenant Colonel Marsden was captured while studying 5th Machine Gun Battalion's targets. It left everyone wondering if the Germans would be waiting for them.

Just before the attack, Monash was given an order which would affect the future of his command. He had to immediately send 800 married men who had been in service since 1914 to Marseille. There was no time to acquire 'fresh clothing from England; they must sail in what clothes they had and would be re-clothed in Egypt.' A second ship would be waiting for another batch of men straight after the attack. It left the attacking battalions weak for the tough task ahead and it was also the beginning of the end of the Australian Corps' contribution to the Advance to Victory.

1st Australian Division, 12 to 18 September, Hargicourt and Villeret

Early on 11 September, 4th Battalion captured and then lost Hill 140 when the mist lifted. The 2nd Battalion occupied an abandoned Jeancourt at the same time. There was a thick fog again on 18 September and 'apart from sounds, flashes were at first the only sign each side saw of the other.'

On the left, 4th Battalion again crossed Hill 140 and was joined by 2nd Battalion en route to Hargicourt. The 11th and 12th Battalions advanced through Grand Priel Wood, rounding up one hundred prisoners. Near Malakoff Farm 3rd Battalion encountered a 'trench full of Germans' but by 'putting a bold face on their surprise they hurled in their bombs and the whole trench-full surrendered'. Two tanks helped them reach Cologne Farm and Villeret.

Both 11th and 12th Battalions lost their barrage but they still cleared Grand Priel Wood with the help of Stokes mortars and Lewis guns. A tank then 'swept over the ground ahead, silencing machine-guns, rolling down the wire and spreading terror among the Germans within sight'. The 10th Battalion rounded up a hundred prisoners in the Hindenburg trenches, leaving Cologne Farm ridge in Australian hands. It meant they could see the St Quentin Canal up ahead when the mist lifted.

4th Australian Division, 12 to 18 September, Le Verguier

On 12 September, the 50th and 51st Battalions met strong resistance in the old British main line. Then on 18 September the 15th and 13th Battalions bypassed Le Verguier: 'fighting like veterans, they simply walked around these places; it was their last fight, and their best.' Sergeant Gerald Sexton rounded up thirty prisoners, including a battalion staff, as he stood 'full height to spray them with bursts from his Lewis gun.' (Sexton's real name was Maurice Buckley; he had been sent back from Egypt suffering from venereal disease in 1915. He deserted from his hospital and re-enlisted under the false name before heading for France.) Buckley or Sexton was awarded the Victoria Cross.

Then 16th Battalion mopped up the ruins of Le Verguier, bringing the total of prisoners to 450. Captain Lynas said, 'if the German had had the fighting spirit of a louse, one battalion on the whole brigade front would

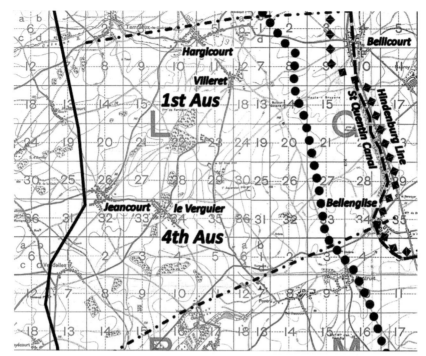

The Australian Corps fought its way through the British trench systems between 12 and 26 September to get in sight of the Hindenburg Line between Bellicourt and Bellenglise.

have made it impossible to go forward; but he never fought an inch, so far as we were concerned.' Private James Woods helped clear and then hold the area south of Le Verguier; he was awarded the Victoria Cross.

Lieutenant Colonel Loutit was hit leading 45th Battalion when the mist lifted, but 46th Battalion cleared the old Outpost Line. The Australian Corps had seized a commanding position, taking nearly 4,250 prisoners, over 300 machine guns, 30 trench mortars and 76 artillery pieces. Its own casualties had been 1,250. Up ahead they could see the 'dense wire belts and white parapets of the Hindenburg Outpost Line'; they could also see the St Quentin canal.

IX Corps

1st Division, 13 to 16 September, Maissemy to Pontruet

On 13 September, the 1st SWBs and 2nd Welsh advanced between Omignon stream and Holnon Wood. Five days later, 2 Brigade moved through

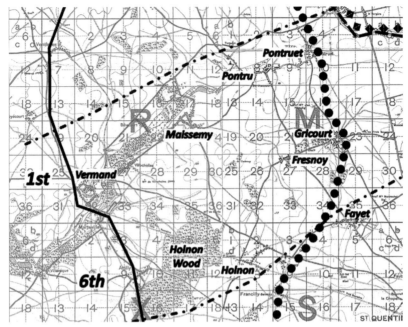

IX Corps pushed through the old British trenches around Pontruet and Gricourt between 12 and 26 September but had trouble around Holnon because the French were held up on Fourth Army's flank.

Vadencourt before zero hour 'in rain and mist so thick that no landmarks could be seen' by accident. The artillery had to wait until the assault troops had been moved back but some short shots still hit Brigadier General Kelly's men. The 2nd Sussex advanced north of Berthaucourt while the 2nd KRRC cleared the village, but were counter-attacked from Pontruet. Meanwhile the 1st Camerons were pinned down south of Berthaucourt, so the 2nd Black Watch had to form a defensive flank. The 1st Loyals soon learnt that 6th Division had been unable to take Fresnoy and Captain Leake was killed organising their exposed flank.

Four tanks helped the 2nd Sussex, 1st Northants and 2nd KRRC clear Pontruet the following morning. One tank was knocked out in Fresnoy-le-Petit but two others helped the 1st Gloucesters and 2nd Welsh establish a line north of Gricourt.

6th Division, 15 to 18 September, Holnon

The 11th Essex advanced towards Badger Copse early on 17 September to secure a jumping off line. The 1st West Yorkshires also took its objective but had to withdraw because the French had been unable to advance on its right. The assault troops were then late because they had to march around a gas-soaked Holnon Wood. Four tanks were disabled as the 2nd York and Lancasters, 1st Shropshires and 1st Buffs 'became hopelessly mixed' in front of Fresnoy-le-Petit the following morning. Some of the 9th Norfolks got lost while the rest were late and became scattered in front of the Quadrilateral. It meant that the 1st Leicesters had to form a defensive flank. The 2nd Sherwoods were unable to enter the Quadrilateral but the 2nd Durhams and 1st West Yorkshires cleared Holnon. Again they had to withdraw because the French had been unable to capture Round Hill on their right flank. The Durhams received reinforcements at dusk,and by midnight the battalion had suffered more casualties than it had started the day with.

There was 'great difficulty circulating the necessary operation orders on time' for an attack on 19 September. Four tanks were hit and both the 1st Shropshires and 2nd York and Lancasters were pinned in front of the Quadrilateral. Later on, the 2nd York and Lancasters cleared Gricourt on the left flank, but some of the Shropshires were cut off in Fresnoy-le-Petit until dusk. Another four tanks were hit by the anti-tank weapons in the Quadrilateral and both the 2nd Durhams and 1st West Yorkshires had to fall back.

IX Corps had taken over 1,400 prisoners in just two days but its two divisions were exhausted. Late on 26 September, 1st Division pushed through Pontruet while 6th Division moved past Fayet. It meant they could both see the Hindenburg Line defences around the St Quentin canal.

46th Division, 24 September, Pontruet

Major General Gerald Boyd's men relieved the 4th Australian Division extending IX Corps' flank north towards Bellicourt early on 22 September. Two days later the 5th Lincolns and 6th Sherwoods struggled to advance north of Pontruet while the 5th Leicesters came to grief around a new trench the Germans had dug during the night south of the village. But the later attack by the 5th Sherwoods took one hundred prisoners in the village. Twenty-one-year-old Lieutenant John Barrett had been wounded twice, silencing two machine-gun posts around Forgan's Trench. He was hit a third time as he organised the 1/5th Leicesters' withdrawal after the mist cleared. Barrett was awarded the Victoria Cross. A night attack by the 6th Sherwoods and 5th Leicesters failed to enter Pontruet only for the Germans to abandon it a few hours later.

Chapter 3

On this Day We Buried all our Hopes for Victory

First Army

27 September to 7 October

Lieutenant General Sir Arthur Currie's men had had over two weeks to 'reorganize, refit and rest' after breaking through the Drocourt–Quéant Line but the Germans had used the time to dig in behind the Canal du Nord. Work on the canal had stopped when war broke out and the length of the half-dug channel was filled with water and thick mud. Patrols reported it was 'practically impassable by any force larger than a platoon'. Aerial observers reported that the new German trenches were still shallow, so Currie decided to forego a preliminary bombardment and told his artillery to focus on wire cutting instead.

Byng set the date of the attack for 27 September and his plan was for the 1st and 4th Canadian Divisions to cross the dry section of the canal around Sains-lez-Marquion and then spread out. The 11th (British) Division could then cross at Marquion and push north-west, while the 3rd Canadian Division crossed at Inchy and headed south-east. It was a tall order and General Byng asked: 'Old man, do you think you can do it?' Currie's reply is not recorded. At the same time both VIII Corps and XXII Corps would probe the line either side of Lens to draw attention away from the Canadian attack.

The RAF's I Brigade deployed twelve squadrons to cooperate with the Canadian Corps. The 236 aircraft worked hard to drive the German planes from the skies but enemy observers could not fail to spot the many columns which had to move up in daylight. One report said it was 'as populous as Coney Island on 4 July (referring to the famous American beach on Independence Day).

VIII Corps, 27 September to 7 October

58th Division, 27 September, Lens

Major General Frank Ramsay had adopted 'a role of peaceful penetration, occupying ground relinquished by the retreating enemy, as and when the opportunity occurred, but avoiding, unless absolutely necessary, a pitched battle'. The 7th and 8th London Regiments moved through an abandoned Cité St Auguste while the 2/2nd and 2/4th London Regiment moved past the north side outskirts of Lens. Brigadier General Cobham's men did not enter Lens because of a gas barrage and 175 Brigade was squeezed into reserve.

20th Division, 27 September to 3 October, Méricourt, Acheville and Fresnoy

Captain Waters led 7th DCLI's attack on the trenches covering Fresnoy early on 27 September, as a diversion to the Canadian Corps. Fires and explosions were seen behind the German line on 2 October and both the 11th KRRC and the 2nd Scottish Rifles reached the Méricourt–Lens railway the following morning. The 6th Shropshires and the 12th KRRC approached Acheville while the 12th King's and the 7th DCLI closed in on Fresnoy.

Captain Campbell's company of the Scottish Rifles failed to capture Méricourt on 4 October and a second attempt on the 6th nearly ended in disaster when Second Lieutenant Jack's patrol was cut off. Five messengers had been hit by the time Private James Towers volunteered to contact them; he made it and would be awarded the Victoria Cross.

8th Division, 21 September to 7 October, Rouvroy–Fresnes Line

Major General William Heneker had started early, organising an attack against the Rouvroy–Fresnes Line for 11 pm on 21 September. The 1st Worcesters, 2nd East Lancashires and the 2nd Berkshires advanced nearly half a mile but a dawn counter-attack drove the Berkshires back. They retook the area early on 23 September after four fake barrages confused the Germans so much they stayed in their dugouts. Early on 27 September the 2nd Northants, 2nd Middlesex and 2nd Devons advanced another half mile towards the Rouvroy–Fresnes Line. A Chinese attack was then made at 5.30 am, again to draw attention from the Canadian Corps' attack.

The trenches north of Oppy were taken on 4 October and then the 1st Sherwoods surrounded the village on 6 October. Early the following morning Lieutenant Colonel Robert's 1st Worcesters bombed along the trenches around Neuvireuil while the 2nd Berkshire, 2nd Rifle Brigade and 2nd West Yorkshires cleared the Rouvroy–Fresnes Line where 'the prisoners all appeared very pleased to be captured'. The gunners fired 'a criss-cross pattern, consisting of two independent but coordinated barrages' as Major Baker's 2nd Middlesex entered Biache St Vaast. That evening they reached the Vitry-en-Artois marshes, next to the River Scarpe.

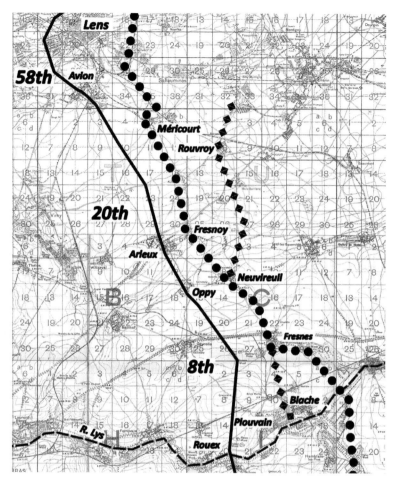

VIII Corps' right penetrated the Rouvroy–Fresnes Line on 7 October as the Germans fell back.

XXII Corps

51st Division, 27 September

The Scots launched a Chinese attack fifteen minutes after the Canadians advanced but some believed it was too dark to see the canvas figures mounted on wooden frames.

Canadian Corps

The Canadians made the final march under heavy rain ready to advance at 5.20 am on 27 September. The small attack front meant the gunners had to be ready to move forward as soon as the engineers had bridged the canal. As the minutes ticked by, there was 'apprehension that a counter preparation by the German artillery might come down on their dangerously dense numbers... Rain began to fall and the cold ground became slippery, adding to the difficulties... Then at 5:20 am came a myriad of flashes from the guns in the artillery areas followed by the crash of bursting shells over the enemy positions.'

Twenty-four Mark IV tanks accompanied two waves of skirmishers but the crews had instructions to return from the third objective so they could be used again. The rest of the infantry and machine gunners followed in section columns.

56th Division, 27 and 28 September, Canal du Nord, Palluel and Arleux

The 5th London Regiment covered the east bank of the Canal du Nord while engineers built bridges for 169 Brigade to cross. But the Germans fought on to Marquion, so Brigadier General Coke had to delay his advance along the east bank until mid-afternoon. The 16th London Regiment cleared Sauchy-Cauchy while the 2nd London Regiment fought their way through Oisy-le-Verger. The 8th Middlesex occupied Palluel and part of Arleux on 28 September, but were driven out of the latter village during the night.

11th Division, 27 and 28 September, Marquion to Épinoy

Brigadier General Winter was in command because Major General Henry Davies had been wounded on 13 September. He received orders to advance mid-morning and the 11th Manchesters led the way across the canal around Sains-lez-Marquion, fanning out on the Canadians' left flank. The Manchesters lost their commander in front of Oisy-le-Verger, so the adjutant deployed his men in a railway cutting south-east of the village until the 8th Northumberland Fusiliers moved up. They had taken 200 prisoners around Oisy by nightfall. The 2nd Green Howards cleared posts along the canal en route to Épinoy, where they were reinforced by the 9th West Yorkshires. The division's line was so far ahead that it did not have to attack on 28 September, but it was clear the Germans were withdrawing across the canal around Aubencheul-au-Bac.

1st Canadian Division, 27 and 28 September, Sains-lez-Marquion, Haynecourt to Abancourt

Two tanks were knocked out as 4th Battalion swarmed cross the Canal du Nord east of Inchy-en-Artois but the Marquion Line was soon cleared allowing 1st Battalion to reach the Green Line. But both 3rd and 2nd Battalions were then pinned down in front of the railway embankment, north of Bourlon. Lieutenant George Kerr silenced two posts and took over thirty prisoners in front of 3rd Battalion; he was awarded the Victoria Cross. Eventually 2nd Battalion reached its objective with the help of a flank attack made by 72nd Battalion (4th Canadian Division).

Four tanks accompanied 14th Battalion past the south side of Sains-lez-Marquion while 15th Battalion faced it across the canal. The barrage then crept back over the village as the Canadians turned on it

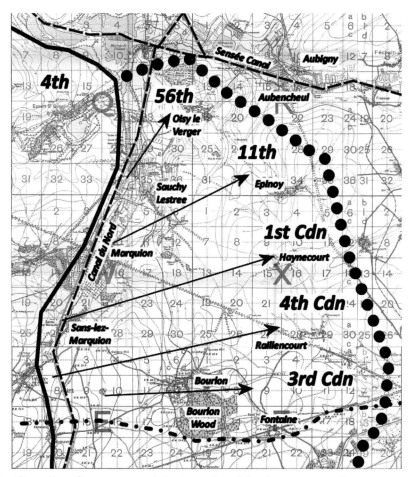

The Canadian Corps crossed the Canal du Nord on narrow frontages on 27 September and then spread out to a position between the Sensée Canal and Cambrai (off the bottom right of the map).

from the rear, taking 350 prisoners. The Stokes mortars supporting 13th Battalion had all been knocked out, so the engineers launched a bridge across the Agache stream. It allowed 15th Battalion to cross and the Germans abandoned Marquion and fell back towards Sauchy-Lestrée.

The 7th Battalion extended their hold on the Blue Line while 5th Battalion cut through wire and advanced through Haynecourt. But the 4th Canadian Division was delayed on the right, so Brigadier General Tuxford had to deploy 8th and 10th Battalions to form a defensive flank facing the Marcoing Line.

Zero hour was delayed until 9 am on 28 September because 1st Canadian Division was ahead of the troops on its flanks. Even so, Lieutenant Colonel Gilson's orders arrived late and it was light by the time 10th Battalion heard it was deployed too far ahead, along the barrage line. Many were hit pulling back towards Haynecourt and there were many more casualties recrossing the same ground; they stood no chance.

4th Canadian Division, 27 and 28 September, Inchy to Bourlon

Eight tanks negotiated the half-dug canal channel as 47th and 46th Battalions overran the Canal du Nord defences north-east of Moeuvres. A smoke screen hid both 50th and 44th Battalions while smoke dischargers attached to exhausts kept the tanks hidden as they crawled towards the Marquion Line; only one was hit. Major General Sir David Watson was then able to order 12 and 11 Brigades across the canal, where they spread out before continuing the advance.

Both the 38th and 85th Battalions suffered many casualties moving past and into the north side of Bourlon village. The 72nd Battalion was delayed because its creeping barrage fell short, and a second one was required so it could reach the Pilgrim's Rest. Lieutenant Samuel Honey took command of 78th Battalion's survivors after all the company officers had been hit advancing. He had to silence a machine-gun post enfilading his position before stopping several counter-attacks and it was dark by the time Brigadier General MacBrien heard that the objective had been secured.

The 87th Battalion cleared the south part of Bourlon village before 54th Battalion could advance through the north end of Bourlon Wood. Lieutenant Graham Lyall captured two strongpoints, taking over fifty prisoners, as 102nd Battalion approached the wood. The Canadians could not outflank the wood to the south until nightfall, so 54th Battalion had to approach Fontaine-Notre-Dame on its own until 87th and 75th Battalions came up on its left flank.

The following morning, 50th and 47th Battalions cleared the Germans from Raillencourt and Sailly, the northern approaches to Cambrai. The 46th and 44th Battalions then moved through the Marcoing Line to the Sailly–Cambrai light railway but came under attack because 3rd Canadian Division was delayed to the south.

3rd Canadian Division, 28 September, Fontaine-Notre-Dame

It was impossible to relieve 4th Canadian Division while Fontaine-Notre-Dame was in enemy hands, so 3rd Canadian Division had to attack through its lines. Three tanks drove towards the Marcoing Line at 6 am but the Royal Canadian Regiment was pinned down in front of the support trench. The Princess Patricia's Canadian Light Infantry advanced through the crossfire coming from Sailly and Sainte Olle towards the outskirts of Cambrai. Lieutenant Milton Gregg eventually found a gap in the wire, so the Royal Canadians could get through, and was then wounded as he killed and captured many during the counter-attacks that followed. He would be severely wounded two days later but he survived to be awarded the Victoria Cross.

A second attack was delayed until dusk because the artillery needed more ammunition. This time 43rd Battalion cleared Fontaine-Notre-Dame while 102nd Battalion covered its right flank but they were then unable to clear the Marcoing Line astride the Bapaume road. The PPCLI negotiated 'unmapped wire' along the Cambrai–Douai road while the 49th Battalion advanced north of Sainte Olle. The 58th Battalion also broke through this time while 116th Battalion reached Ste Olle.

Summary

Late on 27 September Currie wrote, 'today's success jeopardises the hold of the enemy on the Drocourt-Quéant system north of the Scarpe, and he may be expected to fall back to Douai.' At the same time, a German diarist was writing that it had been 'the blackest day of the regiment. Only a little band of men was left at the end of the day... on this day we buried all our hopes for victory.'

First Army, 29 September to 1 October

11th Division, 29 September to 1 October, Sensée Canal

The 2nd Green Howards and the 5th Dorsets were unable to advance north of Épinoy on 29 September despite help from the 2nd West Yorkshires.

Sergeant Frederick Riggs led the 6th York and Lancaster Regiment through the wire the following day to silence a machine gun. He later captured fifty prisoners, but was killed fighting off a counter-attack. Riggs was posthumously awarded the Victoria Cross.

The 5th Dorsets and 8th Northumberland Fusiliers contacted 1st Canadian Division on their right while the 11th Manchesters and 9th West Yorkshires eventually covered a gap opposite Aubencheul-au-Bac. The 11th Division took over the Abancourt sector on 3 October and the 6th Lincolns captured the railway station two days later; it prompted the Germans to withdraw across the Sensée canal.

1st Canadian Division, 29 September to 1 October, Haynecourt to Abancourt

The 8th Battalion took over the line during the night but many men were hit when they had to withdraw from the barrage line in daylight. Zero hour had been set for 8.36 am on 29 September but 4th Canadian Division never appeared and the 8th Battalion had to withdraw. The next attempt by 4th and 1st Battalions was stopped by enfilade fire early the following morning. Sergeant William Merrifield was hit twice while silencing the machine guns in front of 4th Battalion but he still led the advance onto the high ground around Abancourt. He would be awarded the Victoria Cross. The 13th Battalion cleared Blécourt so that 14th and 16th Battalions could reach Bantigny and Cuvillers on 1 October, but it left them in a valley. A counter-attack hit their exposed flanks and drove them out of all three villages.

4th Canadian Division, 29 to 30 September, Raillencourt to Sancourt

Zero hour was set for 8 am on 29 September, so Lieutenant Colonel Kirkcaldy had to assemble 12 Brigade out of sight, in the Marcoing Line. The barrage hit the German position along the Douai railway for twenty minutes, while the assault troops advanced 1,000 yards to catch up with it. The 72nd Battalion captured around 250 prisoners around Sancourt and many were taken by six men who followed a streambed into Blécourt. 'They mounted a Lewis gun in the village square and began rounding up prisoners in the nearby buildings, withdrawing with some eighty to the railway.' They had to leave a similar number of men behind. The 38th Battalion was pinned down on the right and Lieutenant Samuel Honey was mortally wounded attempting to lead 78th Battalion to a railway cutting during the afternoon. It was his second brave deed in three days and he would be posthumously awarded the Victoria Cross.

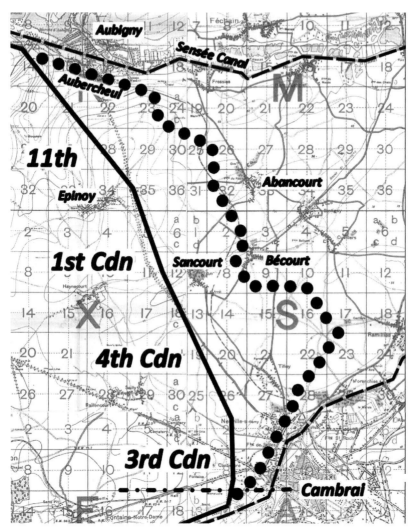

The Canadian Corps struggled to make progress past the north side of Cambrai after 29 September.

A smoke screen failed to cover 75th Battalion's advance towards Blécourt the following day. The 87th and 54th Battalions tried in vain to help but they all had to withdraw. The following morning Lieutenant Graham Lyall captured sixty prisoners during 102nd Battalion's attack on Blécourt. It was his second brave deed in five days and he was awarded the Victoria Cross. The 87th Battalion helped expand the front and the 'prisoners poured in, the identification of a large number of regiments and battalions being evidence that the enemy had thrown in strong reserves.'

3rd Canadian Division, 29 September to 1 October, advance past the north side of Cambrai

The 42nd and 49th Battalions were pinned down in front of the Douai railway cutting around Tilloy but 116th Battalion rounded up 100 prisoners around Ste Olle while 58th Battalion cleared Petit Fontaine. Brigadier General Ormond then let 58th Battalion clear the Marcoing Line for 57th Division on the Canadians' right flank.

The 2nd and 1st Mounted Rifles pushed through the division's centre but the barrage landed too far ahead because the gunners did not know where the front line was. They were then plunged into 'the most desperately fought engagement of the war'. Captain John MacGregor was hit silencing machine guns but he still led the 2nd Mounted Rifles into Neuville-Saint-Rémy, taking 150 prisoners. They too could not reach the Douai railway, north of Cambrai, but MacGregor would be awarded the Victoria Cross.

The Royal Canadian Regiment came under enfilade fire from Blécourt early on 30 September and it had to retire. Two tanks were disabled but a third helped the PPCLI take the south half of Tilloy. The 52nd and 43rd Battalions captured 350 prisoners advancing towards Ramillies early on 1 October but they came under fire from across the l'Escaut Canal. Neither the 58th nor the 116th Battalions could reach Morenchies and all four battalions had to retire at dawn.

Chapter 4

The Most Desperately Fought Engagement of the War

Third Army

27 September to 7 October

General Sir Julian Byng issued the orders for the attack against the Hindenburg Line at 5.20 am on 27 September. However, Lieutenant General Sir Aylmer Haldane was concerned that VI Corps would be advancing along the Grand Ravin valley before IV Corps had taken Highland Ridge on his right flank. So Byng delayed IV Corps' zero hour, meaning that Lieutenant General Sir Montague Harper's men would have to attack in broad daylight.

XVII Corps, 27 and 28 September

52nd Division, 27 September, Moeuvres to Graincourt

The 4th and the 5th Scots Fusiliers had to withdraw a short distance at 4.50 am so that the gunners could shell the German positions around Moeuvres. Thirty minutes later, four tanks accompanied the 4th Royal Scots to the canal in thick smoke. 'Like poachers surprised by hidden snares, they struggled in a ganglion of rusty wire concealed by the jungle-like growth of long, lank grass.' Major Slater's men had lost the barrage, so they followed trenches and took 200 prisoners on the far side of the dry cutting. The 7th Scots Rifles were then able to clear the Hindenburg Support Line.

Major General Francis Marshall's plan included clearing the trenches running parallel to the canal south of Moeuvres. Three tanks were knocked out negotiating tank traps, but the 6th and 7th Highland Light Infantry could turn east to face the Hindenburg Support Line once Lock 8 had been reached.

63rd Division, 27 and 28 September, Hindenburg Line to the St Quentin Canal

Stokes mortars covered the 7th Royal Fusiliers and 4th Bedfords as they charged across the canal before turning south down the Hindenburg support trenches. Four tanks were put out of action clearing the formidable position but the 1/28th London Regiment had been able to clear the canal banks behind them. The Anson Battalion and the Royal Marines could not capture a sugar factory so Brigadier General Coleridge organised an 'artillery crash' ahead of a charge through the complex at 2.15 pm. The Hawke and Drake Battalions could then clear Anneux while the 2nd Irish Regiment helped the Marines take Graincourt.

An evening counter–attack was driven off as the men waited for 57th Division to take over the advance but 189 Brigade was told to advance through 57th Division during the afternoon of 28 September. Brigadier General Curling's men 'came on a scene of incalculable and dangerous confusion' along the canal but Commander Beak led a few of the Drake Battalion across a lock gate. The Hood Battalion had to clear some Germans from La Folie wood but Commander Beak had withdrawn by the time Lieutenant Commander Blackmore caught up with the Hawke Battalion.

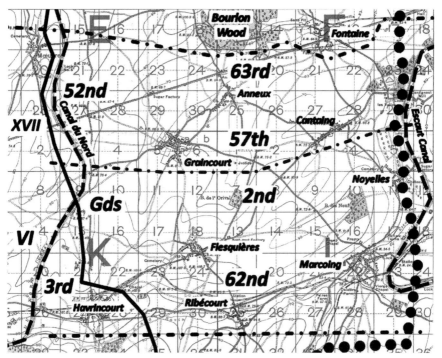

XVII Corps and VI Corps advanced from the Canal du Nord to the Escaut Canal, on Third Army's left between 27 and 29 September.

57th Division, 27 and 28 September, Anneux and Graincourt

The Germans were firing so many flares that no one saw the British ones indicating success, so it was dusk by the time Major General Reginald Barnes issued the order to advance. A counter-attack meant that the 2/7th King's and 8th King's were disorganised by retreating troops while 63rd Division's British SOS barrage prevented them from going beyond Anneux. The 2/6th King's and 9th King's were stopped by machine-fire from the Cantaing Line when they tried again at dusk. The Canadians outflanked Bourlon Wood during the night, forcing the Germans in front of 57th Division to withdraw. The 2/7th King's and the 2/6th King's were able to clear the Fontaine-Notre-Dame area the following morning.

VI Corps, 27 and 28 September

General Haldane's men faced the Hindenburg Line where it ran parallel with the Canal du Nord. The attack was made on a narrow front around Moeuvres and the troops then fanned out to clear the Hindenburg Line down to Havrincourt.

Guards Division, 27 September, Hindenburg Line to Flesquières

Major General Torqhil Matheson had been given a few tanks to cross the dry section of the Canal du Nord, east of Demicourt. The 3rd Grenadier Guards crossed on a narrow front and then cleared the Hindenburg trenches from north to south. Lieutenant Colonel Brand's 1st Coldstream Guards were pinned down in the canal channel until Captain Cyril Frisby and Lance Corporal Thomas Jackson silenced two hidden machine guns. Frisby then rallied a company which had lost all its officers and led them forward. Jackson was killed clearing the trench on the far bank. Both Frisby and Jackson were awarded the Victoria Cross.

The 1st Scots Guards used ladders to cross the channel, but were pinned down in front of the Hindenburg support trenches, under fire from Graincourt to the left. An afternoon attack on the village by 63rd Division encouraged the Germans in front of the Guardsmen to surrender. Lieutenant Colonel Baggallay's 1st Irish Guards then fought their way past the north side of Flesquières until they were stopped in front of a sugar factory. The 2nd Grenadier Guards were supposed to help but Major Harcourt Vernon's men were stopped by enfilade fire from Orival Wood until 57th Division advanced beyond Graincourt.

Brigadier General Follett was killed as the 1st Grenadier Guards led 3 Guards Brigade across the Canal du Nord and past Flesquières. The trenches were filled with the walking wounded and 'severe cases were being carried over the top by prisoners who made no secret of an acute desire to live and jumped among the rest without asking. The men compared the crush to a sugar queue at home.'

Three tanks were knocked out in front of the factory, so Lieutenant Colonel John Vereker directed a platoon to lead a fourth tank along a sunken road and they took the 200-strong garrison by surprise. He then led the 1st Grenadier Guards along Flesquières ridge while Lieutenant Colonel Luxmoore Ball made sure the 1st Welsh Guards covered their flanks. They captured 1 mile of trenches, taking another 200 prisoners and a dozen field guns. A badly injured Vereker refused to go to the aid post until the success signal was fired; he would be awarded the Victoria Cross. (Vereker was Lord Gort, commander of the British Expeditionary Force in France and Belgium during the retreat to Dunkirk in 1940, and then Governor of Malta during the 1942-44 siege.)

2nd Division, 27 September, East of Flesquières

Major General Cecil Pereira's men followed the Guards Division across the Canal du Nord but it was late afternoon before they were ready to continue the advance towards the l'Escaut Canal. The 2nd South Staffords and 1st King's were unable to reach the Cantaing Line despite a smoke barrage.

3rd Division, 27 September, Havrincourt

Major General Cyril Deverell had been given most of VI Corps' tanks because his front line was already across the canal, east of Hermies. The artillery fired a smoke barrage along his right flank where IV Corps would advance along the Hindenburg Line and onto Highland Ridge three hours later.

The 2nd Royal Scots and 7th Shropshires passed though the abandoned trenches west of Flesquières, to find the Germans waiting beyond the first ridge. The 1st Scots Fusiliers outflanked the railway embankment on the right and six out of the eight tanks reached the objective. The 1st Northumberland Fusiliers advanced in line with the 13th King's but they faced a hard time clearing the trenches east of Havrincourt. They then came under fire from Ribécourt, so the 4th Royal Fusiliers attacked its north side while men of 62nd Division came from the south. They took over 600 prisoners between them.

Tanks helped the 8th King's Own and 1st Gordons clear the Hindenburg support trenches south of past Flesquières. Lance Sergeant Thomas Neely silenced three machine-gun posts and captured two bunkers for the 8th King's Own. He was killed in action only three days later but he was posthumously awarded the Victoria Cross.

62nd Division, 27 and 28 September, Ribécourt to Marcoing and Masnières

Major General Sir Whigham's men followed 3rd Division though the Hindenburg Line and the large columns of prisoners marching to the rear indicated that everything was going well. The 2/20th London Regiment and the 1/5th Devons continued the advance east of Flesquières and they took over 800 prisoners between them, including a battalion headquarters. Not everyone wanted to surrender and Lieutenant Slaughter's party was mown down after 'the enemy raised their hands in token.' The fire from the sugar factory to the north stopped when the Guardsmen took it and the 8th West Yorkshires then charged down the slope to the l'Escaut Canal in Marcoing. They were driven back to Orival Wood after losing all their officers.

The 2/4th KOYLIs helped 3rd Division clear Ribécourt while Captain Spencer silenced the machine guns in front of the 4th Royal Fusiliers. The delay meant the barrage was lost and cross fire stopped the advance; the 2/4th York and Lancaster's were also pinned down.

Major General Whigham had two attacks to organise on 28 September but it was difficult to distribute orders in the rain and darkness. Even so, both the 2/4th York and Lancaster's and the 2/4th KOYLIs reached Masnières at 4.35 am. The second advance was made towards the canal at 6.30 am and again there were problems distributing the orders. Lieutenant Colonel Walker's guides failed to turn up after the brigade conference and he was late getting back to the 5th Duke's. Lieutenant Colonel Brook was told to lead the attack with his 2/4th Hampshires and there were just 'a few hasty orders and away the battalion went... And how well it succeeded!' As they swept forward to the canal, the Duke's made 'a regular man-hunt for machine gunners' in Marcoing.

Both Lieutenant Colonel Hart's 2/4th York and Lancaster's and Lieutenant Colonel Chaytor's 2/4th KOYLIs reached the canal on the right but Lieutenant Colonel Peter's 5th KOYLIs had a tough fight for Marcoing Wood on the far bank.

Meanwhile, all was not well in Marcoing where Private Henry Tandey had to rebuild the plank bridge over the lock gates when it collapsed. The 5th Duke's captured the Marcoing Line during the evening but it had cost them dearly and Second Lieutenant Lloyd's platoon was fighting off a counterattack when their prisoners picked up their weapons and surrounded them. Tandey was twice wounded in the bayonet charge which captured thirty-seven prisoners; he was awarded the Victoria Cross.

2nd Division, 28 and 29 September, l'Escaut Canal to Mont sur l'Oeuvre

Major General Cecil Pereira's men relieved the Guards Division east of Flesquières during the night and they cleared the Cantaing Line in a pre-dawn advance at 5.15 am. Nine Wood and Noyelles were also taken but the Germans were ready across the l'Escaut Canal. A few of the 1st King's crossed at a lock but machine-gun fire stopped the rest crossing the canal. The 2nd South Staffords captured 300 prisoners en route to the canal but they too could not cross at Noyelles. Second Lieutenant Water swam across with a rope but his men could not get their raft across, so the rest of 17th Royal Fusiliers had to wait until dusk before filing across another lock. Their slender foothold was first lost and then regained during the night. The 1st Berkshires and 1st King's had had more luck, crossing at the lock north of Marcoing.

IV Corps, 27 and 28 September

42nd (East Lancashire) Division, 27 and 28 September, Trescault Ridge and Highland Ridge

Major General Arthur Solly Flood had to make a two phase attack on 27 September to coordinate with the attacks to the flanks. Two tanks accompanied the 8th and 7th Lancashire Fusiliers when they moved forward on the right at 7.52 am but Lieutenant Colonels MacLeod's and Brewis's men were soon pinned by enfilade fire from Beaucamp.

Six tanks helped the 5th Manchesters clear the Hindenburg trenches on Trescault ridge at 8.20 am on the left. The 7th and 6th Manchesters took many prisoners as they fought their way across Highland Ridge. Three tanks broke down and two were hit; one 'presented a most ludicrous spectacle, hopping around like a wounded rabbit' as its load of thermite bombs exploded. Defensive flanks then had to be made because everyone else was delayed.

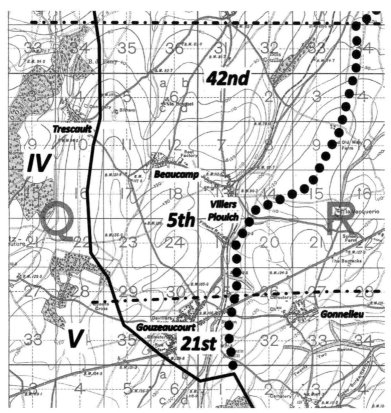

IV Corps cleared the Hindenburg Line trenches as V Corps pushed Third Army's right forward on 28 and 29 September.

The 10th Manchesters and the 5th Lancashire Fusiliers overran the trenches on Highland Ridge at 2.30 am the following morning and then chased the stragglers across Couillet valley. A squadron of the 3rd Hussars joined the pursuit but were stopped by fire from the north end of Welsh Ridge. The 8th Manchesters and 8th Lancashire Fusiliers were sent across Welsh Ridge during the afternoon.

Solly-Flood's division had taken over 1,700 prisoners in two days but there had been so many casualties that there were too few men to provide escorts; 'they simply waved them to the rear and the Boches meekly obeyed, too glad to be out of the fighting to take advantage.'

5th Division, 27 and 28 September, Beaucamp to Banteux

Major General John Ponsonby still had four battalions in each of his brigades because his division had been in Italy when all divisions had been reduced the previous February. They advanced at 7.52 am as drums of blazing oil exploded across the ridge between Beaucamp and Gouzeaucourt. All six tanks were knocked as the 1st Cheshires and 1st Bedfords advanced towards Villers Plouich and most of the tanks with the 14th Warwicks, 15th Warwicks and 1st Queen's Own were hit as they advanced north of Gouzeaucourt. Bombing attacks drove the five battalions nearly back to their start line during the afternoon and Captain Abbott's machine gun teams had to fire thousands of rounds to stop the enemy breaking through.

The 1st East Surreys and 1st Devons renewed the advance at 2.40 am on 28 September but it took them five hours to clear Beaucamp. The East Surreys made good progress onto the south end of Highland Ridge but Major Lock's Devons were stopped by enfilade fire from Villers Plouich. Major General Ponsonby had expected the Germans to withdraw but they fought on and the two battalions had to bomb their way onto Welsh Ridge. Eventually, the Germans began to withdraw and the East Surreys were able to enter Villers Plouich while the Devons cleared African Trench. The 1st Cheshires and the 1st Norfolks then followed up the withdrawal to the railway south of Villers Plouich.

V Corps, 27 and 28 September

21st Division, 27 and 28 September, Gouzeaucourt to the St Quentin Canal

The 12/13th Northumberland Fusiliers advanced towards Gouzeaucourt at 7.52 am on 27 September, but counter-attacks drove 5th Division back on their left, so they too had to fall back at dusk. Lieutenant Chadwell led the 1st Lincolns through an abandoned Gouzeaucourt during the night.

33rd Division, 27 and 28 September, Villers Guislain to Honnecourt

A single tank helped the 2nd Argylls and 1st Middlesex tackle Villers Guislain at 3.30 am while the 4th King's covered the flank. The 1/9th HLI and the 2nd Worcesters advanced down Targelle Ravine in the mist two hours later. A counter-attack retook Villers Guislain, forcing the Argylls and the Middlesex to withdraw, taking their 250 prisoners with them. Brigadier General Baird's messenger was captured so Lieutenant Colonel Menzies and Lieutenant Colonel Stoney did not get the withdrawal order. Most of the HLI and Worcesters were captured.

XVII Corps, 29 September to 1 October

63rd Division, 29 September to 1 October, Crossing the l'Escaut Canal

The Drake Battalion crossed temporary pontoon bridges and the canal locks around Cantaing early on 29 September. The Hood and Hawke Battalions then expanded the bridgehead south of Pronville before the Marines and the 2nd Irish Regiment captured the Marcoing Line. The Anson Battalion, 7th Royal Fusiliers and the 1/28th London Regiment advanced closer to Cambrai on 30 September and 1 October.

57th Division, 29 September, Anneux to Pronville

The Germans had withdrawn across the l'Escaut Canal, so the 1st Munsters moved through Cantaing early on 29 September. Some of the 2/5th King's Own negotiated the Pronville road lock but they were unable to across the river beyond while others crossed to the south, where the canal aqueduct crossed the river. The King's Own fought their way into the Marcoing Line but the 1/5th Loyals were unable to reach them. The 2/6th King's cleared more of the Marcoing Line during the afternoon before crossing the l'Escaut Canal at La Folie wood during the evening. The following day, the 2/7th King's and 8th King's cleared Pronville and the 8th King's and 1st Munsters moved up on their right flank.

VI Corps, 29 September to 1 October

2nd Division, 29 September to 1 October, Mont sur l'Oeuvre

The 17th Royal Fusiliers took 300 prisoners along the Marcoing Line on 29 September. The 1st KRRC and the 1st Berkshires then crossed the canal by two footbridges and bombed along the Marcoing Line beyond. Artillery fire would smash the foot bridges but the bridgehead held. The 23rd Royal Fusiliers failed to capture Mont sur l'Oeuvre early on 30 September but 2nd Ox and Bucks gained more ground at dawn on 1 October. The 2nd HLI and 24th Royal Fusiliers eventually took 400 prisoners on Mont sur l'Oeuvre later in the day.

62nd Division, 29 and 30 September, Rumilly

Major General Whigham planned to expand the bridgehead across the l'Escaut Canal at 7.30 am on 29 September and the fog blinded the Germans in Rumilly Switch. The 2/4th Duke's left was pinned down by fire from Mont sur l'Oeuvre but Lieutenant Colonel Wilson's right cleared the trenches south-west of Rumilly. The 2/4th KOYLIs took 300 prisoners in Masnières while the 5th KOYLIs took more in Les Rues Vertes on the south bank. An evening attack by the 2/4th Hampshires failed because it took them too long to cross the canal, so they lost the barrage.

Captain Cottam was killed when the Germans infiltrated the Hampshires' position in Rumilly Switch but Second Lieutenant Turner's 'daring attack' drove them out. The 2/20th London Regiment were unable to reach Rumilly early on 30 September, again due to fire from Mont sur l'Oeuvre, but the

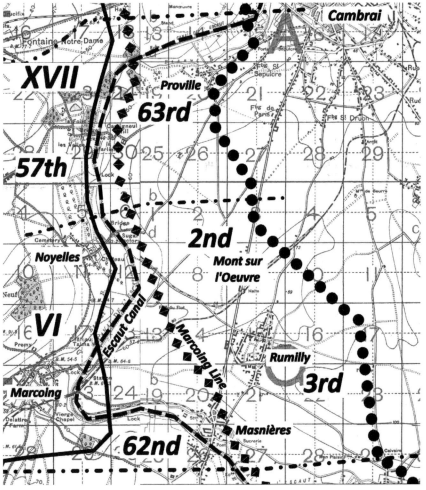

XVII Corps and VI Corps crossed the Escaut Canal and cleared the Marcoing Line on 30 September but they still had a hard fight for Mont sur l'Oeuvre and Rumilly.

1/5th Devons and 8th West Yorkshires advanced south of the village. The Devons and West Yorkshires used forty captured machine guns to stop a counter-attack before withdrawing with their prisoners, so the morning's barrage line could be straight.

3rd Division, 1 October, Rumilly

The 2nd Suffolks and 8th King's Own became disorganised fighting through Rumilly on 1 October but they advanced south of Mont sur l'Oeuvre at dusk while the 7th Shropshires and 1st Gordons cleared Rumilly.

IV Corps, 29 September to 1 October

New Zealand Division, 29 September to 1 October, Highland Ridge to the l'Escaut Canal

The 1st Auckland Battalion and 2nd Wellington Battalion followed old trenches at 3.30 am on 29 September, taking over 500 prisoners and twenty-eight artillery pieces across Welsh Ridge and Bonvais Ridge. The 2nd Otago Battalion came under crossfire because the 1st Canterbury Battalion were delayed around La Vacquerie and one company was taken prisoner because it became lost in the dark. The two battalions reached the Cambrai road under heavy enfilade fire because 5th Division was held up to the south. The 1st Otago Battalion moved to the open flank and Sergeant Foote used two captured field guns to stop a counter-attack. Patrols then approached the l'Escaut while machine-gun teams fired across the canal, 'engaging transport lorries, guns and motor tractors, scattering horses and personnel'.

Major General Andrew Russell wanted to cross the l'Escaut Canal before dawn on 30 September without a barrage. Unfortunately the messengers got lost and the barrage had to be fired at 5.45 am, alerting the Germans. The 2nd Auckland Battalion was pinned down around Crèvecoeur but Private James Crichton was wounded as he swam across with a message. He disarmed the charges under the bridge but the Aucklanders remained pinned down on the island in the middle of the canal. Crichton would be awarded the Victoria Cross.

The first attempt to reach the canal at Les Rues des Vignes was underway before the barrage started. Then the New Zealanders were caught unawares when the guns opened fire for a second time. Patrols later discovered that the Vaucelles bridge had been blown up but the 1st Auckland and 2nd Wellington Battalions crossed at Masnières during the early hours of

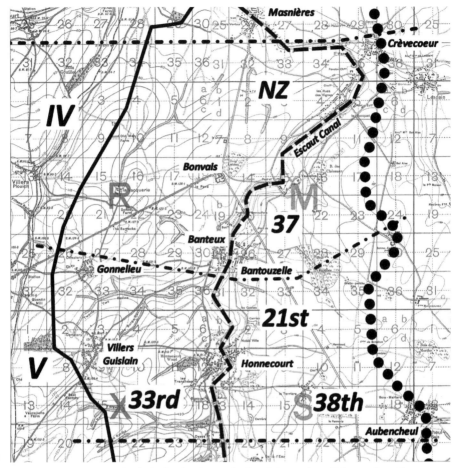

Once Third Army's left had cleared the Marcoing Line, the Germans withdrew rapidly in front of IV and V Corps.

1 October. A counter-attack would drive the Auckland men back but the Wellington men held on to Crèvecoeur.

5th Division, 29 and 30 September, Beaucamp to Banteux

The 12th Gloucesters and 1st DCLI were late for the 3.30 am zero hour, so it was rearranged for 8.30 am. They were both pinned down after half a mile and neither the 14th or 15th Warwicks were able to go much further. Captain Wakefield and some of the 1st Bedfords captured 130 prisoners along the sunken Gonnelieu road but the 1st DCLI were able to capture La Vacquerie after dusk.

Early on 30 September, the 1st Cheshires caught the Germans as they withdrew from the Hindenburg Line towards the l'Escaut Canal. The 1st Norfolks crossed two bridges north of Banteux but were driven back when the Germans returned to the canal. Meanwhile the 16th Warwicks had cleared Gonnelieu, allowing 21st Division to move up.

New Zealand, 4 and 5 October, l'Escaut Canal, Crèvecoeur to Vaucelles

The 4th Rifles crossed the l'Escaut Canal and entered an abandoned Crèvecoeur early on 4 October, taking part of the Beaurevoir Line the following morning. Captain Hutton crossed a demolished bridge to discover that Vaucelles had been abandoned, so the 2nd Canterbury Battalion crossed on a raft made of duck boards and cork.

37th Division, 1 to 5 October, Banteux and Vaucelles

The Germans abandoned Banteux early on 4 October, so the 13th Rifle Brigade and 13th KRRC crossed at Vaucelles and advanced to the Beaurevoir Line the following day.

V Corps, 29 September to 1 October

21st Division, 29 September to 5 October, St Quentin Canal

Order were issued late and then a 'very bad barrage' landed far ahead of the deployment line at 3.30 am on 29 September. The 2nd Lincolns were stopped by machine-gun fire from Gonnelieu while both the tanks with the 1st Lincolns were knocked out. The 6th Leicesters could not take Villers Guislain either, so the isolated Lincolns had to retire.

A heavy barrage on 30 September convinced the Germans to abandon Gonnelieu. The 1st Lincolns and 7th Leicesters followed them to Banteux during the night, only to see the canal bridge blow up in their faces. The Germans fell back 3 miles during the night of 4/5 October and Major General David Campbell's men followed them as far as the Hindenburg Support Line in front of Aubencheul-au-Bois.

33rd Division, 4 October, Honnecourt

The Germans withdrew from the l'Escaut Canal late on 4 October, so Major General Sir Reginald Pinney's men could cross around Honnecourt and advance to the Hindenburg Support line near Aubencheul-au-Bois.

38th (Welsh) Division, 5 October, Aubencheul-au-Bois

Major General Thomas Cubitt's men occupied an abandoned Aubencheul-au-Bois, in front of the Beaurevoir Line.

Summary

Fourth Army had outflanked the Germans, forcing them to fall back to the Beaurevoir Line in front of Third Army's right. All was going well but General Byng's men were tired and he had few tanks left to help them. Casualties had been high (nearly 37,000 over the past four weeks) and three brigadier generals had been wounded: Paynter, Longbourne and Osborn.

Chapter 5

Fighting with Dash and Determination

Second Army

28 September to 2 October

On 16 September, Field Marshal Foch had told General Plumer to prepare to attack east of Ypres and across the Messines Ridge on the 28th; the second of the three BEF strikes over three days. Reports suggested that the Germans were preparing to withdraw to Passchendaele ridge, abandoning the crater field dating back to the Third Battle of Ypres in the autumn of 1917. Plumer had to make a contingency plan in case they did.

Second Army was made part of the Flanders Army Group, which comprised French, Belgian and British troops. Plumer would report to King Albert of the Belgians, instead of GHQ, while his staff would work alongside French General Jean Degoutte. Plumer issued outline instructions to his four corps commanders on 19 September and they submitted their plans three days later. They reported at conference with Belgian commanders forty-eight hours later.

Vice Admiral Sir Roger Keyes, commanding the Dover Patrol, visited Field Marshal Haig and the Belgian King on 24 September to discuss an amphibious raid on Ostend. The plan was to land when the Belgians surrounded the town, to save the docks from demolition. The Dover Patrol also handed over control of 5th Group RAF, and its eight squadrons augmented the sixteen squadrons of II Brigade RAF.

Orders were issued and conferences held while ammunition and supplies were unloaded around Ypres. Everyone was told what to expect and then queues of officers lined up to study a huge scale model of the battlefield at General Plumer's headquarters in Cassel. Rain poured down from the autumn skies as the infantry trudged through and around the ruins of Ypres. Second Army was going to have to take the Passchendaele Ridge once more.

The Artillery Plan

The Belgian artillery were going to fire a three-hour bombardment before zero hour but Plumer preferred to save his ammunition for later. Second

Army's barrage would begin minutes before 5.30 am and then creep forward as the assault troops advanced behind a smoke screen. The infantry would control the speed of the barrage, using flares or contact planes to communicate progress. Brigades would work with infantry brigades, batteries with battalions and sections with companies. Camouflaged battery sites had been built close to the front line, so the gunners could relocate to cover the later stages of the advance. The creeping barrage would end after 4,000 yards and gunners would either shoot at predetermined targets or if the infantry called upon them, to conserve ammunition.

The Germans

A withdrawal from the Lys plain had left the Fourth German Army spread across the crater field dating from 1917. General Friedrich Sixt von Armin had manned an outpost line and it was hoped the old trenches and pillboxes would disrupt any attack.

The Belgians

Seven Belgian divisions attacked across an 8½ mile front at 5.30 am on 28 September. They had fought their way through four lines of defence before midday, crossing 5 miles of craters and old trenches. Houthulst Forest, Passchendaele and Broodseinde had all fallen but there was a tougher task ahead: the Flanders Position I.

II Corps, 28 September

9th Division, 28 September, Ypres to Becelaere

Major General Hugh Tudor's men advanced at 5.25 am over 'slippery and shell-pitted ground' but the 'whole operation went like clockwork'. They worked their way through the maze of dugouts, craters and pillboxes in the pre-dawn gloom. Smoke was used when it became light but there was little resistance because the ground was too difficult to defend.

The 8th Black Watch and 7th Seaforths cleared Westhoek ridge before the 5th Camerons tackled the pillboxes on Anzac Spur and Glasgow Spur. The 2nd Scots Fusiliers, 9th Scots Rifles and Newfoundland Battalion had a similar experience as they bypassed Bellewaarde Lake and cleared Anzac Ridge. There was more resistance when the 11th Royal Scots and 12th Royal Scots advanced onto the ridge between Molenaarelsthoek and Becelaere

during the afternoon. Three German batteries cantered forward to fire at
the 11th Royal Scots but machine-gun fire drove them away; the 12th Royal
Scots also had to stop a counter-attack.

29th Division, 28 September, Zillebeke to Gheluvelt

Lieutenant Colonel Modera's 1st Lancashire Fusiliers followed the Menin
Road 'under a barrage, part of which fell short and inflicted the majority of
the day's casualties'. The 1st Dublin Fusiliers moved past Hooge, finding
that 'enemy opposition had been completely broken.' The 2nd Royal
Fusiliers then found that the bunkers around Polderhoek 'began to fall into
the hands of the troops like ripe fruit'.

On the right, the 2nd SWBs advanced past Zillebeke Lake before the
1st Border Regiment passed through Sanctuary Wood. Lieutenant Beaty-
Pownall's 1st KOSBs crossed Bassevillebeek stream and climbed Tower
Hamlets while the 4th Worcesters completed the advance across 'a maze of

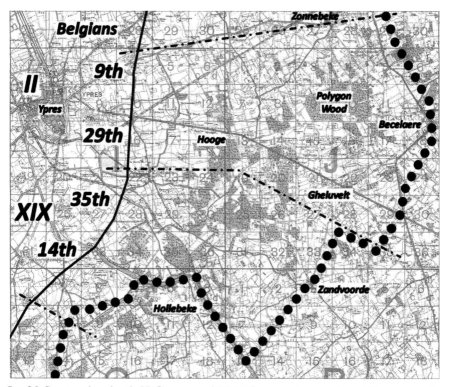

On 28 September both II Corps and XIX Corps advanced rapidly across the
crater field dating from the autumn of 1917.

old trench lines littered with debris and punctuated with craters, mostly full of water'. It only stopped beyond Gheluvelt because the British heavy guns were firing short.

XIX Corps, 28 September

35th Division, 28 September, Zillebeke to Zonnebeke

All three of Major General Arthur Marindin's brigades moved quickly through the outpost line south of Zillebeke, starting at 5.30 am. The 12th HLI led the advance from Zillebeke and then the 18th HLI cleared Shrewsbury Forest. The 18th Lancashire Fusiliers and 19th Durhams crossed Hill 60 and the Caterpillar astride the Comines Canal before Lieutenant Colonel Jones led the 17th Lancashire Fusiliers through a 'soft spot' in the enemy line to reach Zandvoorde. On the right, the 15th Sherwoods and 4th North Staffords captured 650 prisoners, including a battalion staff, in Battle Wood. The advance had been a complete success but the artillery had been hampered due to 'horses treading on tin canisters filled with explosive buried in the roadways'. It would take most of the night to clear the booby traps.

14th Division, 28 September, astride the Comines Canal

Captain Leeming outflanked the spoil heap called the Bluff as the 12th Suffolks advanced along the north side of the Comines Canal. The position 'bristled with machine-guns and trench mortars' but Lieutenant Lloyd's men took 200 prisoners while the 20th Middlesex approached the White Chateau on the south bank. The 6th Wiltshires and 14th Argylls won a fierce battle for the St Eloi craters, only to be pinned down by the machine guns along Damm Strasse.

41st Division, 28 September, Kortewilde

Major General Sydney Lawford told Brigadier General Adlercron to start moving when he heard that the Germans were falling back in the afternoon. The 26th Royal Fusiliers advanced from Hill 60 to Kortewilde while the 23rd Middlesex covered the Comines Canal facing Hollebeke.

X Corps, 28 September

34th Division, 28 September, Wytschaete

Sergeant Louis McGuffie captured many during the 1/5th KOSB's advance west of Wytschaete. He then escorted a number of escaping prisoners to the rear before rescuing some captured comrades. McGuffie later took more prisoners but would be killed in action on 4 October; he was posthumously awarded the Victoria Cross.

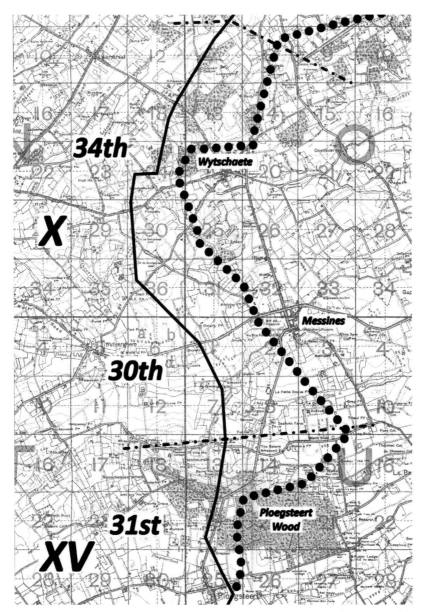

X Corps struggled to clear the Messines ridge while XV Corps could not enter Ploegsteert Wood on 28 September.

The 1/5th Argylls advanced through Bois Quarante and Grand Bois, coming under enfilade fire from Damm Strasse where 14th Division had been held up. Lewis gunners had subdued the defence by the time Brigadier General Rawson organised a second barrage and the Argylls were hit by it as they advanced north of Wytschaete. They also came under fire from the village area because the 2nd Loyals had been unable to reach it. Orders to attack again at dusk did not reach the Argylls in time and the Loyals could not clear Wytschaete on their own.

30th Division, 28 September, Messines

There was little opposition to 2/17th London Regiment's advance and then the 2/16th and 2/15th advanced up the slopes onto the Messines Ridge. The Germans withdrew during the evening but it was impossible to clear the Messines area in the dark.

XV Corps, 28 September

31st Division, 28 September, advance along the Douve Stream

The 10th East Yorkshires advanced north of Ploegsteert Wood during the afternoon but the 11th East Lancashires struggled to clear it. Lieutenant General Beauvoir De Lisle ordered Major General John Campbell to send troops north of the Douve stream, to get behind Messines, but traffic congestion and shell fire made it difficult to get forward in the dark. The 15th West Yorkshires then encountered many machine-gun teams sheltering in pill-boxes. Green flares controlled a confused retirement and at one point the Yorkshiremen found German units marching on both their flanks.

Second Army, 29 September to 2 October

The 28th of September had been a day 'of uninterrupted successes'. The German infantry had been 'left in the lurch by its artillery and, save at isolated points, made no serious resistance'. The Fourth German Army was on the back foot and 'in one day considerably more ground had been won than during months of furious fighting in 1917. Nothing could have revealed in a stronger light the unmistakeable change that had come over the character of the war.' General von Armin was shocked by the collapse and told Crown Prince Rupprecht that his troops could 'no longer stand up to a serious attack'.

All was going well but Plumer still faced many problems. Bad weather continued to interfere with RAF operations, so he had to rely on prisoner reports. They suggested the Flanders I and II lines would be held until a new line had been prepared behind the River Lys. The rain restarted in the afternoon, making it difficult to get wheeled transport forward along the few roads, so pack mules loaded with ammunition and food were sent to the front.

II Corps, 29 September to 2 October

The artillery batteries struggled to get forward along the overcrowded roads, leaving Lieutenant General Claud Jacob short of guns. Instead he organised a smoke barrage to cover the advance towards the Flanders I Line at 9 am.

9th Division, 29 September to 2 October, Broodseinde Ridge to Ledeghem

The Newfoundland Battalion and the 9th Scottish Rifles 'suffered grievously' as they battled through the Flanders Position I on 29 September. The 5th Camerons reinforced the left flank, where the Belgians were struggling, while the 11th Royal Scots and 6th KOSBs tackled Terhand on the right. The Germans withdrew as soon as Lieutenant Colonels Campbell and Smyth had forced a way through.

Major General Tudor had to wait for the divisions on his flanks to catch up before attacking the Flanders II Line on 1 October. The 8th Black Watch and 7th Seaforths cleared the pillboxes around St Pieter while the 12th Royal Scots and 6th KOSBs fought their way into Ledeghem; they had to withdraw because their flanks were exposed. Field guns worked in close cooperation with the infantry and Lieutenant Robert Gorle's crew manhandled their weapon forward to support an unsuccessful attack on Hill 41. He then rallied the infantry to make a second attempt. Gorle would be awarded the Victoria Cross. Ground had been gained but the Newfoundland Battalion were in a salient between the Belgians and Hill 41 which was under attack.

36th Division, 29 September to 2 October, Becelaere to Dadizeele

Major General Clifford Coffin was to take over the line between 9th and 29th Divisions but 109 Brigade could not reach Becelaere until 5 am on 29 September. 'The roads were choked. The only tolerable ones among them were the Menin and Zonnebeke roads. Upon each was a solid mass of transport, which often for hours at a time remained immobile.' The German Gotha bombers which frequently flew over could hardly miss.

The 9th Inniskillings encountered machine-gun nests 'cleverly disposed in depth behind hedges or buildings', but they still pushed through the Flanders I Line to Dadizeele. Lance Corporal Ernest Seaman silenced two machine-gun posts holding up the 2nd Inniskillings around Terhand. He was killed tackling a third and was posthumously awarded the Victoria Cross.

The 12th Irish Rifles nearly reached the Flanders II Line early on 30 September. However, the artillery were too far behind to help the 9th Irish Fusiliers take the bunkers on Hill 41. Two attempts to outflank the position from the south also failed. Heavy artillery supported a third attack early on 1 October but neither the 12th Irish Rifles nor the 2nd could help the 1st Irish Rifles take Hill 41. Lieutenant Colonel Bridcutt was killed organising a fourth attack with the help of the 1st Inniskillings but it too failed. It would take until the morning of 12 October to clear Hill 41.

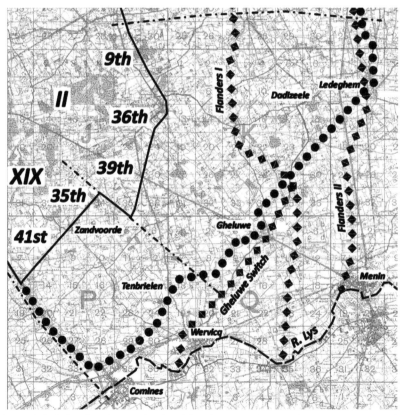

II Corps' left broke through the Flanders I Line and even penetrated the Flanders II Line by 3 October, but its right could not get through the Gheluwe Switch. XIX Corps had moved close to the River Lys.

29th Division, 29 September to 1 October, Menin Road

The attack on 29 September was delayed until 7 am but the artillery was still not ready, so Stoke mortars had to give support. The 1st Lancashire Fusiliers, 1st Dublin Fusiliers, 4th Worcesters and 2nd Leinsters then faced 'heavy machine-gun fire from the ridge across the Menin road'. The 2nd SWBs captured ground on the right but they then had to fall back under fire from America Cabaret. Major General Douglas Cayley's men spent 30 September driving rearguards out of farms and pillboxes in pouring rain. Then came 'the hardest day's fighting yet experienced in the new offensive' as they fought to establish a foothold in the Gheluwe Switch.

XIX Corps, 29 September to 2 October

35th Division, 29 September to 2 October, Zandvoorde to Wervicq

The 15th Cheshires advanced in the wrong direction in the mist at 8 am on 29 September and came under fire from Hollebeke chateau. Brigadier General Turner made Lieutenant Colonel Johnstone do an about turn but his men could not take Zandvoorde from the west. It was down to the 4th North Staffords and the 15th Sherwoods to clear the village during the afternoon. The two battalions then headed for Ten-Brielen, 'a maze of disused trenches and neglected wire', while the 17th Royal Scots covered their left flank.

The gunners could do little on 30 September due to the heavy rain and high winds, so the 18th HLI and 12th HLI were hit by heavy fire from Wervicq when they advanced at 6.15 am. The 17th Royal Scots reinforced the left flank where 29th Division had been delayed but the Highlanders could not hold on to the village, despite help from the 15th Cheshires.

Neither the 18th Lancashire Fusiliers nor the 19th Durhams could dislodge the Germans from America Cabaret so they had to spend two days clearing the Gheluwe Switch pillboxes instead. In four days, casualties and sickness had reduced 105 Brigade from 2,280 to 900 men and 106 Brigade from 2,050 to just 500.

41st Division, 29 September to 2 October, Comines Canal to the Gheluwe Switch

The 4 am advance on 29 September surprised the Germans and the 10th Queen's Own captured a battery of howitzers. Some of the 23rd Middlesex then crossed the canal to help the 10th Queen's clear the Houthem area. The Germans were withdrawing across the River Lys but the 26th Royal Fusiliers faced 'numerous small and fierce encounters' with rearguards along the north side of the Comines Canal on 30 September. They eventually entered the town, finding many buildings filled with abandoned stores.

Lieutenant General Herbert Watts wanted to help 29th Division, so Major General Lawford deployed 123 and 122 Brigades around Kruiseecke, ready to advance early on 1 October. Machine-gun fire from the Gheluwe Switch pinned down the 11th Queen's and 15th Hampshires when the mist cleared while orders to make a second attack arrived too late to be acted on. The Germans withdrew during the night and their rearguards were driven from their pillboxes the following morning.

X Corps, 29 September to 2 October

14th Division, 29 September, Damm Strasse to the Comines Canal

The withdrawal from the Messines Ridge meant that Major General Percy Skinner was able to push 42 and 43 Brigades to the Comines canal, around Hollebeke. The 34th Division then passed through their lines, en route to Houthem.

34th Division, 29 September, Wytschaete to the Comines Canal

The Germans abandoned Wytschaete during the night, so the 2nd Loyals occupied the ruins at dawn. Lieutenant Colonel Moir was then wounded leading the 1/7th Cheshires through Oosttaverne en route to the Comines Canal.

XV Corps, 29 September to 2 October

30th Division, 29 September to 1 October, Messines Ridge to the Comines Railway

The 2/17th London Regiment advanced through the mist at 3.40 am on 29 September and the 2/15th London Regiment joined in when they were in line. They both moved over Messines Ridge, 'fighting with dash and determination, still making steady progress but not a little disorganised.' There was no sign of any troops on the right flank, so Lieutenant Colonel Ogilvy deployed the 2/14th London Regiment south of the Douve. A line was taken up along the Comines railway but Lieutenant General De Lisle's orders to take Warneton did not reach Brigadier General Goodman in time to deploy 21 Brigade. The 2/14th London Regiment occupied the village the following morning. On 1 October the division's line was extended east along the railway as far as the northern outskirts of Comines.

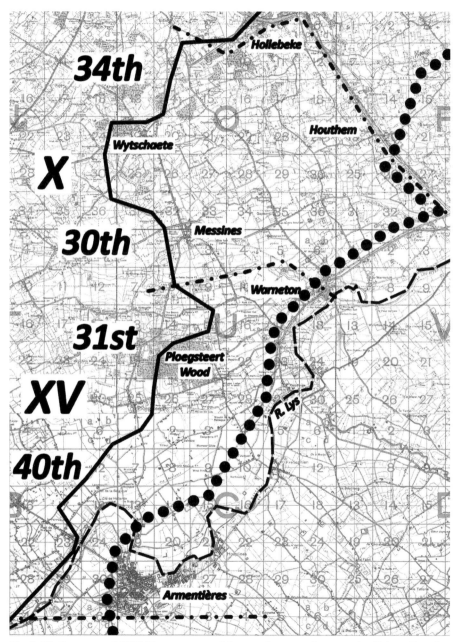

Both X Corps and XV Corps were able to advance close to the River Lys by 3 October.

31st Division, 29 September and 1 October, Advance to the Lys

The 15th West Yorkshires and 18th Durhams were supposed to advance towards Warneton on 29 September but they drifted north into 30th Division's area. The 10th and 11th East Yorkshires emerged from Ploegsteert Wood to find rearguards waiting along the Warnave stream, but the 11th reached the River Lys around La Basse Ville. The 12th Norfolks moved close to the Warnave stream the following day.

40th Division, 29 September to 1 October, Armentières

Major General William Peyton's men pushed closer to the large loop in the River Lys north of Armentières between 29 September and 1 October. No one dared to enter the abandoned town in case the Germans had booby trapped the buildings.

Chapter 6

An Orgy of Fighting and Killing

Fourth Army

29 September to 3 October

Fourth Army had spent two weeks clearing the old British trenches and it now faced the Hindenburg Main Line, where it ran parallel with the St Quentin Canal. Major General Charles Budworth had assembled 593 medium and heavy howitzers and they started targeting the Hindenburg Line at 10.30 pm on 26 September.

The artillery had been firing small quantities of captured mustard gas shells for months but 30,000 British ones had just been delivered to Fourth Army. 'It was thought that the Germans would be confused by this first use of their own implement against them.' High-explosive shells would be used once the ground had been soaked in gas. Budworth had also assembled 1,044 field guns but the crews were waiting for zero hour.

The Hindenburg Line had been built in secret over the winter of 1916-17 and then a rapid withdrawal was made from the Somme battlefield to the line of fortifications in March 1917. It had three lines of trenches studded with pillboxes, machine-gun posts and shelters, all protected by vast aprons of barbed wire. The Outpost Line would break up and delay an assault while the Support Line stopped the advance. The Reserve Line (later known as the Beaurevoir Line) would contain any breakthroughs.

The RAF had been busy photographing the Hindenburg Line so the artillery could locate targets while the infantry made their plans. An old plan of the German trenches had been captured some months before and, while modifications had been made, the basic layout remained the same. The trenches were 'zig-zagging across it, like sepia-coloured zebra stripes; thick, dark, wide lines, all wire, treble rows, and behind this deep lines of trenches, one mass of dug-outs as one knew, as hopeless looking a proposition as one was ever likely to see'.

General Rawlinson issued the order to attack on 22 September. It would start on 29 September, as the Germans sent their reserves north to counter First and Third Armies' attacks. III Corps would take Vendhuille on the St Quentin Canal while the Americans and Australians crossed the Bellicourt tunnel. IX Corps had to cross the St Quentin Canal around Bellenglise. Attempts to empty the canal by shelling an embankment had failed, so plans were afoot for how to get across. Troops started assembling on the night of 23 September, and while steps were taken to hide all movements and hide everything under camouflage, the Germans knew an attack by Fourth Army against the Bellicourt tunnel was imminent; the question was when?

The American II Corps had just joined Fourth Army and both divisions were double the size of a British division. As one observer note, 'they were full of beans but lacked experience.' A composite Australian and American Corps was formed under Lieutenant General Monash and Major General George Read. Major General Edward Lewis's 27th Division relieved III Corps' right in front of the Bellicourt tunnel while Major General John O'Ryan's 30th Division relieved the Australian Corps' left opposite Bellicourt village.

Late on 26 September, Rawlinson reported that Fourth Army was ready to attack. The Hindenburg Outpost Line had been taken and all three of his corps had secured good jumping off positions. The RAF had been photographing the Hindenburg Line for some time and the gunners had ground observers all along the line. The artillery started hitting targets in earnest at 10.30 pm on 26 September. Rawlinson's plan was to attack along a 10 mile front at dawn on 29 September.

Meanwhile Ludendorff was unhappy that Fourth Army had been able to take the Hindenburg Outpost Line and he had blamed General Georg von der Marwitz. The reverse on 18 September was the final straw and Marwitz was relieved of his command of the Second German Army.

III Corps, 29 September to 2 October

Lieutenant General Richard Butler was to clear the ground around Vendhuille once the Americans had taken the Hindenburg Outpost Line.

12th Division, 27 to 30 September, Vendhuille

The 27th American Division had taken the Knoll, south-west of Vendhuille, on 27 September but Major General Harold Higginson's men had been unable to capture Lark Post or the nearby quarry. Early on 29 September Lieutenant Colonel Dawson's 6th Queen's Own captured Swallow and Catelet Trenches while Lieutenant Colonel Smeltzer's 6th Buffs could clear the quarry. The Germans fell back during the night, so the Queen's Own and Buffs moved up to the west bank of the St Quentin Canal.

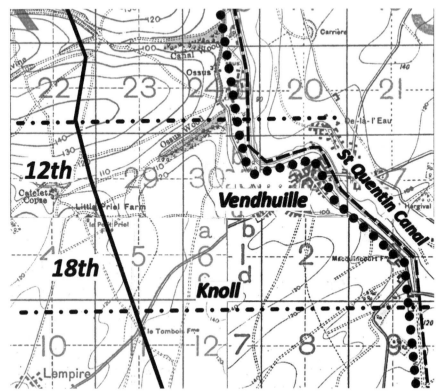

III Corps inched towards the St Quentin Canal around Vendhuille.

18th Division, 29 September to 1 October, Vendhuille

The 11th Royal Fusiliers and 6th Northants advanced from the American sector at 5.40 am to capture Macquincourt Trench. But Lieutenant Colonel Turner's men had become mixed up with the American troops in the mist so they were unable to get closer to Vendhuille. Brigadier General Wood had to tell the 7th Queen's to just reinforce the line because machine-gun fire was sweeping Macquincourt valley. The division's senior staff officer, Colonel Blewitt, organised a defensive flank where the Americans should have been, and the 7th Buffs would reinforce it later on. The 8th East Surreys and 7th Buffs would enter the ruins of Vendhuille the following morning. The division was relieved late on 1 October.

II American Corps, 29 September

Six weeks of hard fighting had left the Australian Corps short of men while the no-conscription policy in Australia meant there were no replacements.

Lieutenant General John Monash asked 'for the loan of two strong divisions' so he could break the Hindenburg Line around the Bellicourt tunnel and Major General George Read's II American Corps had been offered. Sixty American tanks would help the 27th and 30th American Divisions take the first objective and then the 5th and 3rd Australian Divisions would pass over the tunnel around Bony and Bellicourt. The American divisions could then fan out to widen the break in the Hindenburg Line.

Monash planned a prolonged barrage by over 800 guns and howitzers to smash the wire and lower German morale. Zero was set for 5.20 am but 27th Division had to advance an hour earlier to get in line with 30th Division. The addition of the two American divisions was welcomed; each was twice the strength of a British division and the soldiers were fresh, fit and strong. They were inexperienced but Monash had seen them in action at Hamel back in July, where their performance had been 'eminently satisfactory'. But they faced 'five or six successive trenches, the main ones 10 feet wide and 7 or 8 feet deep, with concrete blockhouses and tunnelled dugouts, the open ground between being crossed by belts of dense wire.'

The Bellicourt tunnel was the ultimate dugout and it was believed that the 'Germans had moored barges inside as barracks and had excavated many stairways to it from Bellicourt and the area around. It was expected that considerable forces might shelter inside the tunnel and try to emerge after the Americans had passed.' It meant the Americans had to find and guard every stairway.

There was, however, a complication because the Outpost Line still had to be taken in front of the tunnel. On 25 September, Monash asked if he could change the starting line, but it was too late, there would have to be a preliminary operation. Haig wanted to save the Americans for the main attack but Rawlinson insisted on using them. It meant the main attack was being planned on the assumption the start line would be captured during a preliminary operation.

27th American Division, 27 September, preliminary attack towards Bellicourt Tunnel

Colonel Taylor's 106th Regiment was covering a 2-mile-wide sector and he was concerned that so many of his officers were away on training courses. Major General John O'Ryan asked for support but Monash refused because he was saving the Australians for the main attack.

Eight tanks accompanied the advance through thick mist at 5.30 am but an eagerness to avoid the counter-barrage meant the waves ended up too close together. The Americans could not hold the Knoll nor capture Gillemont Farm or Quennel Copse. All the tanks had been knocked out apart from the ones which never caught up with the right hand battalion. Sergeant Reidar Waaler was awarded the Medal of Honor for rescuing two men from a burning tank under fire.

The shortage of officers and the poor visibility meant inadequate steps were taken to search for dugouts. Lieutenant William Turner was injured three times as he led his men across four lines of trenches. He silenced three machine-gun teams en route, but was killed during a counter-attack on his objective. Turner was posthumously awarded the Medal of Honor.

As the mist cleared they came under fire from 'enemy detachments which had come out from cover after the attacking waves had passed over or which had been fed into such positions aided by covered ways'. Casualties were high while the survivors were pinned down with few leaders and little ammunition.

27th American Division, 29 September, Knoll, Gillemont Farm and Quennel Wood

The incomplete success meant that zero hour was moved forward an hour, to 4.50 am, while the barrage had to start 1,000 yards into no man's land to avoid hitting the American soldiers. The premature advance would put all the Germans in the area on standby. The forty-five Mark V tanks of Major Harrison's 301st Tank Battalion had been allocated to support 108th and 107th Infantry Regiments, but many would be hit as they negotiated the Hindenburg trenches. Sergeants Alan Eggers and John Latham and Corporal Thomas O'Shea were sheltering in a shell hole when they heard shouts for help from a disabled tank in 107th Regiment's area. They rescued three crew members before turning one of the tank's machine guns on the enemy to keep them at bay. All three were awarded the Medal of Honor.

Machine-gun fire swept Colonel Hutchinson's 107th Regiment as it advanced across the Knoll. Private Michael Valente silenced two machine guns pinning down his comrades before rounding up sixteen prisoners. He would be awarded the Medal of Honor.

The barrage landed so far ahead that Colonel Jennings's 108th Regiment were soon pinned down. Many dugouts were missed due to the fog during 'an orgy of fighting and killing' around Gillemont Farm. Private Frank Gaffney single-handedly silenced one machine-gun team and then rounded up eighty prisoners hiding in nearby dugouts. His one-man crusade meant the Americans could reach the Hindenburg Support Line at Bony. Gaffney would be awarded the Medal of Honor.

30th American Division, 29 September, Bellicourt

Thirty-three tanks accompanied Major General Edward Lewis's men as they cleared the Hindenburg Line in front of Bellicourt. Sergeant Joseph Adkison charged a machine gun nest, kicking the weapon into the trench before taking the crew prisoner. He was awarded the Medal of Honor. Sergeant Milo Lemert silenced another three machine-gun teams during the advance but was killed as he charged a fourth. He was posthumously awarded the Medal of Honor.

The advance was going well until the mixture of fog and smoke 'made it impossible to see more than six yards'. Colonel Metts' 119th Regiment cleared the first line of trenches but the left flank came under fire from the north and some had to turn to face the threat. Half the armoured cars and Whippets which drove up the Bony road were knocked out as the mist cleared, so the rest withdrew. The right flank reached the Hindenburg Support trenches east of Bellicourt but heavy casualties and the need to cover the exposed left flank had stretched the Americans too thin. General Lewis had to send a battalion each from the 117th and 118th Infantry Regiments to reinforce the front line.

Colonel Minor's 120th Regiment crossed the Hindenburg Main Line around the south end of the tunnel trapping many prisoners inside the tunnel. 'The road from Bellicourt to Hargicourt was practically filled with them during the entire day' and German officers were saying 'all is lost; there is nothing between you and the Rhine.' However, elsewhere, the Americans again failed to spot the dugouts in the mist and were again pinned down when the mist cleared. The tanks were then picked off one by one; only eighteen would rally.

Australian Corps, 29 September

The 3rd and 5th Australian Divisions had left their assembly places at dawn and were unaware of the problems the Americans were having as they marched towards the front line.

3rd Australian Division, 29 September, The Knoll, Gillemont Farm and Quennel Copse

On the left, eight tanks were disabled when they drove into an old British minefield. The 40th and 38th Battalions then came under fire from Gillemont

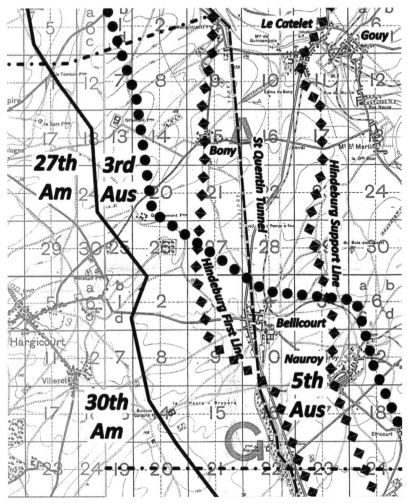

The failure to clear the first objective during the preliminary attack on 29 September left the Australians struggling to clear the trenches around the St Quentin canal tunnel.

Farm, which was supposed to have been taken by the Americans. Another eight tanks were hit accompanying 41st and 44th Battalions towards Malakoff Wood. Brigadier General Goddard's 9 Brigade was sent into 3rd Australian Division's area to outflank the Germans. After 59th Battalion became mixed up with Lieutenant Colonel Clark's 44th Battalion, Lieutenant Colonel Scanlan veered east through chaotic scenes en route to Bellicourt. 'Many lay dead or wounded among the yellow half-trampled wheat. Small parties, clearly Americans, were seen ahead.'

It was clear that there were many Germans amongst the Australians as the mist cleared. Even so, Lieutenant Colonels Lord and Henderson decided to push on with 40th and 38th Battalions while Captain Fairweather led his men along Dog Trench towards Gillemont Farm. Captains Ruddock and Findlay eventually secured the Knoll on the left while the 39th Battalion helped 40th and 38th Battalions hold on. Again there was chaos as the Americans they came across admitted 'they did not know what had happened except that they had failed: they had lost their way in the smoke, were without officers, did not know what to do and were anxious to find anyone who could tell them.'

Hobbs instructed Brigadier Generals Jess and Rankin to try again at 3 pm but there could be no artillery support because of the many Americans up ahead. This time 44th Battalion and part of 41st captured Quennemont Farm while Captain Longmore and the rest of 44th Battalion joined 59th along the line of the tunnel north of Bellicourt. But the situation was desperate because the Australians had been split into two groups and 'the bodies of many Americans lay around. The wire sparkled where bullets hit. The men sank into shell holes.'

5th Australian Division, 29 September, Bellicourt and Nauroy

Major General John Gellibrand had to stop the advance towards Bellicourt because of the heavy fire from the Hindenburg Main Line. So Brigadier General Elliott's men reorganised and made a second attempt in thick mist. The 59th Battalion cleared the trenches east of Malakoff Wood but both 58th and 57th Battalions found 'it was impossible to see more than a few yards. But the troops closed up in file, each able to tap the back of the man ahead.' The officers worked hard to keep moving, encountering groups of Americans and Germans en route, but they eventually reached the tunnel embankment.

Major General Gellibrand wanted Brigadier General Elliott to renew the advance at 3 pm while Brigadier General Tivey reinforced his right flank with 8 Brigade. A barrage was arranged but it was so weak that it did nothing more than alert the Germans. Four tanks were hit as Lieutenant Colonel Derham's 29th Battalion encountered a 'tank fort' north of Nauroy. The infantry cleared the area but it was too dangerous to go any further, so they waited for 32nd Battalion to enter the village from the south.

Major Blair Wark had guided a tank crew to silence two German machine guns shooting at the rest of 32nd Battalion. He then rallied 200 leaderless Americans gathered at a tunnel entrance before commandeering several tanks to help them. His new command then followed the east bank of the St Quentin Canal towards the Riqueval bridge where he captured a battery of field guns and fifty prisoners. Wark was awarded the Victoria Cross for capturing part of the Hindenburg Support Line.

IX Corps, 29 September

46th Division, 29 September, Crossing the St Quentin Canal at Bellenglise

Major General Boyd's men faced St Quentin Canal, which was filled with 'stagnant, fetid water, uninviting for an early morning dip'. They had to run down an open slope, clamber down the canal wall, cross the 10 metre wide waterway and then climb the other side under fire from machine-gun posts at Riqueval bridge and Bellenglise. The Staffordshire men then had to negotiate the wire and trenches of the Hindenburg Line on the far bank. Brigadier General Campbell's 137 Brigade had been chosen to make the assault and they practised crossing the Somme in Fourth Army's rear area the day before.

The barrage began at 5.50 am and, 'though fired without registration, it was described as one of the finest ever seen', even if the men could see little more than flashes through the smoke and mist. One party of the 1/6th North Staffords rushed the machine-gun post covering Riqueval bridge preventing the demolition party from blowing it up. Captain Charlton's company then crossed, taking 130 prisoners.

The rest of the 1/6th North Staffords and some of the 1/5th South Staffords were wearing life belts and they jumped in the water and paddled across. The rest of the 1/5th South Staffords and the 1/6th South Staffords crossed north of Bellenglise, where shallow water covered thick mud. Some paddled across on rafts while others ran across a plank bridge left by the Germans. Plenty of lifelines were installed and while some were hauled across on rafts, the rest 'swarmed up the farther wall and took the German trenches on the far bank'. The engineers then launched piers made of petrol tins and cork slabs to make it easier to cross.

After reorganising in the sunken road east of the canal, some continued up the slope while others attacked Bellenglise. There they heard that 800 men were hiding from the bombardment inside Bellenglise tunnel, 'a veritable trap', so they were rounded up and sent to the rear. They discovered there were plans to demolish the tunnel so tunnellers were ordered up to disarm the charges.

The mist and smoke meant observers could see nothing and the first good news was given to 46th Division's staff by a wounded sergeant who was heading for a dressing station. Major General Boyd ordered 138 and 139 Brigades to cross the canal at once and he was so optimistic he asked IX Corps to send a cavalry brigade forward.

Brigadier General Rowley's men crossed Riqueval bridge and found themselves having to help the Americans clear their area. It made the 1/4th Leicesters late and the mist had cleared by the time the attack on Magny-la-Fosse was made. Four tanks helped the 1/5th Lincolns surround the ruins but two had been hit by the time the 1/5th Leicesters advanced towards the Beaurevoir Line.

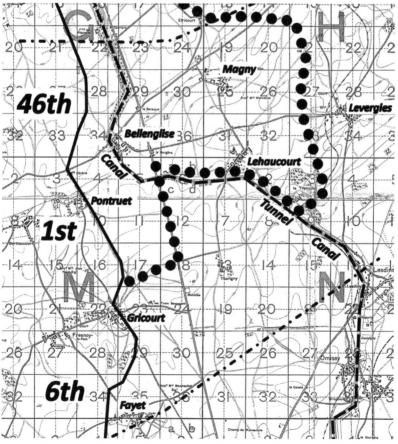

As 46th Division dashed across the St Quentin Canal and the Hindenburg Line beyond, 1st Division had a tougher time clearing the area south of Bellenglise.

Meanwhile Brigadier General Harington's men had crossed the canal at Bellenglise and deployed facing Lehaucourt. The 8th Sherwoods advanced at 11.20 am only to see their four tanks knocked out by a battery of field guns. The 1/6th Sherwoods were next but they were hit by machine-gun fire coming across the canal, where 1st Division had been delayed. Lieutenant Colonel Bernard Vann ran forward to rally his men, so they pressed home the attack. He would be killed on 3 October and was posthumously awarded the Victoria Cross. A few 6th Sherwoods recrossed the canal to silence the machine guns, so their comrades could clear the Hindenburg Support Line and reach Lehaucourt. The 5th Sherwoods were then able to advance towards Flèche Wood.

Major General Boyd's men had taken 4,200 prisoners while their own casualties were less than 800. 'The whole operation was characterised by the freedom with which the enemy troops surrendered.'

32nd Division, 29 September, Hindenburg Support Line

Major General Thomas Lambert had set up his headquarters alongside 46th Division's, so he could coordinate his orders with Major General Boyd. His men marched towards the St Quentin Canal at dusk and Brigadier General Minshull-Ford's men crossed the Riqueval bridge while Brigadier General Evans used Bellenglise bridge. Three tanks were knocked out as the 2nd KOYLIs and 10th Argylls were pinned down in front of Levergies. The 1st Dorsets captured 400 prisoners in the Hindenburg Support Line while the 15th HLI rounded up another 300 Germans around Le Tronquoy and Flèche Wood.

1st Division, 29 September, Pontruet

Major General Peter Strickland's men were to clear the east bank of the St Quentin Canal. The 1st Loyals fought their way to the canal at Bellenglise while the 1st Black Watch and 1st SWBs took 300 prisoners in 'the maze of trenches' east of Pontruet. Captains Cheney and Merrick led the 1st Gloucesters onto the high ground around Sycamore Wood only to come under enfilade fire from the right where there was no attack.

6th Division, 29 September, Gricourt and Fayet

Major General Thomas Marden's men tried to draw the attention of the Germans around Gricourt and Fayet.

29 September Summary

The attack on the Hindenburg Line had only been a partial success. The 46th Division had taken a staggering 4,200 prisoners and 72 guns around Bellenglise and Magny-la-Fosse. However, the mistake of making Americans carry out a preliminary attack on 27 September had caused many problems for the Australians in front of Bony; they had only taken 900 prisoners and eighteen guns. Most of the Hindenburg Outpost Line had been cleared but a large part of the Hindenburg Support Line was still in German hands.

Australian Corps, 30 September to 2 October

3rd Australian Division, 30 September to 2 October, Bony

Major General Gellibrand's men were to carry out a flank attack at 6 am but it got off to an inauspicious start. All the infantry and eleven out of eighteen tanks were late, the Australian barrage was 'very weak, a desultory gun fire', but the German artillery and machine guns around Bony were blazing away.

Both the 38th Battalion and 34th Battalion discovered that the Germans had abandoned the Hindenburg Outpost Line when they advanced at dawn. In the centre the tanks explored Bony and then returned to find that 44th Battalion had still not assembled. The Germans were ready for the Australians when they finally advanced and they could get nowhere.

For the third day in a row the Australians were going to try to reach the Hindenburg Support Line. Again artillery support was limited because of the large number of Americans out in no man's land, while poor weather meant that the RAF observers could neither locate the enemy nor drop food parcels to the stranded men. The 37th, 39th and 38th Battalions cleared the Hindenburg Support Line and the tunnel mound north of Bony. Fortunately the Germans had had enough and were withdrawing.

5th Australian Division, 30 September

Lieutenant Colonel Cheeseman's 53rd Battalion and a group of men gathered by Captain Loughman were also late on 30 September. They could not advance over the top because the barrage had moved on, so they bombed along the tunnel mound and the Hindenburg Support Line. The Germans exploited the gap between the two positions and were about to surround 55th Australian Battalion when Private John Ryan counter-charged. All the group were killed and Ryan would be posthumously awarded the Victoria Cross. Neither 57th nor 29th Battalion could make any progress east of

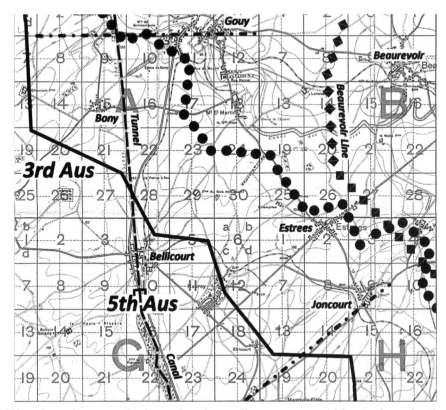

The Americans and then the Australians were unable to breach the Hindenburg Line around Bony. But they had reached the Beaurevoir Line between Estrées and Joncourt by 1 October.

Nauroy when they attacked at 4 pm but 32nd Battalion advanced over half a mile towards Joncourt.

Mist prevented the contact planes from locating the front line, so it made it difficult to provide adequate artillery cover for the dawn attack on 1 October. Ten Whippets led the advance and while 57th and 58th Battalions secured Folemprise Farm and Mint Copse, 54th and 56th Battalions cleared Estrées and Mill Ridge.

Again the Germans were soon withdrawing. As soon as he heard, Brigadier General Elliott told his battalion commanders, 'Damn it! If you can do it, do it now!' They pushed beyond the summit of the ridge overlooking the Beaurevoir Line but came under intense artillery and machine-gun fire. As they withdrew to a safe distance, 30th and 31st Battalions cleared Mill Ridge while 32nd sent patrols into an abandoned Joncourt.

IX Corps, 30 September to 2 October

1st Division, 30 September and 1 October, Le Tronquoy

The 1st Camerons and 1st Loyals took over the north bank of the St Quentin canal as far east as Le Tronquoy while 1st Black Watch crossed the tunnel and cleared the south end of the village. Two tanks later accompanied the 1st SWBs as they rounded up 300 prisoners between Talana Hill and Thorigny, finding that the 'enemy's opposition lacked the determination of the previous day'.

32nd Division, 30 September, Levergies

Major General Thomas Lambert's men attacked the Beaurevoir Line beyond Levergies at 8 am on 30 September. Captain Townend was seriously wounded leading the 15th Lancashire Fusiliers while three Whippets were knocked out around Joncourt. A second attempt by Lieutenant Colonel Alban's men and five Whippets also failed but the Germans decided to withdraw soon afterwards.

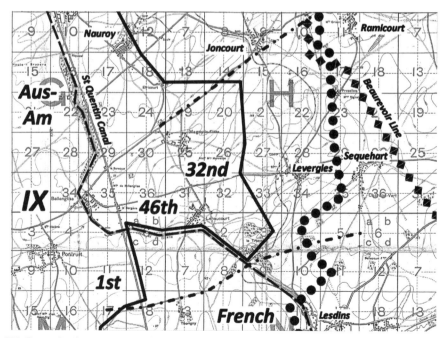

IX Corps' advance towards the Beaurevoir Line was hampered by the lack of progress by the French on its right flank.

Both the 2nd KOYLIs and 10th Argylls were pinned down north of Levergies because the 1st Dorsets had failed to capture the village. A 'crash barrage' at dusk convinced the 400-strong garrison to surrender. The 15th HLI cleared Le Tronquoy tunnel on the right flank while eight Whippets waited in vain for the French to cross the canal at Lesdins.

32nd Division, 1 and 2 October, Ramicourt and Sequehart

Major Mandleburg discovered that Joncourt had been abandoned early on 1 October, so the 15th Lancashire Fusiliers were able to support the Australian attack to their left. Major General Lambert organised a coordinated attack with the 5th Australian Division against the Beaurevoir Line for 4 pm. Three tanks were knocked out crawling through the wire east of Joncourt but the five survivors helped the 2nd Manchesters round up over 200 prisoners in trenches beyond.

A squadron of the 20th Hussars was sent forward, but machine-gun fire from Ramicourt stopped it going any further than the infantry. The 1/5th Border Regiment then entered the trenches next to the Manchesters while the 5/6th Royal Scots took around 150 prisoners in Sequehart. They were both driven out by counter-attacks.

Both the 16th Lancashire Fusiliers and 10th Argylls failed to capitalise on their foothold in the Beaurevoir Line and they were unable to reach Ramicourt on 2 October. The 5/6th Royal Scots again suffered many casualties trying to secure Sequehart, so Major General Lambert asked if the French could cross the canal at Lesdins.

Fourth Army Summary

Rawlinson had issued orders to get close to the Hindenburg Reserve Line (also known as the Beaurevoir Line) on 1 October because he wanted to let the Cavalry Corps loose. Haig visited Fourth Army headquarters the following day to hear that it was doing all it could. Rawlinson had asked General Debeney to help, to no avail, so Haig had to speak to Foch instead. Their attack on 3 October would fail but the Germans retired to the St Quentin Canal during the night.

Chapter 7

The Reception Accorded
the Troops was Historic

Fifth Army

5 to 23 October

The attacks to the north and south made General Ferdinand von Quast nervous and the German Sixth Army was preparing to pull back to the Haute Deule Canal. General William Birdwood's artillery started shelling the German positions astride the La Bassée canal on 28 September and his infantry had been raiding the trenches. It was only a matter of time before the withdrawal began.

XI Corps, 2 to 4 October

61st Division, 2 October, Fleurbaix to Bois Grenier

The 2/8th Worcesters and 2/4th Berkshires advanced slowly through the old trenches and bunkers around Fleurbaix and Bois Grenier.

59th Division, 2 to 4 October, Picantin to Ennetières

The 13th Duke's took over the line south of Bois Grenier and advanced east. Major General Nevill Smyth VC (awarded for bravery during the battle of Omdurman, 1898) then added 61st Division's sector to his own. The 25th King's, then the 26th Welsh Fusiliers and finally the 17th Sussex 'followed the slow and deliberate retirement of the enemy' towards Wez Macquart over the next two days. Meanwhile the 2/6th Durhams and then the 11th Somersets had moved through Radinghem before the 15th Essex advanced to Erquinghem-le-Sec.

47th Division, 3 October, east of the Aubers Ridge

The Londoners advanced through the abandoned Fromelles Line on 3 October until the 18th London Regiment was stopped by fire from the railway around Ennetières and Erquinghem-le-Sec. The following day 19th London Regiment reached the embankment while the 22nd London

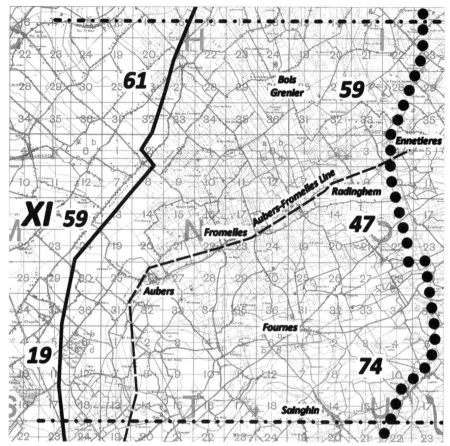

XI Corps followed up the German withdrawal beyond the Aubers–Fromelles Line on 2 October.

Regiment seized Beaucamp. Further operations were called off because General Birdwood had no intention of attacking such a strong position.

19th Division, 1 and 2 October, Aubers and Illies

The German gunners fired all their surplus ammunition before withdrawing and then the 8th North Staffords and 9th Welsh Fusiliers 'discovered that the enemy had gone' from the Aubers–Fromelles Line.

74th Division, 3 October, Sainghin

The 10th Buffs took over from part of 19th Division's line and moved through Sainghin to the flooded Haute Deule Canal on 3 October.

I Corps, 1 to 14 October

55th Division, 1 to 14 October, La Bassée to the Haute Deule Canal

The 4th Loyals cleared the outposts from the north bank of the La Bassée canal on 1 October. The 2/5th Lancashire Fusiliers and the 4th King's Own bombed their way into La Bassée the following day. The 10th King's struggled to clear Marquillies while the 6th King's had an easier time getting to Hantay on 3 October, but again the Haute Deule Canal had been flooded; 'our troops found the marshy country impassable; the water being eight feet deep in places.'

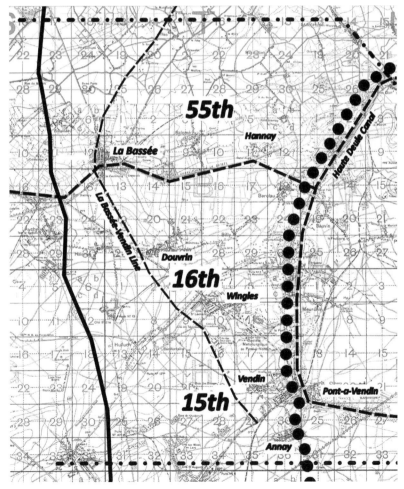

I Corps cleared rearguards from the La Bassée–Vendin Line to reach the Haute Deule Canal by 3 October.

16th Division, 2 to 4 October, Auchy-la-Bassée to the Haute Deule Canal

Major General Archibald Ritchie's men advanced from Auchy-la-Bassée on 2 October, only to find the Germans had abandoned the fortifications protecting Douvrin. They advanced through the village the following day, coming under fire from Beauvin, beyond the flooded Haute Deule Canal.

15th Division, 2 to 3 October Hulluch to the Haute Deule Canal

A prisoner reported that the Germans had withdrawn late on 1 October, so the 4/5th Black Watch, 8th Seaforths and 1/8th Argylls advanced to the Vendin-La Bassée position. The 13th Royal Scots relieved the Argylls during the night and the three battalions then drove the outposts back to the Haute Deule Canal.

East of the Haute Deule Canal, 14 to 31 October

Fifth Army spent nearly two weeks along a 15-mile-wide sector, waiting for the next withdrawal. Poor weather hampered flying but enough planes got off the ground to spot that Sixth Army was heading east on the morning of 15 October. General William Birdwood ordered his corps commanders to follow up across the flooded fields, aware that his left flank faced the ancient forts surrounding Lille. The town was full of civilians, so the gunners could only target the surrounding roads to interfere with the withdrawal.

XI Corps, 14 October to 1 November

59th Division, 14 October to 1 November, advance past Lille to the Schelde Canal

Second Lieutenant James Johnson time and again stopped German attacks against the 36th Northumberland Fusiliers on 14 October. After six hours fighting he was ordered to withdraw from Wez Macquart but made sure everyone had escaped before carrying a wounded man to safety. He returned to rescue three more under fire and would be awarded the Victoria Cross.

Brigadier General Cope's men followed the German withdrawal past Fort Senarmont on 16 October. The 11th Scots Fusiliers 'received an enthusiastic welcome' in La Madelaine the following day and then bypassed the rest of Lille's old forts. The 176 Brigade crossed the Basse Deule stream north of the town in the early morning fog on 18 October while RAF spotters could see the column of German troops up ahead when the mist cleared.

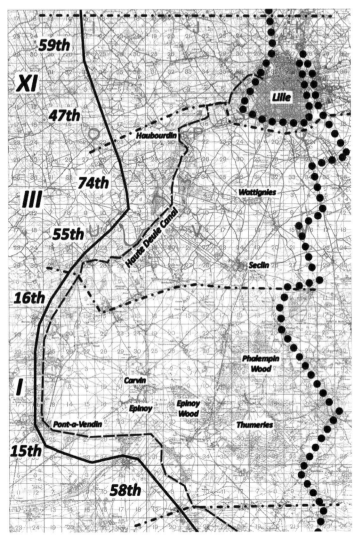

XI Corps entered Lille on 18 September while both III and I Corps followed up the German withdrawal from the Haute Deule Canal.

There were no encounters during the 4-mile advance towards Nechin and Templeuve on 19 October and German engineers blew up the only bridge across the Schelde Canal before it could be taken. Several attempts to cross the mile-wide floods were made over the days that followed. Second Lieutenant Paton 'succeeded in getting a footbridge in position by means of a strong telephone wire' while others of the 11th Scots Fusiliers scrambled across the ruined Pont-à-Chin bridge. They then used the telephone line to pull a pontoon back and forth while 25th King's used a chain to pull themselves across at Esquelmes. The 2/4th Loyals and 2/5th King's Own crossed using rafts and a footbridge balanced on a line of barrels. But all three battalions discovered that the east bank was also flooded and they had to withdraw because they could not dig in. The King's eventually found that a loop of the original river formed an island, where they could establish a bridgehead north of Esquelmes.

47th Division, 16 October, west of Lille

The Londoners outflanked the 'tremendous earthwork, Fort d'Englos, one of the biggest forts that girdle Lille'.

57th Division, 17 to 22 October, Lille to the River Schelde

The 2/7th King's deployed machine guns along the Haute Deule Canal where it ran through the Canteleu suburb of Lille on 16 October. 'Patrols reported the enemy had gone and simultaneously civilians came in with the news that the Germans had evacuated that great city which had groaned under their rule for four long years.' The 2/6th King's found that all the bridges were down, so the 9th King's scrambled across the ruins of the main bridge and entered the old town. 'The reception accorded the troops was historic. The men were decorated with French and Belgian colours and flowers by the civilian population, who cheered and shouted in delight.' It turned out the Germans had fled after an orgy of destruction, but, for once, they had left a week's supply of food for the people. Prisoners were made to disarm any booby traps and the town was clear by dawn.

Lieutenant General Richard Haking made a formal entry into Lille on 18 October while his troops pushed east of the town. The 2/7th King's and 8th King's moved through Hellemes, Ascq and Tressins, on the Le Marque stream. The two battalions then followed the Germans through Blandain to Froyennes over the next two days, coming in sight of the River Schelde. The 2/6th King's replaced the 2/7th King's on 21 October but they could not reach the river and even came under fire from a convent flying a Red Cross flag. A German rearguard abandoned Froyennes during the night, so posts could be established close to the river bank.

III Corps, 16 to 22 October

74th Division, 16 to 22 October, Haute Deule Canal to the River Schelde

The 16th Devons and 14th Black Watch crossed damaged bridges and footbridges around Haubourdin early on 17 October and then advanced

from the Haute Deule Canal to the ancient walls of Lille. The 15th Suffolks
went as far as the Douai railway to the south-east. The occupation of the
town was left to 57th Division while the La Marque stream was crossed
around Austaing on 18 October. There was a rapid advance through Baisieux
and Camphin the following day but it stopped around Marquain on the
20th. Prisoners reported that the Germans planned to hold high ground
overlooking the River Schelde while they took everything of value from

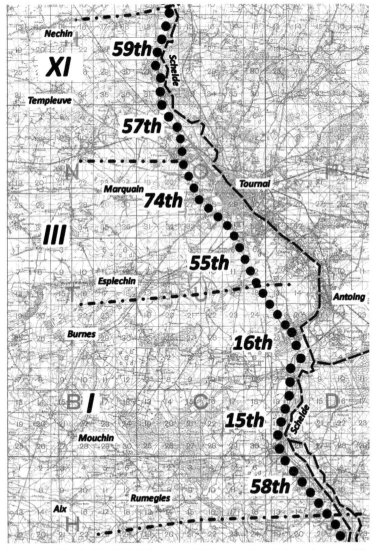

Fifth Army reached the Schelde around Tournai and Antoing on 20 and 21
October, finding it flooded and the bridges down.

Tournai. After two days hard fighting, the 14th Black Watch still could not get close to the town.

55th Division, 16 to 22 October, Haute Deule Canal to the River Schelde

The 1/6th King's crossed the Haute Deule Canal at Don early on 16 October and then advanced to Gondecourt. Second Lieutenant Ferguson of the 2/5th Lancashire Fusiliers crossed near Warvin later that night, so the rest of Lieutenant Colonel Brighten's men could widen the bridgehead. They discovered the Germans were withdrawing, so the 1/6th King's crossed the Seclin canal and kept moving east on 17 October. The 5th and 7th King's cleared Bouvines and then used ladders to cross the La Marque stream the following night. The 4th King's Own cleared Fort Sainghin and Peronne before crossing the stream as soon as it was dark.

The Germans fell back 5 miles on 19 October and the villagers helped the engineers build a bridge so the artillery could follow the 4th Loyals. It was the turn of the 2/5th Lancashire Fusiliers next and they captured dozens of abandoned ammunition wagons near Froidmont. They then encountered the rearguards covering the west bank of the Schelde and neither the 1/5th South Lancashires nor the 4th Loyals could make any progress on 22 October.

I Corps, 16 to 22 October

16th Division, 16 October to 22 October, Annoeulin to Antoing

Lieutenant Colonel Cruickshank led the 9th Black Watch through the south part of Annoeulin on 16 October while the artillery smothered the north part with mustard gas. The Germans then fell back rapidly through Camphin and Phalempin to the Lille railway, covering 9 miles in two days. Bois de Tassonière was abandoned on 19 October and Taintignies was reached the following day but the rearguard holding Mont de la Justice, overlooking the Schelde, held on. Major General Ritchie cancelled an attack on Antoing on 21 October, after hearing that the Germans were already evacuating the village.

15th Division, 15 to 22 October, Haute Deule Canal to the Schelde Canal

The 9th Royal Scots established a bridgehead over the Haute Deule Canal at Pont à Vendin on 12 October. Three days later Major General Hamilton Reed VC's (awarded during the Boer War) men crossed, 'cheered by a light barrage, to find that the bird had flown'. Major Sutherland halted the 7/8th KOSBs east of Carvin while the 1/9th Royal Scots moved through Épinoy Wood. The 13th Royal Scots and 1/8th Argylls met little resistance as they advanced 18 miles over the next four days. They cleared rearguards from Flines Wood late on 20 October, only to find that the Schelde canal and river had been flooded south of Antoing. Patrols found that 'both were wide and deep and, to make matters worse, there was a strip of marshy ground intersected by wide ditches on the western bank.'

58th Division, 15 to 22 October, Haute Deule Canal to the Schelde Canal

Major General Frank Ramsay extended his sector as far south as Dourges. The 9th London crossed the Haute Deule Canal east of Courrières and cleared the Bois d'Harponlieu on 15 October. The 7th London continued the advance through Oignies to the Douai–Lille railway before the 8th London moved rapidly through Bois de l'Offlarde. The Londoners had covered 15 miles in just four days and the final stage of the advance was to clear the rearguards from Bois de Flines on 21 October.

The Schelde around Maude was flooded and 2/24th London were unable to cross a footbridge at Bléharies while the 2/2nd London Regiment struggled to paddle across with a barrel raft. A few men made it and reported that the far bank of the river was flooded. The rearguard in Fort de Maulde left late on 22 October and patrols crossed on rafts the following morning. The 9th London cleared Maulde while the 10th London entered the fort.

Chapter 8

Reorganise, Push On and Get the Objective

Fourth Army

3 to 19 October

Rawlinson issued orders to capture the Beaurevoir Line on 3 October. Prisoners believed there were few reserves left while all the civilians in the area were being evacuated. XIII Corps would form a defensive flank east of Vendhuille while the Australian Corps advanced towards Beaurevoir. IX Corps would expand its foothold in the Beaurevoir Line and push towards Montbréhain. The Cavalry Corps was on standby in case there was a breakthrough.

XIII Corps, 3 to 7 October

50th Division, 3 to 7 October, Le Catelet to Prospect Hill

The first attack against Le Catelet by the 13th Black Watch, 2nd Dublin Fusiliers and 4th KRRC failed, but a second bombardment convinced the Germans to abandon the village. Major Greville's 6th Inniskillings faced a tough battle to clear Gouy while Major Hoghton led the 1st KOYLIs across Prospect Hill. They had to withdraw from the forward slopes when the mist cleared while a counter-attack drove the 4th KRRC out of Le Catelet.

Major General Jackson had given Brigadier General Rollo two extra battalions to clear XIII Corps' left flank at 6 am. But the 2nd Dublin Fusiliers were unable to advance north-west of Le Catelet, forcing Lieutenant Colonel Nicholson to withdraw the 3rd Royal Fusiliers from the area north of the village. Lieutenant Colonel Tonson-Rye's 2nd Munsters cleared Gouy while the 7th Wiltshires advanced over Prospect Hill. Major Freeman's 2nd Northumberland Fusiliers then followed an old trench, 'for the most part by crawling on hands and knees', and took 250 prisoners. Major General Jackson threw in his third brigade during the evening. This time the 4th KRRC helped the Royal Fusiliers push north of Le Catelet while the 2nd Munsters advanced beyond Gouy with help from the 1st KOYLIs.

The 7th Wiltshires and Munsters were able to advance north from Prospect Hill the following afternoon because 25th Division had cleared the area north of Beaurevoir. The Germans pulled back to the Beaurevoir Line during the night and the 2nd Northumberland Fusiliers and 2nd Munsters moved close on 6 October. A few men entered the enemy positon to find 'the enemy trench was only twelve inches deep and under the fire of machine guns sited on the high ground to the east.' The 13th Black Watch and 2nd Dublin Fusiliers twice failed to increase their hold on the Beaurevoir Line the following day and it was down to the 1st KOYLIs to take it during the early hours of 8 October.

25th Division, 4 to 6 October, Beaurevoir

Brigadier General Hickie had taken over responsibility for the line facing Beaurevoir early on 4 October. But the artillery orders were late and the 9th Devons 'did not then know whether they were to attack', until ten minutes after the 6 am zero hour. The 20th Manchesters attacked Beaurevoir 'which was strong and well-sited and defended by numerous machine guns concealed in buildings and along the railway'. They then fought their way into Ponchaux but had to withdraw from their exposed position due to heavy losses.

The 11th Sherwoods captured nearly 200 prisoners around Guisancourt Farm early on 5 October, but were driven back when the mist cleared. Three tanks helped the 9th Green Howards advance north-west of Beaurevoir but they too fell back when the fog lifted, leaving Captain Blow isolated around Bellevue Farm. Five tanks silenced the machine guns in the village but they then had to withdraw because the 13th Durhams were pinned down. At the same time, the 20th Manchesters cleared the cemetery south-east of Beaurevoir.

Guisancourt Farm held out during a second attack at dusk but the 1/5th Gloucesters cleared the railway embankment west of Beaurevoir, taking the Germans holding the south side of the village by surprise. They then helped the 1/8th Worcesters clear the rest of the ruins.

The 8th Warwicks finally captured Guisancourt Farm before dawn on 6 October. At the same time the 11th Sherwoods and 13th Durhams cleared the area north of Beaurevoir before the 9th Green Howards took it over. Neither the 20th nor the 21st Manchesters could make any progress towards Ponchaux.

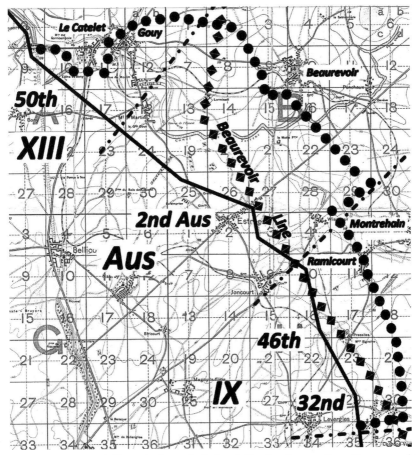

XIII Corps secured Fourth Army's left while the Australian Corps and IX Corps had broken through the Beaurevoir Line by 6 October.

Australian Corps, 3 to 7 October

2nd Australian Division, 3 to 5 October, Beaurevoir

Major General Charles Rosenthal's men had to cut the Beaurevoir Line wire by hand because the tanks were late. Three tanks joined the 25th and 27th Battalions as they crossed the Torrens stream and they fought through 'pill-boxes along and between the trenches'. It seemed the 'Germans must have had so many defeats that they must have given up in spirit as soon as our line started.' But one captured German officer had a different opinion: 'You Australians are all bluff. You attack with practically no men and are on top of us before we know where we are.'

The 28th Battalion headed for Prospect Hill while the 26th Battalion fought 'from blockhouse to blockhouse' and the slope was soon 'dotted with fleeing Germans and those who remained were captured'. A counter-attack from Beaurevoir drove 26th Battalion behind the Torrens stream, where it was joined by 28th Battalion.

Six Mark V tanks and eight Whippets came crawling past Estrées as the 19th and 18th Battalions cut through the wire. But five of the Whippets were knocked out in quick succession, so the rest of the tanks hung back as 19th Battalion cleared the support trench. The 18th Battalion needed a second bombardment to help it catch up and they took over 200 prisoners between them.

Lieutenant Joe Maxwell silenced two machine guns in front of 18th Australian Battalion but was captured. He pulled out a concealed revolver, shot two of his guards and led his group to safety before returning to capture the post; he would be awarded the Victoria Cross.

Tanks silenced the Germans holding the north end of Estrées and then Lewis gunners fired along the main road while the 20th and 17th Battalions pushed men forward on the flanks. Three of the tanks were hit during the advance but the Australians discovered that the trenches 'had merely been spit-locked a foot deep, except for short lengths beside the pill-boxes'. Major General Rosenthal wanted to keep pushing, so 24th, 22nd and 23rd Battalions advanced to the crest overlooking Beaurevoir at dusk, prompting a withdrawal in front of 26th and 28th Battalions. The Australians had captured 1,200 prisoners and 11 field guns around the Beaurevoir Line.

The 22nd and 23rd Battalions became disorientated in the fog while advancing north-west of Montbréhain early on 4 October but Lieutenant Colonel Wiltshire's order was typical: 'Reorganise, push on and get the objective.' The Australians could not capture Ponchaux but they could see across the German line when the mist cleared. 'All day German transport or guns were seen withdrawing but again the lack of direct communication from battalions to artillery caused many opportunities for shelling the movement to be missed.'

The II American Corps could not take over the line in time, so Major General Rosenthal was told to attack with the 2nd Australian Division at 6.5 am on 5 October. The artillery fired late, hitting 24th and 21st Battalions and four tanks were knocked out but seven more crawled around Montbréhain. Sergeant George Ingram silenced nine machine-gun teams and then Lieutenant Colonel James rallied enough of 24th Battalion to keep pushing past the north-west side of the village. Meanwhile Lieutenant

Colonel Duggan's men went through the south side while Lieutenant Colonel Annand's 2nd Pioneer Battalion covered the right where IX Corps was behind.

Ingram would be awarded the Victoria Cross for his part in what was the Australians' last battle of the Great War. A few hours later the Americans took over and Sergeant Edward Talley silenced a machine-gun post while securing his position in 117th Regiment's line before stopping another team moving forward to fire on his men. He was awarded the Medal of Honor.

IX Corps, 3 to 7 October

46th Division, 3 October, Beaurevoir Line

Five tanks helped the 8th Sherwoods and 5th Sherwoods clear the Beaurevoir Line before they made a pincer movement around Ramicourt. Sergeant William Johnson was wounded silencing the two machine-gun posts which had delayed the 5th Sherwoods' advance; he would be awarded the Victoria Cross. Lieutenant Colonel Vann of the 6th Sherwoods then made sure 400 prisoners were rounded up.

The 8th Sherwoods cleared Wiancourt on the left flank where the Australians were delayed, while six tanks helped the 6th Sherwoods clear several sunken roads; one even silenced a strongpoint bristling with sixteen machine guns. The field guns around Montbréhain hit all six tanks and Lieutenant Colonel Vann was one of the many casualties but his men eventually trapped 1,000 men in the ruins.

There were reports that the Germans were in full retreat after the fall of Montbréhain, so Major General Boyd asked for cavalry to advance towards Branscourt-le-Grand. Brigadier General Haig had moved his 5 Cavalry Brigade across the St Quentin Canal, as arranged, but the front had stabilised by the time he received the pursuit order.

Two tanks were hit crossing the Beaurevoir Line with the 6th South Staffords, so Captain Charlton's Lewis guns silenced two field guns and the surviving tank could follow Lieutenant Colonel Storey's men. The 5th South Staffords reached Mannequin Hill on the right, but it was under fire from Sequehart because 32nd Division had been delayed.

The 1/6th North Staffords were helping Storey's men reach the Sherwoods when a counter-attack hit Montbréhain. There was no way of contacting the artillery, so Brigadier General Harington ordered the Sherwoods to retire to Ramicourt. Lieutenant Colonel Evans was killed during a second counter-attack which drove the 5th South Staffords off

Mannequin Hill. Lance Corporal William Coltman would be awarded the Victoria Cross for rescuing many of the 1/6th South Staffords' wounded.

32nd Division, 4 October, Sequehart

A smoke screen covered the left flank while Brigadier General Tyler (the division's senior artillery officer) controlled a pincer attack against Sequehart early on 4 October. Two tanks led the 2nd KOYLIs south down the main street while another two led the 1st Dorsets' attack from the west. The 15th HLI helped them secure the village following a counter-attack. Tyler's men used some of the 200 German machine guns they had found to stop a second attack at dusk.

1st Division, 4 October, Sequehart

The 1st Loyals covered 32nd Division's right flank during the attack on Sequehart, driving off a counter-attack from Cerise Wood.

46th Division, 5 October, Mannequin Hill

Major General Boyd's men took over the line between Montbréhain and Sequehart on 5 October and they found the Germans along the ridge between Doon Hill and Mannequin Hill. The 1st Gloucesters managed to get onto Mannequin Hill but they could not hold the summit.

Fourth Army, 8 October

The 30th American Division took over the Montbréhain sector during the night. The Australian Corps had suffered over 25,000 casualties since 8 August but Monash's men could be proud of the fact that they had captured 22,850 prisoners and over 330 artillery pieces in just two months.

Fourth Army had taken over 14,500 prisoners breaking through the Beaurevoir Line, but it had taken longer and been more costly than expected. Haig had issued new orders to Generals Horne, Byng and Rawlinson late on 4 October, warning them that they would be fighting across countryside unscarred by war, seeing 'unfamiliar sight of towns and villages showing no trace of shell fire; fields without craters; woods not reduced to mere branchless stumps of trees'.

Haig and Foch discussed French newspaper reports of armistice requests made by Germany, Austria and Turkey on 8 October. Foch wanted to push the German armies behind the River Rhine before the meetings began and he was going to make his thoughts known. He sanctioned Haig's attack plans but was unable to give him another three American divisions because Pershing was refusing to hand over any.

Haig then met Horne, Byng and Rawlinson to discuss the next attack. Horne had to move First Army across the Schelde, outflanking the Germans facing Third Army's left. They were already unsteady in front of Third Army's right and Fourth Army, so Byng and Rawlinson were told to push towards the Selle stream. The RAF observers could see that the Hermann Line was incomplete but the Selle was swollen by heavy rain and damming.

XIII Corps, 8 to 10 October

50th Division, 8 October, South of Villers Outreaux

The 4th KRRC captured one hundred men around Marliches Farm but it had to withdraw because 38th Division had been unable to capture Villers Outreaux to the north. Two tanks helped the 2nd Dublin Fusiliers stop a counter-attack before they reoccupied the farm.

66th Division, 8 to 10 October, Serain to Le Cateau

Major General Keppel Bethell had spent the summer rebuilding his division with British, Irish and South African battalions. Third Army's early attack against the Beaurevoir Line had alerted the enemy, so 198 Brigade and the South African Brigade came under artillery and machine-gun fire as they marched towards Beaurevoir under a smoke screen created by phosphorus bombs dropped by the RAF.

Five heavy tanks accompanied the 5th Inniskillings and 6th Dublin Fusiliers to Villers Outreaux. Whippets led Lieutenant Colonel MacLeod's 4th South African Regiment and Major Sprenger's 2nd South African Regiment along sunken roads and into the Usigny ravine, where over 500 prisoners were taken.

The Inniskillings and Dublin Fusiliers continued the advance towards Serain while 199 Brigade took over from the South African Brigade. The 18th King's drew the attention of the Germans in Serain while the 9th Manchesters and 5th Connaughts made a pincer attack. It had been a tough battle in which most of the Whippets had been lost while only seven out of nineteen Mark V tanks rallied.

A mistimed barrage hit the 6th Lancashire Fusiliers as they advanced through the fog towards Élincourt early on 9 October. Lieutenant Colonel Gross had to reorganise his men so they could drive the rearguards out of

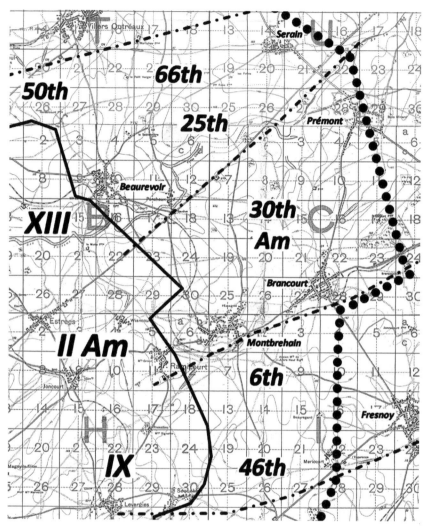

Fourth Army advanced 4 miles on 8 October, sparking a general retirement to the Selle stream.

Pinon Wood and Iris Copse but the 18th King's had no trouble clearing Maretz on the Le Cateau road.

Rawlinson thought the time had come to pursue the Germans and 3rd Cavalry Division was pushed through XIII Corps' line (see the cavalry account below). The South Africans followed and while Captain Tomlinson's company of the 4th South African Regiment cleared Bertry, the 2nd South African Regiment encountered rearguards in Gattigny Wood and Maurois. Lieutenant Colonel Jenkins's 1st South African Regiment eventually relieved the cavalry around Honnechy and Reumont, where 'they were received with enthusiasm by the French inhabitants'.

Major General Bethell's right had to advance first on 10 October, so it could catch up with the left flank. But the 18th King's advance onto the heights overlooking Cambrai alerted the Germans and they spotted the 6th King's advancing from Reumont in the half-light of dawn. The 6th Lancashire Fusiliers and 18th King's reached Montay, finding 'the banks of the Selle heavily wired'. The 5th Connaughts advanced through the north part of Le Cateau but they soon had to withdraw from the exposed position.

25th Division, 8 to 10 October, Along the Le Cateau Road

The 9th Devons advanced on a narrow front through Ponchaux while seven tanks helped the 20th Manchesters round up nearly 300 prisoners as they mopped up behind. The 21st Manchesters captured a similar number of men and a dozen field guns along the Le Cateau road. Brigadier General Hickie then spread his frontage to contact the Americans on his right flank.

The 1/5th Gloucesters and 1/8th Worcesters advanced along the Le Cateau road to Maretz early on 9 October. There was little resistance but 66th Division's artillery was firing short, driving the Gloucesters out of the village for a time. The 9th Green Howards and 11th Sherwoods came under fire from the railway cutting beyond Honnechy while the 6 Cavalry Brigade was stopped by wire fences.

'Intelligence reports indicated the enemy would probably make a stand on the Selle' and they were right. They were erecting wire entanglements and digging in on the far bank. The advance down to the stream started at 5.30 am on 10 October, but the 13th Durhams were pinned down as they approached St Benin. It forced the 1/8th Warwicks to halt their advance on St Souplet while Captain Rogers's 1/5th Gloucesters could get no further. A second barrage helped the 9th Green Howards enter St Benin, forcing the Germans to abandon St Souplet.

II American Corps, 8 to 10 October

30th American Division, 8 to 11 October, Montbréhain to St Souplet and Vaux Andigny

Major General Edward Lewis set zero hour for 59 Brigade at 5.10 am on 8 October. There was plenty of machine-gun fire but the 'the enemy's reply to the artillery bombardment was very weak and towards the end of the day almost absent.'

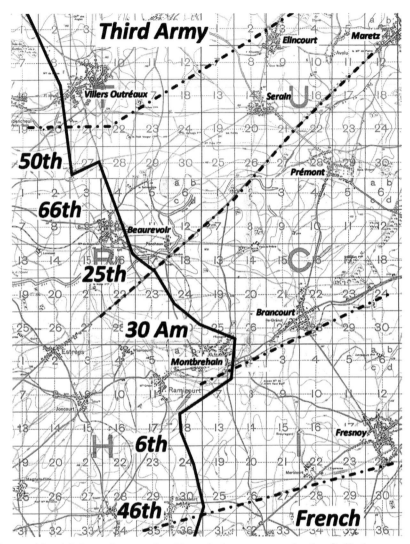

The rapid withdrawal opposite Fourth Army towards the Selle began on 9 October.

Around ten Mark V tanks supported the attack on Vaux le Prêtre Farm in which no less than five members of the 118th Regiment carried out deeds worthy of the Medal of Honor. A badly injured Lieutenant James Dozier silenced one machine-gun team, Sergeant Thomas Hall dealt with another with his bayonet, while Sergeant Richmond Hilton was seriously injured tackling a third. Both Sergeant Gary Evans and Corporal James Herriot were mortally wounded knocking out yet more machine-gun posts.

A similar number of tanks helped 117th Regiment reach Brancourt. Sixteen Whippets then fired into Prémont while infantry moved around the flanks; they took 1,500 prisoners and thirty artillery pieces. During the fighting, Sergeant James Karnes and Private John Ward decided they had 'had all they could take' of being pinned down, so they fixed bayonets and silenced the machine-gun team pouring enfilade fire into the flank of their company. They were both awarded the Medal of Honor. 'The enemy were reported to be in full retreat', but casualties had been high and less than half the tanks rallied.

It was the turn of 60 Brigade at 5.30 am 10 October. Colonel Metts's 119th Regiment cleared Escaufourt before heading down the slope to the Selle under enfilade fire from St Benin. St Souplet was cleared but the Americans could not cross the stream. Private Robert Blackwell volunteered to take an important message back despite the heavy fire but was killed en route. He was posthumously awarded the Medal of Honor.

Colonel Minor's 120th Regiment cleared the outposts around Vaux Andigny but they had to pull back to a safe distance due to fire from the far bank; they cleared the village the following day. Corporal John Villepigue's comrades were hit as they patrolled the area on 15 October but he carried on alone and had silenced a machine-gun team by the time his platoon had caught up. He was severely wounded later in the day but survived to receive the Medal of Honor.

Cavalry Corps, 8 to 10 October

All three cavalry divisions crossed the Canal du Nord and deployed along the Le Cateau road early on 8 October. During the afternoon, General Rawlinson warned Lieutenant General Charles Kavanagh to 'be prepared to take advantage of any break in the enemy's defence'.

1st and 2nd Cavalry Divisions, 8 and 9 October, Montbréhain

Major General Richard Mullens instructed Brigadier General Legard to push ahead of II American Corps' line to engage the Germans falling back to the Selle. It was difficult moving the three cavalry brigades forward along the busy roads and even harder to push squadrons through the infantry line between Ponchaux and Montbréhain. Only the 19th Hussars got through and they were stopped by machine-gun fire along the Le Cateau road. The only success came when a few troopers 'got among some field guns with the sword' near Brancourt.

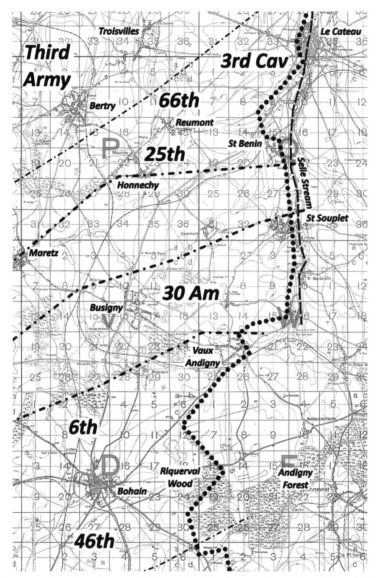

Cavalry were deployed several times in the hope of turning the withdrawal into a rout, but the Germans were able to dig in along the Selle between Le Cateau and St Souplet.

Brigadier General Haig had also been given orders to move through 6th Division's line south of Montbréhain. But neither the 2nd Dragoons nor the 20th Hussars could get to Brancourt; as one observer said, 'you cannot have a cavalry charge until you have captured the enemy's last machine gun.'

Lieutenant General Kavanagh had to report that his troopers had been unable to achieve much, so Rawlinson told him withdraw them. The cavalry had in fact snarled up the roads, delaying the advance rather than speeding it up. Hundreds of horsemen behind Fourth Army's lines also made a tempting target for German bombers. Despite the problems, Rawlinson wanted the cavalry to try again the following day. Brigadier General Haig again had to report that the 12th Lancers had been unable to get through 6th Division's line north of Sequehart.

3rd Cavalry Division, 9 to 10 October, Maretz to Le Cateau

Major General Anthony Harman was told to make a second attempt to disrupt the German retreat to the Selle. Nine armoured cars of 17th Armoured Car Battalion joined the cavalry as they advanced along the Le Cateau road past Maretz. Two helped Lord Strathcona's Horse and the Fort Garry Horse round up 230 prisoners in Gattigny Wood. However, 6 Cavalry Brigade had to be recalled because wire fencing blocked the route to Honnechy.

A second advance towards Le Cateau in the afternoon was more successful. Lord Strathcona's Horse and Royal Canadian Dragoons passed through Bertry and Troisville before sending patrols into Neuville and Montay along the Selle. The Fort Garry Horse moved onto the high ground west of Le Cateau.

Aircraft attacked the 1st and the 3rd Dragoon Guards as they moved through Honnechy south of the main road. The remaining armoured cars helped them drive the garrison back towards Le Cateau where they were intercepted by the Royal Dragoons.

Rearguards remained at Neuvilly, Montay and Le Cateau and so the Cavalry Corps withdrew during the night. The troopers had captured over 500 prisoners, 10 artillery pieces and 60 machine guns but they had suffered nearly 600 casualties, both in horses and men.

IX Corps, 8 to 16 October

6th Division, 8 October

Zero hour was set at 5.10 am on 8 October. The French planned to advance fifty minutes later, so Major General Thomas Marden decided to clear the ridge north of Méricourt before turning south into the Sequehart valley. The 139 Brigade (attached from 46th Division) would hold Sequehart in case the Germans tried to counter-attack out of the valley.

Three Whippets suppressed fire from Brancourt while the 9th Norfolks advanced steadily. Meanwhile the 2nd Sherwood Foresters captured nearly 700 prisoners and six field guns around Doon Hill. Lieutenant Colonel Meynell's 1st Shropshires captured many prisoners on Mannequin Hill before the 1st Buffs advanced to Beauregard in the centre. There were, however, many problems on the right flank where the 1st Monmouths (Pioneers) struggled to silence the machine guns covering the jumping off line. Two Whippets were knocked out helping the 1st West Yorkshires clear the area before zero hour and they were also under fire from their right flank where the French were supposed to be. The 2nd York and Lancasters were pinned down when they advanced into the Sequehart valley at 8.37 am because no one had told the artillery to fire the creeping barrage.

Marden had to make arrangements to enter the French sector under cover of a smoke screen at 1.20 pm to outflank the German position. This time the 1st West Yorkshires took 450 prisoners between Mannequin Wood and Cerise Wood, allowing the French to move up on 6th Division's right flank. The 2nd York and Lancasters could then enter Méricourt.

Early the following morning, the 9th Norfolks and 1st Leicesters found the Germans waiting along the railway west of Bohain. The Norfolks outflanked the village only to find it had been abandoned once the morning mist cleared. It was full of civilians and 'vast quantities of war materials but few prisoners'.

The 2nd Sherwoods and 1st Leicesters reached Riqueval Wood on 10 October. Two tanks helped the 9th Norfolks go further the following morning but the British gunners fired short, forcing them to withdraw.

46th Division, 9 to 16 October, Fresnoy-le-Grand to Riquerval Wood

Major General Boyd took over 6th Division's right late on 8 October and the dawn patrols discovered that the Germans had withdrawn from Méricourt. Captain Nichols's men moved through Fresnoy-le-Grand but the rest of the 5th Lincolns came under crossfire because the French were held up around Étaves Wood. There was no movement on 9 October because the artillery had to catch up.

The Lincolns were pinned down by fire coming from Riqueval Wood when they tried again early on 10 October. Dummy tanks and figures had been deployed to draw fire while a real tank helped the 6th North Staffords clear the west edge of Riqueval Wood. Cyclists found the main German line on the far side of the wood but repeated gas barrages made it unwise to occupy it.

Chapter 9

More Anxious to be Accepted as Prisoners than to Fight

Second Army

14 to 27 October

Foch had wanted the advance in Flanders to move as soon as possible but the roads were so bad that one man said, 'it's not the Army they are needing here but Admiral Beatty and the bloody Navy!' The Flanders Army Group was finally ready to attack on 14 October, giving the Germans time to plan their withdrawal to the Schelde. Second Army had cleared most of the Flanders I Line but it now faced the Flanders II Line. The creeping barrage started at 5.32 am and the infantry advanced three minutes later.

II Corps, 14 to 19 October

9th Division, 14 to 18 October, Ledeghem to Courtrai

The 2nd Scots Fusiliers and Newfoundland Regiment negotiated eight wire entanglements and then crossed the bridge over the Wulfdambeek stream. But Major King's Scots were pinned down in front of Laage Kepel Wood while the Newfoundlanders could not enter Bois de Heule. Time and again field gun teams cantered up, unhooked, and gave the infantry support. There was fierce fighting around Ledeghem and Private Tommy Ricketts ran back for ammunition when his Lewis gun section ran out. They were able to capture a battery of guns but neither the 5th Camerons nor the 8th Black Watch could break the deadlock. Ricketts would be awarded the Victoria Cross; he was just 17 years old, the youngest army recipient of the award in the war.

The 11th Royal Scots were pinned down on Hill 40 on 15 October until 19-year-old Corporal Roland Elcock silenced three machine guns with his Lewis gun. He too was awarded the Victoria Cross. Lieutenant Colonel Murray had led the 12th Royal Scots past Steenbeek and through Bois de Heule before the 11th Royal Scots moved up on the left. Cyclists and motorbikes mounting machine guns then pursued the Germans to the River Lys.

The artillery spent 16 October silencing the machine guns across the river but the 11th Royal Scots were unable to scramble over the demolished Harlebeke bridge. Lieutenant Colonel Ker's 6th KOSBs crossed a boat bridge at Cuerne but they were unable to clear Harlebeke. The 12th Royal Scots crossed during the night but the engineers had to build a barrel bridge after the original one was smashed by artillery fire. In the meantime, Major Diarmid swam across and organised his men into a human chain, standing waist deep in water on the bridge rubble, so they could pass ammunition forward. The Germans eventually withdrew from the river line south-west of Courtrai on 18 October, so Major General Tudor prepared to cross the Lys later that night.

29th Division, 14 to 19 October, Terhand Line to the River Lys

At 5.35 am on 14 October, the 2nd Royal Fusiliers went 'straight through' the Flanders II Line around Ledeghem while a company of the 1st Lancashire Fusiliers mopped up the village. But Lieutenant Colonel Moore was killed leading the 1st Dublin Fusiliers across the Heulebeek stream while the rest of the Lancashire Fusiliers were pinned down in front of Steenbeek.

The 2nd Leinsters advanced 'through mist, somewhat thickened unnecessarily by our smoke shell' into the Flanders II Line. Sergeant John O'Neill's men captured an artillery battery and two machine guns while Private Martin Moffat rushed through a hail of bullets to capture thirty men in a house. Both men were awarded the Victoria Cross. The Germans then started falling back towards the Lys with the 4th Worcesters and 2nd Hampshires in pursuit. They often found that men were 'more anxious to be accepted as prisoners than to fight' as they mopped up. Both the 2nd SWBs and 1st Border Regiment ran into their own barrage but the 1st KOSBs were able to push along the north bank of the Heulebeek stream to Cuerne.

Major Crawshaw's men crossed the Lys between Harlebeke and Courtrai during the night but the engineers had to keep repairing their bridges because of heavy shellfire. Planes dropped supplies to the 2nd Hampshires but Brigadier General Freyberg eventually had to admit defeat and he deployed Lewis gunners late on 18 October to cover Lieutenant Colonel Westmoreland's withdrawal. The Germans abandoned their positions when the divisions to the flanks crossed the Lys and four ferries carried the 2nd Hampshires across after dusk on 19 October.

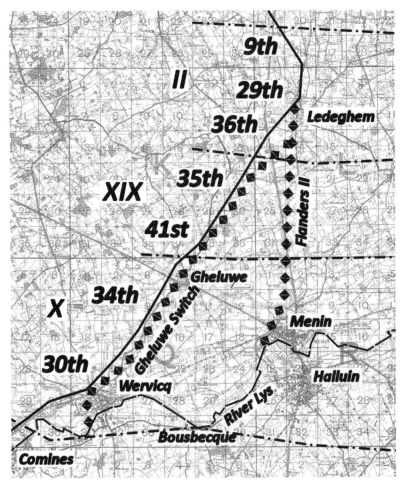

Second Army's left cleared both the Gheluwe Switch and the Flanders II Line on 14 October and could then advance astride the River Lys.

36th Division, 14 to 16 October, Moorslede to Courtrai

The 15th Irish Rifles had 'swept in with the bayonet' over Hill 41 and into Moorslede. The 1st Inniskillings then moved up on the left. The second stage of the advance along the Heulebeek stream was stopped in front of Gulleghem. The 2nd Inniskillings and 1st Irish Rifles continued the advance the following day and then the 9th Inniskillings took over en route to the railway line north of Courtrai. Lieutenant Adams had lived in Courtrai before the war so he was sent on a reconnaissance early on 16 October. He reported that the Germans had withdrawn, so the barrage was stopped and the 12th Irish Rifles marched into the town here they were met by 'scenes of great enthusiasm among the citizens, who came forth into the streets from their cellars'.

A smoke screen covered two pontoons full of troops on the river and they 'leapt ashore exultantly and drove the Germans from the bank. They had had scarce a casualty.' The engineers rigged up a footway across the damaged bridge but artillery fire soon brought it down and the Irishmen had to be withdrawn. Lieutenant General Sir Claud Jacob had decided to outflank the town to avoid civilian casualties.

XIX Corps, 14 to 19 October

35th Division, 14 October, Gheluwe Switch to the River Lys

Lieutenant Colonel Jones was mortally wounded leading the 17th Lancashire Fusiliers through the Gheluwe Switch around Kezelberg. The 15th Sherwoods and then the 18th Lancashire Fusiliers advanced through Moorseele. Meanwhile Lieutenant Colonel Johnstone's 15th Cheshires cleared the rest of the Gheluwe Switch, so the 19th Durhams and 18th Lancashire Fusiliers could head for Wevelghem.

The 36th Division finally caught up on the left on 15 October, so the 19th Durhams and 18th Lancashire Fusiliers could advance from Poeselhoek toward Heule. The 15th Sherwoods and the 4th North Staffords were soon pinned down but they managed to send patrols into Wevelghem during the night. The British artillery had often struggled to keep up with the infantry but the German gunners had paid dearly for staying forward with theirs; seventy-seven guns had been lost in just two days.

The 12th and 18th HLI advanced through Wevelghem early on 16 October, coming under heavy fire from the far side of the Lys. The river banks were open and flat so the men spent the day collecting building material. Heavy fire stopped the engineers launching their two bridges late on 17 October but Lieutenant Stranack managed to build a plank bridge between two sunken barges so the 18th HLI could cross. Lieutenant Inroan's patrol of 17th Royal Scots then found that Marcke was full of civilians, so an attack was postponed.

The 19th Durhams, 18th Lancashire Fusiliers and 17th Lancashire Fusiliers cleared the area south of Courtrai early on 19 October. The Durhams' patrols were 'the first British troops to enter the town and they received an ovation from the inhabitants. Coffee was freely offered to the men; it was all they had to offer.'

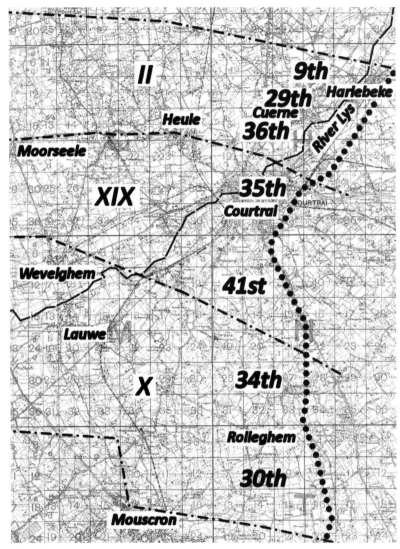

XIX Corps and X Corps continued to follow up the German withdrawal south of Courtrai and then II Corps crossed the Lys north of the town on 19 October.

41st Division, 14 to 19 October, Terhand Line to the River Lys

The 12th East Surreys, 15th Hampshires and 12th KRRC fought their way through the Terhand Line and Flanders II Line on 14 October. 'The men by now knew how pillboxes should be tackled and did not let themselves be held up.' The 20th Durhams then followed up the Germans as they fell back to the Lys around Wevelghem. The 23rd Middlesex and 11th Queen's crossed the river on boats on 19 October, finding the Germans had withdrawn from the east bank.

X Corps, 14 to 19 October

Lieutenant General Reginald Stephens faced the Terhand Line on his left and the Gheluwe Line on his right. Zero hour had been set for 5.25 am. Troops had to move along congested roads 'in full view of the enemy's positions but fortunately the Hun was fully occupied'. The 'only line of supply was along a plank road, unfit for lorries' and it had soon been smashed.

34th Division, 14 to 16 October, Gheluwe to Menin

The 1/5th KOSBs and 8th Scottish Rifles advanced along the north side of the Reutelbeek stream while the 1/4th Cheshires and 1/7th Cheshires followed the south bank. They followed a smoke and thermite barrage 'reminiscent of a London fog' through Gheluwe and the Flanders I Line, sometimes 'advancing holding each other by the belt'. The 1/5th Argylls broke through the Flanders II Line but a counter-attack from Menin drove Lieutenant Colonel Drage's 1/4th Cheshires back.

German rearguards kept patrols at bay while others removed or burnt supplies before withdrawing through Menin and across the Lys during the night. Second Lieutenant Thomson's patrol of the Argylls reached the damaged Marathon Bridge while Lieutenant Montague led a patrol of the 1/4th Cheshires through the deserted town. The 1/5th Argylls and 1/1st Herefords crossed the river and checked out Halluin returning before dawn. Meanwhile Thomson's men had made a bridge out of barges so the 1/8th Scottish Rifles could cross.

On 16 October, the 1/4th Sussex cleared the west bank of the Lys ready for the Argylls and Scottish Rifles. At the same time, the 2nd Loyals crossed 'one man at a time, on an improvised ferry raft'. The Germans retired again on 18 October, so Lauwe was cleared and it was 'the first town we had entered which was still inhabited. The enemy was in full retreat and the crowds of liberated civilians were met on all sides.' The 2/4th Queen's spotted the Tricolour flying from Reckem church tower the following morning so they occupied it.

30th Division, 14 to 16 October, crossing the Lys at Wervicq

The 7th Irish Regiment and 2/23rd London Regiment cleared the Switch Line south of Gheluwe, finding the main German line along the Menin–Comines railway. Meanwhile the 2/14th and 2/15th London Regiments fought their way through the same defensive line to reach the Lys.

The 6th Cheshire crossed the river west of Wervicq late on 15 October while the 2/15th London Regiment crossed a damaged bridge early the following morning. They both spread out to form a bridgehead at Bousbecque where a loop in the river formed an island. There was a shortage of building material, so the engineers tied duckboards to a line of rafts and the men crossed in single file to secured the area east of Wervicq.

XV Corps, 14 to 19 October

14th Division, 14 to 19 October, Comines to Dottignies

The engineers bridged the River Lys at Bas Warneton, where an old curve in the river formed an island, on 14 October. The 29th Durhams crossed and discovered that the Germans had abandoned Comines. Engineers then built bridges either side of the town so the 29th Durhams and 33rd London could cross to the east and west respectively. A rearguard held the switch trench north of Linselles until late on 17 October and then the 20th Middlesex and 10th HLI moved past the north side of an abandoned Tourcoing. The advance was along the railway around Mouscron until nightfall. The advance continued to an abandoned Dottignies on the 20th.

31st Division, 15 to 19 October, crossing the Lys around Warneton to Tourcoing

A few of the 10th East Yorkshires paddled across the Lys before dawn on 15 October after hearing Comines had been evacuated. A rearguard stopped others crossing south of Warneton until late in the afternoon but others got over at Deulemont. The 11th East Yorkshires then secured the bridgehead so the rest of the division could cross.

The Germans had left during the night, so the two East Yorkshire battalions 'advanced in company columns preceded by cyclist screens' over the next two days, halting in front of Tourcoing. An RAF spotter plane flew over, looking for signs of life during the afternoon, and while it saw little movement, the fact that no one had shot at it was encouraging. The 11th East Lancashires were greeted by 'enthusiastic demonstrations of gratitude from the freed inhabitants' early on 18 October. Rearguards came under fire from Herseaux and Wattrelos during the afternoon and again around Toufflers the following day but the Germans were anxious to get across the River Schelde.

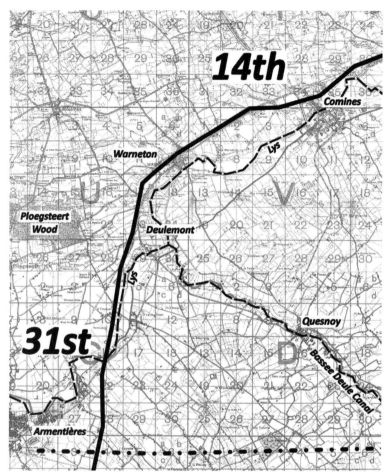

XV Corps crossed the Lys between Comines and Armentières on 15 October and joined Second Army's pursuit east.

40th Division, 15 to 18 October, Houplines on the River Lys to Roubaix

Rearguards kept the 8th Royal Irish at bay, and the 23rd Lancashire Fusiliers 'tried to gain touch with the Germans, who were then withdrawing rapidly' on 16 October. The Lancashire Fusiliers crossed the La Basse Deule stream by abandoned footbridges during the night, but the Wambrechies canal bridge had been blown up: 'The troops had to get down to water level by stepladders, cross on rafts and clamber up the steep bank on the other side, encouraged by crowds of cheering children who lined the towpath.' Engineers then had to build a footbridge across the Roubaix Canal because the water was too shallow to float their pontoons. The Lancashire Fusiliers

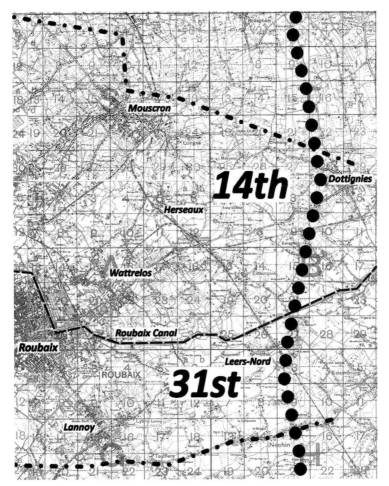

XV Corps had caught up between Second Army's left and Fifth Army by 19 October.

continued through the southern outskirts of Roubaix, reaching Lannoy on the Lille railway.

Second Army's Advance Continues

Prisoners reported the Germans planned to flood the Schelde valley and dig in on higher ground beyond. X Corps had reached the canal on the right flank but II Corps and XIX Corps were struggling on the left and in the centre. Plumer would have liked to have kept pushing but bridges had to be built over the Lys so his heavy artillery could move forward. Lieutenant

Generals Watts and Jacob were told to wait until XIX and II Corps were ready to continue the advance on 25 October.

II Corps, 19 to 31 October

36th Division, 19 to 27 October, crossing the Lys north of Harlebeke

Lieutenant Brunyate's patrol forced the Germans to abandon the east bank early on 19 October, so the engineers could build a footbridge. The 9th Inniskillings started crossing as soon as it was dark, some by the bridge and some by pontoons. The 1st Inniskilling Fusiliers used a second temporary bridge to get across and the two battalions discovered the Germans were falling back. The 15th and 1st Irish Rifles followed and they advanced south-east.

The 12th Irish Rifles cleared Dries the following day but they then had to form a defensive flank because the French were held up. It was 'the custom to lop the lower branches off the trees' so the machine gunners could see long distances and the 1st Irish Rifles and 1st Inniskillings came under fire as they advanced north-east of Deerlyck. They could not ask the artillery for help because the engineers were struggling to find material to bridge the Lys canal.

On 22 October, the 15th Irish Rifles had to extend the defensive flank even further, leaving Lieutenant Colonel Belcher's 2nd Irish Rifles to fight for the objective. The 1st Irish Fusiliers reached Heinweg the following day but they still had to extend their left flank back over 2 miles to stay in contact with the French. The 2nd Irish Rifles captured a lost German messenger carrying orders to retire, so 107 Brigade headed for the Schelde. A squadron of French dragoons made 'a spirited dash' for the Berchem bridge, but were driven back by machine-gun fire from the far bank.

The 12th Irish Rifles, 2nd Inniskillings and 1st Inniskillings encountered 'the most determined opposition' on the low ridge north of Ingoyghem during the morning of 25 October. 'Repeatedly the men charged houses defended by machine guns and bayoneted the detachments.' But the Irish Rifles had to pull back to Heinweg after hearing the French had not moved again. Major General Coffin wanted to try again but the Inniskillings' orders were late so they missed the barrage and were pinned down. Nineteen-year-old Private Norman Harvey silenced three machine-gun posts so the 1st Inniskillings could get moving again; he was awarded the Victoria Cross.

There was little movement on 27 October until a civilian reported that the Germans were retiring towards the Schelde. So Major General Coffin

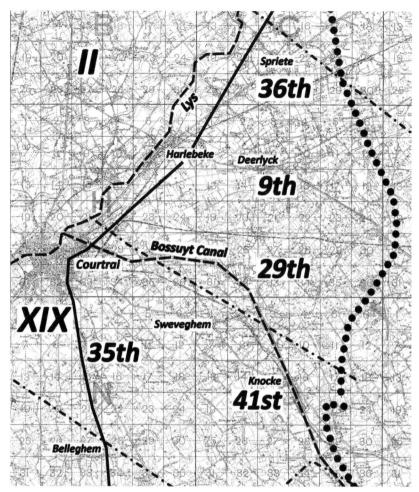

Once across the Lys, Second Army continued to push east rapidly, starting on 20 October.

ordered Brigadier Generals Vaughan and Hessey to push patrols forward north of Tieghem.

34th Division, 31 October, Anseghem and Tieghem

Major General Lothian Nicholson had taken over Second Army's left but the RAF could not fly due to the bad weather, prisoners knew nothing, and patrols could not get across the Schelde. 'Tanks and infantry were mutually pleased with each other' as they advanced through the early morning mist between Anseghem and Tieghem. But 'the wily Boche machine gunners remained silent until the tanks had gone away and then became troublesome.'

The 1/8th Scottish Rifles came under enfilade fire while Captain Nuttall's liaison squad of the 2/4th Queen's reported that the French were held up. Meanwhile the 1/5th KOSBs had a straightforward advance to their objective. The Germans fell back across the Schelde that night and 34th Division handed over the line to the French.

9th Division, 20 and 26 October, River Lys to Ooteghem

Late on 20 October, the 2nd Scots Fusiliers and 9th Scottish Rifles filed over a bridge made of duckboards and barrels while the 5th Camerons used boats and rafts to cross the Lys. A bridgehead was established at Harlebeke and Cuerne by the early hours and then motorcycles mounting machine guns accompanied the 1/1st Green Howards cyclists through Deerlyck. Major King was wounded leading the 2nd Scots Fusiliers into Vichte while the Newfoundland Battalion captured the station to the south-east. A counterattack overwhelmed Captain Glass's Scots Fusiliers and while some 'broke through the German cordon after dark, others sheltered in cellars with the Belgian civilians'.

Major General Tudor had to stand fast on 21 October because the failure of the French to advance to the north had left 36th Division lagging behind. A mixture of German gas and British smoke allowed Lieutenant Colonel Ker's 11th Royal Scots to sneak into Vichte the following day and the Scots Fusiliers came out of hiding. Captain Andrews then galloped ahead to reconnoitre Hill 50 but the 6th KOSBs' advance was stopped by fire from Ingoyghem and the 8th Black Watch had to cover their right flank.

The advance restarted at 9 am on 25 October and the 9th Scots Rifles and 2nd Scots Fusiliers soon reported they had reached their objective. But the 7th Seaforth and 5th Camerons said they were unable to make progress because 'every farm was a centre of resistance and furious conflicts were being waged behind the objective. But they persisted and the high ground around Ingoyghem was eventually cleared by dusk. The Germans fell back across the Schelde during the night and while Major General Tudor's 'men were keen to follow up their victory, they had now reached the limit of their physical endurance'. Ooteghem was occupied and patrols reached the canal but battalions were too weak to do any more, so the division was withdrawn from the line. It would not be engaged again.

31st Division, 27 October

The 11th East Yorkshires and 11th East Lancashires had fought their way onto the high ground around Avelghem by nightfall. The Germans retired across the Schelde late on 30 October and Sergeant Thomas Caldwell led a Lewis gun section of the 12th Scots Fusiliers against the rearguard covering the Rugge bridge. He was awarded the Victoria Cross for rounding up seventy prisoners.

29th Division, 20 to 22 October, River Lys to the River Schelde

The 2nd Hampshires went 'forging ahead over rather difficult country, seamed with small streams and dotted with farms and cottages surrounded by hedges and gardens'. Most of the Germans 'could be seen retiring in disorder' but a few decided to fight. Sergeant John O'Neill silenced a machine-gun position pinning the 2nd Leinsters down; he was awarded the Victoria Cross. Major Rigg was wounded leading the 1st Dublin Fusiliers alongside the Bossuyt Canal towards St Louis. At the same time the 2nd Royal Fusiliers made a flank attack through Banhout Wood and 'they fired from the hip with good results' as they advanced.

The orders to attack at 9 am on 22 October arrived late and then the enemy artillery hit the assembly area. So the 1st KOSBs and 1st Border

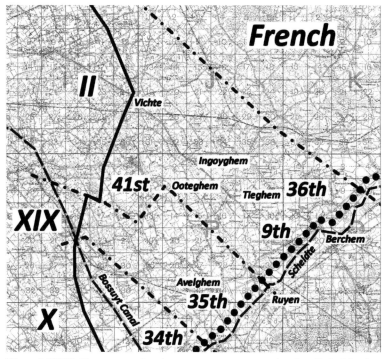

Both II and XIX Corps made slow progress towards the Schelde but they had reached the river by 27 October.

Regiment missed the barrage and had to follow ditches and hedges to get to their objective. Lieutenant David McGregor's machine guns were mounted on a limber and he made the driver gallop forward so he could direct fire onto an enemy position. The Germans soon spotted McGregor and he was killed; he would be posthumously awarded the Victoria Cross.

XIX Corps, 20 to 31 October

35th Division, 20 October, South-east of Courtrai

The 4th South Staffords, 15th Sherwoods and 15th Cheshires reached Sweveghem while the 19th Durhams, 18th Lancashire Fusiliers and 17th Lancashire Fusiliers got close to Beekstraat. Major General Marindin decided to outflank the Courtrai Switch but the heavy rain meant it was dark before the 12th HLI could advance. They cleared the line by dawn only to find the Germans were preparing to hold the Bossuyt Canal opposite the division's left flank.

41st Division, 21 to 26 October, Bossuyt Canal to the Schelde Canal

On 21 October, the 18th KRRC crossed the Bossuyt Canal at Pont Levis No 2 while the 15th Hampshires scrambled over a demolished bridge at Knokke. The 12th East Surrey and 10th Queen's faced considerable resistance around the canal tunnel but the 26th Royal Fusiliers and 20th Durhams managed to get beyond it.

Major General Sydney Lawford had planned to give his men a rest on 26 October but civilians told Brigadier General Kemp-Welch that the Germans had left, so the 20th Durhams occupied Avelghem. The 12th East Surreys, 15th Hampshires and 11th Queen's Own then moved close to the river between Rugge and Avelghem. The rest of the division moved up on the flanks to find a single temporary bridge near Autryve still standing.

35th Division, 27 to 31 October, River Schelde

Major General Marindin's men took over the line around Rugge and Avelghem on 27 October to find rearguards waiting along the west bank of the Schelde. Sergeant Sweeney of the 17th Lancashire Fusiliers risked dressing as a civilian so he could locate the machine gun positions for the artillery. It also helped that the machine gunners were using tracer ammunition, making it easy to spot their positions. On 31 October, the 18th and 17th Lancashire Fusiliers and the 19th Durhams carried out their 'finest achievement of the war' as they helped the French reach the Schelde. 'An almost unique amount of artillery' covered the 3 mile advance as Germans were 'blasted off the bank of the river'.

X Corps, 20 to 26 October

30th Division, 20 and 21 October, advance to the Schelde around Helchin

The 1/6th Cheshires were unable to clear the rearguards from the Courtrai Switch where it crossed the St Genois spur while the 2/14th London Regiment was pinned down in front of the railway near Coyghem. But the Londoners could move closer to the Schelde during the night, while the Cheshires advanced towards Bossuyt the following morning. Rearguards stopped the 2nd South Lancashires entering Helchin and then the German engineers blew up the bridge before escaping on rafts.

41st Division, 22 to 26 October, Bossuyt Canal towards Ooteghem and Avelghem

Brigadier General Weston faced several problems before the 9.30 am zero hour. A counter-attack threatened to overrun part of the 18th KRRC while the 15th Hampshires were driven back from their deployment line. Weston wanted a postponement but Major General Sydney Stopford told him to attack at all costs. He then heard that the 12th East Surreys were pinned down, so the Hampshires had to cover their sector. The KRRC and Hampshires eventually crossed the Bossuyt Canal but machine-gun fire from the south tunnel entrance stopped them. A second attempt to reach Hoogmolen in the afternoon also failed, despite help from the 10th Queen's.

The 23rd Middlesex tried in vain to clear Hoogmolen ridge but it took until 25 October to reach Herstert. Artillery and machine-gun fire then raked the 26th Royal Fusiliers but the 20th Durhams advanced south of Ooteghem. Lieutenant Colonel Robinson was one of the many casualties as the Royal Fusiliers dug in for the night.

34th Division, 24 October, Schelde Canal at Bossuyt

A preliminary attack by Captain Flunder's 1/7th Cheshires crossed the Schelde canal at Bossuyt but they failed to secure Lock 4. Major Morris's men then advanced along the east bank of the Courtrai canal, passing through Moen en route to the Schelde. The 1/1st Herefords covered Autryve on the left flank while a smoke barrage hid the engineers as they bridged the three locks for the 1/4th Cheshires.

XV Corps, 20 to 29 October

14th Division, 20 to 29 October, Dottignies to the Schelde around Warcoing

The Germans had abandoned Courtrai Switch so the 12th Suffolks advanced astride the Espierres Canal to the River Schelde north of Warcoing on 20 October. The 16th Manchesters crossed the river close to the mouth of Espierres Canal late on 29 October.

31st Division, 20 October

There was a rapid advance along the south bank of the Espierres Canal to Warcoing on the Schelde canal.

Summary

On 24 October, Haig asked Foch if he could have Second Army back so he could coordinate the crossing of the Schelde with the rest of the BEF. Foch refused because he wanted the King of the Belgians to command the allied troops which liberated Brussels. Haig referred the matter to London only to be told to ask the Ambassador to France, Edward Stanley, Earl of Derby. He in turn put the request to Prime Minister Georges Clemenceau who agreed that Second Army would be returned to Haig as soon as it reached the Schelde. It did so on 4 November and Plumer was told he had to cross the river a few days later.

The Hindenburg Line's trenches and entanglements zig-zag across the landscape.

Machine-gun teams were the backbone of the German defence until the ammunition ran out.

A Mark V tank carries a crib forward to the deployment area, so it can bridge a stream.

Men of 46th Division cross the St Quentin Canal near Bellenglise.

Lines of men snake across the landscape as the reserves move up to exploit the early successes.

Prisoners help to evacuate the wounded from the battlefield.

Australian soldiers search for documents, weapons and valuables, otherwise known as contraband.

A column of prisoners heads to the prison cage unescorted.

The pursuit was often delayed by demolished bridges, cratered roads and flooded waterways.

Time and again, the civilians helped the engineers clear away wreckage so they could bridge the many rivers and canals.

The people of Lille turn out to meet the soldiers of 57th Division.

Children who had known nothing but hunger and deprivation for most of their short lives welcome their liberators.

Tricolours hang from windows as the crowds gather to hear an army band play the national anthems.

An artist's impression of the Allied representatives reading the armistice terms to the German delegation.

Smiles all round as news of the Armistice sinks in. Soon these men will be able to go back home to their families.

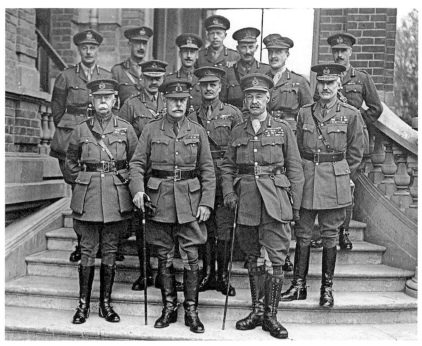

Field Marshal Haig with his army commanders and their chiefs of staff on 11 November.

Chapter 10

A Most Enthusiastic Reception

First Army

8 to 29 October

Third Army advanced past the south side of the town early on 8 October, so the Canadian Corps prepared to attack the angle between the Sensée and the Schelde at 1.30 am the following morning. As hoped for, the Germans began withdrawing towards the Selle stream opposite First Army's left flank.

I Corps, 10 to 13 October

58th Division, 10 to 13 October, Lens to the Haute Deule Canal

The Germans evacuated Loison and Noyelles early on 10 October and the 2/2nd, 3rd and 2/24th London Regiments advanced astride the Lens canal spur the following morning. Annay Switch was abandoned during the night, so the Londoners could reach Harnes Fosses by dawn on 12 October. The 9th, 2/10th and 12th London Regiments then discovered that Annay had also been evacuated, but the Germans stopped them crossing the Haute Deule Canal. The 7th London cleared Courrières on 13 October and the 2/22nd London Regiment crossed the waterway two days later.

VIII Corps, 8 to 16 October

12th Division, 8 to 16 October, advance to the Haute-Deule Line, east of Lens

Major General Harold Higginson took over the Acheville sector early on 8 October and his patrols soon discovered the Germans were withdrawing. The 6th Queen's and 6th Buffs advanced beyond Avion while the 7th Sussex and 9th Royal Fusiliers moved close to Méricourt. The 1/1st Cambridgeshire Regiment and the 7th Norfolks cleared Acheville Trench.

On 9 October, the 6th Queen's and the 6th Buffs advanced towards Sàllaumines while the 7th Sussex and 9th Royal Fusiliers moved close to the

German defences around Rouvroy. The 1/1st Cambridgeshire Regiment and 7th Norfolks moved up on their right. They occupied the Rouvroy–Fresnes Line around Rouvroy the following morning but the Germans in Noyelles held out until evening.

Early on 10 October, the 6th Queen's and 6th Queen's Own entered Billy Montigny and Noyelles. Captain Duff stopped a counter-attack, so the 9th Royal Fusiliers could hold on to Rouvroy while the 7th Norfolks cleared Drocourt. Patrols later discovered that the Drocourt–Quéant Line had been evacuated so the 6th Queen's and 9th Royal Fusiliers advanced to Fouquières.

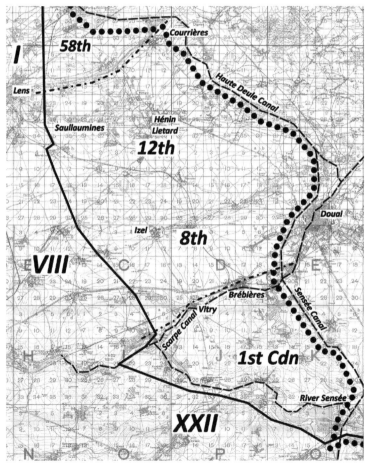

VIII Corps reached the Haute Deule Canal between Courrières and Douai on 13 October while XXII Corps was along the Sensée Canal on the right flank the following day.

The Germans fell back to the Haute Deule Canal during the night and the 9th Essex encountered a rearguard in Courrières early on 12 October. The 1/1st Cambridgeshire Regiment also came under fire from houses surrounded by floods but Lieutenant Ellard guided the 9th Royal Fusiliers through Noyelles Godault as Sergeant Baum led the 9th Essex into Courcelles. The 5th Berkshires cleared Dourges and Cité Bruno while the 9th Essex cleared Courcelles the following day. Company Sergeant Major then took his men into Auby on 14 October.

8th Division, 8 to 13 October, Fresnoy to Douai on the Scarpe

On 8 October, the 1st Worcesters and 1st Sherwoods pushed through Neuvireuil while the 2nd Devons and 2nd East Lancashires made a pincer attack against Fresnoy. The following day they all moved closer to the Rouvroy–Fresnes Line. Floods made it difficult to get the artillery forward, so only the 2nd Middlesex and 2nd Devons advanced to the Scarpe early on 11 October. Lieutenant Colonel Baker sent two platoons of the Middlesex across the canal at Vitry-en-Artois, forcing the Germans to withdraw from the high ground opposite the 1st Canadian Division. The barrage then moved along the German line as Lieutenant Colonel Isaac's 2nd Berkshires advanced to Cuichy and Faubé.

Brigadier General Brand had to wait until the 2nd Worcesters came up on his left flank before he could advance to the Haute Deule Canal north of Douai. Brigadier General Grogan VC (awarded the previous May) then waited for the artillery to shell the town before he moved up to the edge of the floods. The 2nd East Lancashires could then capture the prison.

The Germans breached the bank of the Scarpe on 13 October, forcing Grogan to withdraw part of 23 Brigade and the 1st Worcesters to withdraw from the water-logged area. Captain Prosser was taken prisoner while reconnoitring the canal while his men returned to report that the ground was too wet to cross.

XXII Corps, 8 to 15 October

1st Canadian Division, 8 to 14 October, Sailly-en-Ostrevent to the River Sensée

Major General Archibald Macdonell's men carried out a 'Chinese Attack' along the La Trinquise stream on 8 October to test the German reaction. Two days later, 13th Battalion probed the Drocourt–Quéant Line (D-Q Line) north of Sailly-en-Ostrevent, to find the Germans were still there.

Macdonell heard that 8th Division was advancing on his left flank on 11 October, so Brigadier General Tuxford was told to check the area south of the Scarpe Canal. The 15th and 16th Battalions crossed La Trinquise stream to find that the Germans had finally abandoned the D-Q Line. Men from 8th Division then crossed the Scarpe Canal at Vitry-en-Artois to outflank the rearguards around Noyelle. The 7th Battalion crossed the Senseé stream to discover that the Germans had also abandoned Estrées, Bellonne and Hamel.

On 12 October, the artillery shelled Férin across the Sensée while 3 Brigade ran up to the embankment, only to find that all bridges were down. At the same time 2 Brigade made a pincer attack on Arleux where the Sensée and Canal du Nord Canals met. Two days later, 1 Brigade's patrols crossed cork floating bridges but the 'enemy's retaliation was too strong for a permanent bridgehead' around Férin. Prisoners suggested a withdrawal to the Schelde Canal was being prepared, so Macdonell called off further attacks.

56th Division, 11 to 13 October, Crossing the Sensée Canal

The 1/13th London crossed the Sensée canal at Fressies on the division's right flank on 11 October. Then the 1/7th Middlesex crossed at Palluel on the left flank the following day. Lieutenant Arnold's engineers of 416th Field Company built an 'unstable affair with no handrail' at Aubigny-au-Bac late on 13 October. The 1/2nd London then crossed in silence; they had taken 200 prisoners by the time Captain Sloan ordered a withdrawal. When the bridge broke, Corporal James McPhie told his men that 'we have got to make a way for them; it is a death or glory job.' He jumped into the water and held the two halves of the bridge together while his comrades repaired it. McPhie was mortally wounded and posthumously awarded the Victoria Cross.

4th Canadian Division, 15 October, Sensée Canal

The Canadians took over the Sensée Canal sector early on 15 October but lost the Aubigny-au-Bac bridgehead later that night.

Canadian Corps, 8 to 14 October

11th Division, 8 October, along the Sensée Canal and Schelde Canal

Brigadier General Winter (Major General Davies was recovering from a wound) was responsible for a long sector along the Sensée and Schelde canals. Brigadier Generals Spring and Clay moved close to the Sensée Canal on 10 October, occupying Paillencourt, while the 6th Lincolns and 7th South Staffords took Hem-Lenglet the following night. The 9th West Yorkshires

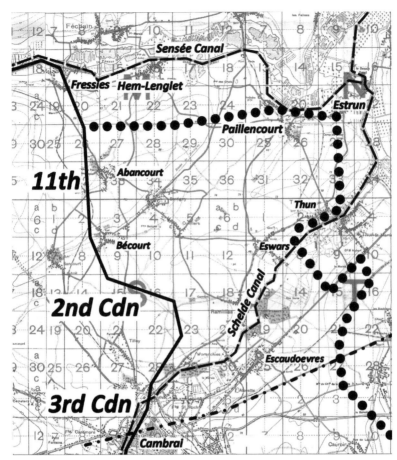

The Canadian Corps cleared the area between the Sensée Canal and the Scarpe Canal on 8 and 9 October.

had already taken Thun l'Évêque and Thun Saint Martin, freeing up 2nd Canadian Division's front. They then cleared the west bank as far as Estrun the following day while the 6th York and Lancasters and the 2nd Green Howards supported the Canadian attack on Iwuy.

2nd Canadian Division, 8 to 12 October, North of Cambrai to Hordain

Late on 7 October, drums filled with phosgene and tear gas exploded in Bantigny ravine. Major General Sir Henry Burstall then had to stop the Germans escaping across the Sensée and Schelde Canals. The attack at 1 am on 9 October 'was a complete surprise and it caught the enemy in the midst of preparing for a withdrawal'. As 31st Battalion moved through Bantigny and Cuvillers, 27th Battalion cleared Ramillies and Cuvillers. Men also ran up to the Pont d'Aire bridges over the Schelde Canal. Captain Norman Mitchell (1st Canadian Tunnelling Company) had cut the leads at the first bridge and was securing the main crossing when he was attacked. He held them at bay until reinforcements arrived and then disarmed the explosives as the Canadians crossed. Mitchell would be awarded the Victoria Cross.

The 25th Battalion then cleared Escaudoeuvres while 22nd and 26th Battalions entered the north-east suburbs of Cambrai. Machine-gun fire from Iwuy and Naves stopped the Canadian Light Horse interfering with the withdrawal so the 23rd Battalion had to advance astride the Schelde but the 26th Battalion reached the 'strong wire defences' covering Naves.

Early on 10 October, 31st Battalion learnt that 11th Division had already cleared Thun l'Évêque next to the Schelde Canal. First the 28th Battalion and then the 29th passed through Thun St Martin but were pinned down along the Ereclin stream leaving 18th Battalion under fire south of Iwuy. The 19th Battalion had less trouble clearing Naves before advancing along the Saulzoir road.

The 49th Division took over the southern part of Major General Burstall's line on 11 October. But it still took 28th and 31st Battalions all day to clear Iwuy, leaving 20th Battalion's flank exposed to enfilade fire. Lieutenant Wallace Algie silenced two of the machine guns before turning one on the enemy. He was killed shortly afterwards and was posthumously awarded the Victoria Cross. Meanwhile 21st Battalion was making good progress towards Avesnes-le-Sec until it was attacked by half a dozen tanks. A battery of field artillery cantered forward, unhooked, and forced them to retire.

3rd Canadian Division, 9 to 10 October, Cambrai

The 4th Mounted Rifles discovered the Germans were withdrawing early on 9 October, so the Canadians crossed the Schelde Canal and entered Cambrai:

> Evidence of pillage and wanton destruction by the retreating Germans met the Canadians as they advanced. For some days they had seen columns of smoke rising from Cambrai and it was apparent the enemy had determined to destroy the city by fire but the rapid progress of the Canadians defeated these plans. Piles of combustible material were found unignited, and detachments of engineers extinguished the fires which were raging in many areas.

51st Division, 12 and 13 October, Lieu St Amand and Avesnes-le-Sec

The 7th Argylls were pinned down in front of Lieu St Amand but the 4th Seaforths and 5th Seaforths were able to clear Avesnes-le-Sec. The Germans used their artillery and planes to stop the Scots reaching the Selle, so 'it was decided to attempt to gain this objective by exploitation'.

49th Division, 12 to 14 October, North of the Cambrai to Saulzoir Road

The late start of 9 am on 12 October surprised the Germans while a 'magnificent' barrage made the whole ridge 'disappear rapidly in smoke and exploding shells'. The 7th and 6th West Yorkshires advanced south of Avesnes-le-Sec while the 4th and the 7th Duke's advanced north of Villers-en-Cauchies. They were fighting to cross a railway line when eight A7V tanks drove the Yorkshiremen back. The attack was resumed when the tanks withdrew and then followed the withdrawal towards the Selle. Casualties had been high but many prisoners and two batteries had been taken during the 3 mile advance.

Dawn brought a 'strange stillness' because the Germans had withdrawn during the night, so the barrage was cancelled and zero hour was postponed

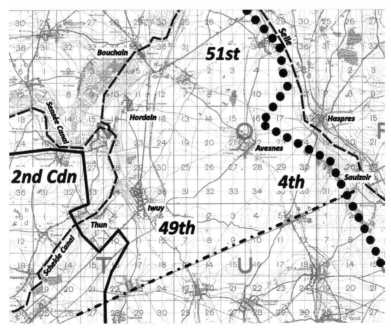

The Canadian Corps followed up the German withdrawal, reaching the Selle stream by 14 October.

to 11.15 am. The 5th West Yorkshires, 4th Duke's and 6th Duke's had soon reached the high ground overlooking Haspres and Saulzoir and could see the Germans waiting for them across the Selle stream.

Major General Neville Cameron had been told to push across the Selle but there had been no time for artillery registration so the barrage missed the German positions. There had also been no time to locate the enemy machine-gun posts, so fire raked the 4th KOYLIs, the 4th York and Lancasters and the 5th York and Lancasters when they advanced towards the stream at 9.30 am. There were over 700 casualties and no one crossed the Selle between Haspres and Saulzoir. Patrols crept into Saulzoir during the night and established two small bridgeheads.

Summary

Haig met his army commanders on 11 October to hear that they thought the Germans would withdraw opposite Second Army and Fifth Army but hold on to the Hermann Line opposite Third Army and Fourth Army. The plan was for Second Army to renew the new offensive in Flanders on 14 October. First Army would cover Third Army's flank as it crossed the Selle while Fourth Army advanced alongside the French towards the Sambre and Oise Canal. The problem was Third Army only had two single railway lines to move its supplies forward while the bad weather increased the time to carry all the required ammunition forward, so the attack across the Selle was postponed until 17 October.

The Germans fell back towards the Haute Deule Canal, between Pont-à-Vendin and Douai, opposite I Corps and VIII Corps on 17 October. Two days later the retirement extended as far south as Anneux, to where the Scarpe Canal joined the River Sensée, so XXII Corps could move forward. Heavy rain and artillery fire on 21 and 22 October hampered the preparation for the attack against the Hermann Line, but the situation elsewhere along the line was changing rapidly. Fifth Army was held up along the Haute Deule Canal but Third Army was across the Selle and outflanking the Germans opposite First Army's right flank.

VIII Corps, 16 to 31 October

12th Division, 16 to 28 October, Haute Deule Canal to the Scarpe

The 7th Sussex crossed the Haute Deule Canal on trench boards tied to slabs of cork on 16 October and 'received a most enthusiastic reception' in Oignies. The 7th Norfolks also crossed to find the Germans had gone and 'the French Tricolour was displayed everywhere'. The 5th Berkshires crossed Dourges' damaged railway bridge to be greeted by civilians clutching bottles of cognac they had kept hidden for over four years. By evening Major General Higginson's men were 4 miles beyond the canal.

The 4th Hussars encountered enemy cavalry patrols over the next two days, and then found infantry waiting for them around Orchies. The 7th Norfolks negotiated ditches and hedges while the engineers repaired bridges and filled craters so the artillery could follow them. It was the turn of the 9th Essex and the 6th Buffs and then the Cambridge Regiment and 6th Queen's to advance through Saméon and Lecelles. They reached the Schelde late on 21 October and Brigadier General Incledon-Webber took advantage of the bright moon to cross on barrel rafts. The 9th Royal Fusiliers cleared Fresnoy but the 6th Queen's Own found that the Nivelle bridge had been blown up. They both discovered that the fields flanking the Schelde Canal were flooded.

On 23 October, the 9th Royal Fusiliers reached the Schelde, east of Flagnies, under fire from Fort de Maulde. Machine-gun fire delayed the engineers work on the pontoon bridge at Nivelle so it was dusk before the 6th Buffs reached Haute Rive. Lieutenant Colonel Dawson of the 6th Queen's was mortally wounded during the crossing – his seventh wound after three years at the front. 'The whole division mourned the loss of such a gallant soldier.'

The 9th Royal Fusiliers were unable to get past Fort de Maulde on 25 October, but the 6th Buffs charged through Bruille, taking the Germans by surprise. They abandoned Fort Justice the following day, so the 7th Sussex could enter Chateau de l'Abbaye on 28 October. The engineers were then able to launch a bridge across the Schelde.

8th Division, 17 to 31 October, Haute Deule Canal to the Schelde Canal

Major General William Heneker heard that the Germans were withdrawing from the Haute Deule Canal on 17 October, so he decided to explore the far bank. The 1st Worcester and 2nd Rifle Brigade crossed under fire and then cyclists and field guns accompanied the 4th Hussars as they pushed ahead. The Rifle Brigade entered an abandoned Douai during the afternoon and Lieutenant Colonel Baker accompanied Brigadier General Grogan when the Union Jack and the Tricolour replaced the German flag. The citizens had been evacuated some time before and the Germans had given them little warning. They had left no booby traps but everything else of value had been smashed, even the cathedral organ.

The 1st Sherwoods and 2nd East Lancashires pushed along the north bank of the Scarpe through Marchiennes Forest on 19 October. 'Everywhere our troops were received with tears of joy. Gifts of flowers were pressed upon us but there was no food. The Germans had carried off everything edible with them and the townspeople were starving.'

The advance slowed down on 20 October because 'the roads were crowded by civilians who, with the poor pitiful possessions left to them pilled on carts, hand barrows or carried on their back, trudged wearily, yet hopefully, back to what might remain of their homes.' Lieutenant Willison entered St Amand at the head of the Sherwoods, finding it crowded with the refugees from Douai. German artillery fire had caused casualties while everyone

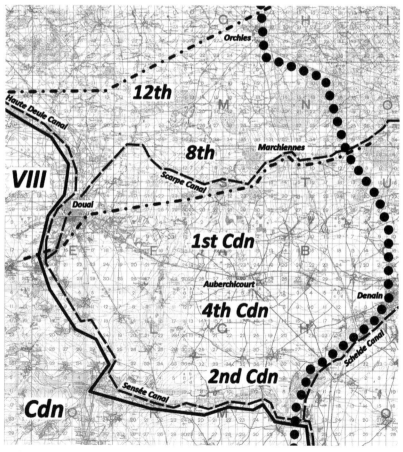

The Germans abandoned the Haute Deule and Sensée Canals on 17 October and both the VIII Corps and the Canadian Corps followed up the withdrawal.

was suffering from the effects of poison gas. The 2nd East Lancashires also discovered that every bridge over the Scarpe had been blown up and the ruins were covered by German machine-gun teams.

The Sherwoods filed across the canal on a plank bridge during the night and then moved up to Raismes Forest on 22 October. The 1st Northants were unable to capture Odomez the following day but the Germans soon abandoned it. The floods had receded by 26 October, so patrols could move up to the Schelde Canal.

Major Prior tried to cross the Schelde at dusk on 27 October. A few of the 2nd Devons crossed at Odomez but the Germans counter-attacked and only three escaped. Another attempt late on 30 October was compromised when one of the Jerusalem pontoon bridges collapsed. Others crossed by rafts and another bridge,but came under fire from across the Canal du Jard. Everyone withdrew when it was dark because the area between the canals was water-logged.

Canadian Corps, 17 to 23 October

1st Division, 17 October, Sensée Canal to the Schelde Canal

The gunners fired 'an artillery barrage along its front each morning, as a test for the presence of the enemy'; there was no response on 17 October. Both 2 Brigade and 1 Brigade crossed the Sensée Canal between Corbehem and Cantin to find that Douai had been abandoned. Brigadier General Clark pushed his 8th Battalion onto the ridge around Erchin.

A mixed group of the Canadian Light Horse, cyclists, armoured cars and machine guns mounted on motorcycles led the pursuit through Pecquencourt and Écaillon on 18 October, 'finding themselves in a new role; that of liberators.' In Pecquencourt they had found '2,000 civilians whom the retiring enemy had left without food; before they departed the Germans had combed the countryside bare of cattle, sheep, pigs and poultry'. They found the same in Warlaing and Hélesmes the following day. On 21 October, 1 Brigade and 3 Brigade passed through Vicoigne Forest, driving the Germans from Vicoigne and Raismes before handing over their sector.

3rd Canadian Division, 23 October Raismes Forest

Both 7 and 9 Brigades advanced through the Raismes Forest, to find the Germans waiting behind the Schelde between Fresnes and Thiers. The canal was overflowing because the sluices had been opened but the rearguards had been driven from the west bank by nightfall.

4th Canadian Division, 17 to 23 October, River Sensée to the Schelde Canal

The withdrawal from the River Sensée began later on 17 October and rear guards stopped patrols crossing until Major General Sir David Watson ordered 87th Battalion to cross the Sensée Canal in 1st Canadian Division's sector. They cleared the north bank, starting from Arleux, so the engineers could build bridges for 11 and 10 Brigades to cross between Palluel and Fressies. A mixed group of the cavalry, cyclists, armoured cars and motorcycles then followed the Germans through Auberchicourt and Émerchicourt, en route to Denain, on 18 and 19 October. Throughout the day, 'long hidden Tricolours appeared as if by magic along the route of the marching troops, who were greeted with embraces, cheers and shouts of Vive la France!'

The race was now on and while 11 Brigade passed through an abandoned Haveluy, 10 Brigade had to drive a rearguard out of Denain. On the left, 11 Brigade found the Germans waiting around Bruay, Anzin and Valenciennes on the west bank of the Schelde on 22 October. The 78th and 85th Battalions had a difficult time negotiating the marshes and floods before fighting their way into the outskirts of Valenciennes during the night.

2nd Canadian Division, 17 October, Crossing the Sensée Canal

The 6 Brigade crossed the Sensée Canal at Hem Lenglet late on 17 October and then advanced beyond Wasnes-au-Bac but it was another twenty-four hours before 4 Brigade could cross Pont Rade at Paillencourt. On 19 October, 29th Battalion reached Marquette, where it was joined by 19th Battalion, but 18th Battalion could not clear Hordain on the east bank of the Sensée.

On 27 October, Billy Barker was flying his Snipe fighter plane above the Schelde when a large group of Fokker DVIIs pounced on him. He was badly injured but managed to crash land near the front line, where he was rescued by Canadian troops. Barker had shot down nearly forty planes during his flying career and his Victoria Cross would make him the most decorated Canadian of the war.

XXII Corps, 20 to 21 October

51st Division, 18 to 21 October, Selle Stream to Mont Houy

The 7th Argylls and the 6th Seaforths could not reach Lieu St Amand while the 6/7th Gordons and the 5th Seaforths struggled to advance north of Avesnes-le-Sec on 18 October. The Germans withdrew in the morning mist and it was dark by the time the 7th Black Watch and the 6th Argylls reached Dochy-les-Mines and Noyelles. The 7th Argylls and 4th Gordons had already crossed the Selle between Fleury and Noyelles.

The Germans were worried they would get trapped against the Schelde Canal east of Denain, so they withdrew and the 7th Black Watch followed them up. Machine-gun fire from the Valenciennes railway pinned the 1/6th Argylls down until it was dark but the 7th Argylls and 4th Seaforths kept up the pressure during the night. They found the Germans waiting for

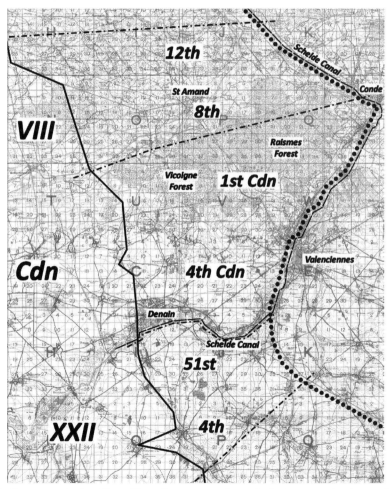

VIII Corps and the Canadian Corps continued their pursuit through the Raismes Forest, finding the Germans waiting for them behind the flooded Schelde Canal. Meanwhile, XXII Corps encountered fierce resistance south of Valenciennes.

them behind the Écaillon stream around Thiant. Other attempts to cross the Écaillon stream were all stopped by fire and while the 7th Argylls had to abandon their foothold, the 4th Seaforths held onto theirs.

It was impossible to find out how wide the Écaillon was, so the engineers found that some of their foot bridges were too short. The 1/7th and 1/6th Black Watch had to wade or swim across the flooded stream before the attack began at 4 am on 24 October. The delay meant they lost the barrage and then faced a tough fight for Maing.

The 6th Argylls, 6th Seaforths and 6/7th Gordons advanced to Mont Houy and Famars early the following morning but counter-attacks drove the Gordons and then the Seaforths back to the railway. The 1/6th Argylls were running out of ammunition when the Germans turned on them, so Lieutenant William Bissett led a bayonet charge over the embankment and saved the line. He was awarded the Victoria Cross.

On 26 October, the 1/6th Black Watch failed to hold onto Mont Houy while the 1/4th Gordons and 6/7th Gordon Highlanders faced a long battle in which Famars was 'to change hands for a fourth and fifth time'. The 1/4th Seaforths captured nearly 200 prisoners around Le Poirier and Mont Houy on 28 October but they 'were weakened by serious losses and had one half company surrounded and isolated'. First the 1/7th Argylls reinforced the Seaforths and then the 1/6th Argylls took over the Mont Houy sector. The Scots could not capture the hill but 'it could no longer be used as an observation post.'

The Highlanders right section was relieved by 49th Division but Lieutenant General Arthur Currie refused to take over their left until Mont Houy was taken. It would give the Canadian heavy artillery a 'full and proper opportunity to do their work free from the hysteria of a suddenly improvised attack.'

4th Division, 20 to 24 October, Selle Stream to the Rhonelle Stream

Major General Cuthbert Lucas ordered Brigadier Generals Webb-Bowen and Greene to start moving after he heard the Germans were withdrawing from the Selle. The 1st Rifle Brigade and 1st Hampshires moved through Haspres early on 20 October and 'received a wonderful welcome from the inhabitants, wild with joy at being delivered from Germans hands'. They then pushed to Monchaux, on the Écaillon stream. The 2nd Duke's moved through Saulzoir while the 2nd Seaforths advanced alongside Third Army to Verchain. Lucas then waited for Third Army to prepare its attack across the stream.

The Écaillon stream was 'a troublesome obstacle, four feet and more deep in places, with a muddy bottom and 20 feet wide, with steep banks and running quite fast.' Captain May and Second Lieutenant Holmes of the 1st Hampshires 'hauled themselves over along a wire' so their men could take one hundred prisoners. Second Lieutenant Rayner also waded across and persuaded a German officer who spoke English to surrender Monchaux and its garrison. The 1st Somersets were then able to advance to Maing. The 2nd Duke's and 1st Warwicks also negotiated the Écaillon only to find that Third Army's advance was delayed on their right. So it was late afternoon before they had rounded up 900 prisoners on the high ground beyond the stream.

The 1st King's Own and 2nd Essex took over the division's right flank during the night and then advanced through Quérénaing early on 25 October. The 2nd Lancashire Fusiliers helped the 2nd Essex clear Artres the following morning and then Second Lieutenant Henshall's platoon crossed the Rhonelle by the demolished bridge and held a bridgehead while the rest of the Lancashire Fusiliers scrambled over. The 1st Rifle Brigade then expanded the bridgehead northwards.

Chapter 11

What is the Good of Going On?

Third Army

8 to 24 October

General Byng issued his orders for 'a full dress attack' on 7 October, but postponed it to the following day after consulting General Rawlinson. There would be a preliminary operation at 1 am to clear the Beaurevoir Line in front of Villers Outreaux to get in line with Fourth Army. The rest of Third Army would attack at 4.30 am.

XVII Corps, 8 to 16 October

57th Division, 8 and 10 October, South of Cambrai

Cambrai 'was burning so fiercely that the spire of one its churches stood out black against the background of flame.' The 2/5th King's Own and 1/5th Loyals moved up to the outskirts and patrols entered early on 9 October, meeting Canadian patrols in the centre. The 2/6th King's and 8th King's cleared the rest of the south half the following day. Major General Barnes' division was then squeezed out of the line.

63rd Division, 8 October, tank battle at Niergnies

The Hawke Battalion formed a defensive flank as the Drake Battalion and the 2nd Irish Rifles cleared the first objective. The Anson Battalion outflanked Niergnies, and the Marines and the Hood Battalion were clearing the village when four Mark IV tanks crawled towards them in the gloom. No one saw the Iron Cross markings until it was too late and the German crews knocked out four British tanks in quick succession. Commander Pollock knocked out one of the enemy tanks with a captured field gun while Commander Buckle accounted for another with a captured anti-tank rifle; the other two withdrew. The Hood Battalion had taken Niergnies by the time there was another attack, this time with just one tank. The division had taken over 1,150 prisoners and 'the way was now open for the advance of Third Army's left.'

24th Division, 9 to 16 October, Cambrai to the Selle Stream

The 9th East Surrey and 1st North Staffs advanced towards Awoingt early on 9 October. Up ahead were 'smoke shells bursting in profusion, while big crumps falling continually in the village were sending up huge clouds of red dust. The town of Cambrai seemed to be one huge bonfire.'

A squadron of Carabiniers led the 9th Sussex through Cauroir but Captain Pearson's patrol was captured in Cagnoncles ahead of the 7th Northants. Lieutenant Colonel Grune's men took the 'best defended locality encountered during the final advance' the following morning. German resistance then collapsed and the Northants had reached Rieux by the time the 13th Middlesex passed through. Cavalry and cyclist patrols found their enemy waiting beyond the Ereclin stream.

The 1st Royal Fusiliers and 3rd Rifle Brigade were pinned down by machine-gun fire when they tried to cross the Ereclin at 5.45 am on 11 October. Brigadier General Thorpe delayed the next attack until the artillery were ready at noon the following day, only to find the Germans had fallen back to the Selle.

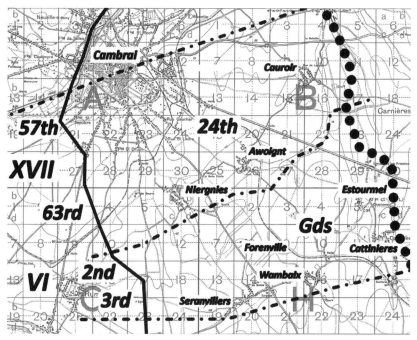

XVII and VI Corps faced a counter-attack with tanks as they pushed past the south side of Cambrai on 8 and 9 October.

The 8th Queen's cleared Montrécourt late 12 October and a few men scrambled across the demolished bridge only to find that 'the enemy was holding the railway embankment beyond with a considerable number of machine guns.' The engineers installed two pontoon bridges south of the village during the night. The Queen's turned their attention to Haussy on 14 October, fighting their way to the river bank. The locals 'gave information as to the whereabouts of the enemy, they concealed our men in their houses and fed them on coffee and eggs'. Captain Selfe even led some men across the broken bridge and they returned with prisoners. Second Lieutenant Thomas 'spoke French like a native' and he led the 150 inhabitants of Montrécourt to safety before the attack began.

The 1st North Staffords cleared the area around Montrécourt bridge early on 16 October, so the 8th Queen's Own could cross the stream. They took 200 prisoners during a tough battle for the railway embankment beyond while the 9th East Surreys took a similar number in Haussy. However, failures on the flanks invited counter-attacks and the two battalions were forced to abandon the bridgehead during the night. A barrage of high explosive and gas shells then caused many casualties before Haussy could be evacuated.

VI Corps, 8 to 13 October

2nd Division, 8 October, Forenville

Two tanks led the 1st KRRC and 23rd Royal Fusiliers towards Forenville at 4.30 am but their prisoners turned on the 1st Berkshires who were following; 'these treacherous Germans were suitably dealt with.' A counter-attack supported by three captured tanks was stopped but the KRRC and Royal Fusiliers had to withdraw because the men to their flanks had fallen back. A second attempt failed but the 17th Royal Fusiliers reached Forenville at dusk.

3rd Division, 8 October, Séranvillers

Incendiary shells hit Séranvillers while the 4th Royal Fusiliers and the 1st Northumberland Fusiliers advanced to the Hindenburg Reserve Line. The 13th King's and 2nd Suffolk then moved into the ruined village but they were unable to clear it. Two tanks were spotted and 'a plucky corporal ran forward to ask their assistance. On nearing the tank he saw they had small iron crosses painted on them and at the same moment they opened fire.'

The counter-attack threatened to surround the 13th King's until two friendly tanks drove them away and the eighty survivors escaped the ruins.

A second attack in the afternoon failed due to enfilade fire because 2nd Division had been given a different time to advance. The 8th King's Own and 1st Gordons reached the German trench west of Séranvillers at dusk but the 2nd Suffolks had difficulty clearing it.

Guards Division, 9 October, Advance to the Selle Stream

Major General Matheson's men took over the line south-east of Cambrai late on 8 October and he allocated four field guns to each brigade to act in an anti-tank role. But the Germans had gone and the 1st Coldstream and 3rd Grenadier Guards marched to Estourmel, encountering 'no trouble at all, except for some of our guns firing short; it seemed a pity one could not switch off the barrage but it was not possible.' The 2nd Grenadier Guards and 2nd Coldstream Guards, however, came under machine-gun fire and Private William Holmes rescued several injured men as the 2nd Grenadier Guards approached Cattenières. He was mortally wounded and would be posthumously awarded the Victoria Cross.

Matheson eventually decided 'to discontinue the advance until darkness set in. There was no need for useless loss of life.' The 1st Scots Guards

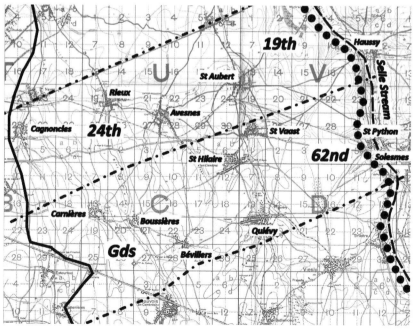

The Germans fell back rapidly ahead of XVII Corps and VI Corps to the Selle around Haussy, St Python and Solesmes between 10 and 12 October.

and the 1st Irish Guards renewed the advance early the following morning and they drove rearguards around Carnières, Boussières and Bévillers back beyond St Hilaire and Quiévy. A squadron of the Oxfordshire Hussars and motorbikes mounting machine guns led the 1st Welsh, 2nd Scots Guards and 1st Grenadier Guards on to the ridge around St Vaast on 11 October. They could across Solesmes where rearguards covered the bridges until their comrades had crossed the Selle. Matheson was preparing to cross the stream on 12 October when RAF spotters reported that the rearguards had pulled back behind the railway. The Guardsmen discovered that dams had created deep pools which would need longer bridges to cross.

The 2nd Scots Guards entered St Python early on 14 October 'but the clearing operations were hampered by the presence of many civilians'. Corporal Harry Wood dragged a lump of masonry into the road and gave covering fire while his platoon crossed the bridge. He later stopped a counter-attack and would be awarded the Victoria Cross. The 1st Scots Guards and the 3rd Grenadier Guards cleared the rest of village on 15 October while the 1st Coldstream Guards established a foothold on the far bank the following day.

62nd Division, 13 October, St Python

The West Yorkshire men took over the line facing Solesmes on 13 October and cleared the west part of St Python, ready to cross the Selle.

IV Corps, 8 to 13 October

New Zealand Division, 8 to 13 October, Crèvecoeur to Briastre on the Selle Stream

The 2nd and 1st Rifles advanced from Crèvecoeur at 4.30 am while four tanks helped the 4th Rifles round up 300 prisoners in Lesdains before knocking out two German tanks. The 2nd Canterbury Battalion and the 1st Otago Battalion headed for Esnes and were able to stop the same counter-attack. The 3rd Rifles, 1st Canterbury and 2nd Otago continued the advance early the following morning only to find the Germans had gone 'and the 38,000 shells of our barrage were wasted.' A squadron of the 3rd Hussars cantered ahead as the 3rd Rifles took over the lead beyond the Cambrai railway. 'Disdaining to use low ground, they presented an excellent target,' and the machine guns in Fontaine forced them to retire.

Patrols discovered that the Germans had evacuated Fontaine during the night and the few civilians left in Beauvais 'gave their liberators a rapturous welcome when day dawned'. The 2nd Canterbury and 1st Otago came under enfilade fire from Quiévy but still reached the Selle around Briastre. The 2nd Auckland and 1st Wellington then cleared the west bank during the night, evacuating 200 civilians while the engineers built a footbridge. Some of the 1st Wellington crossed the Selle only to discover the Germans dug in along the railway south of Solesmes.

42nd Division, 13 October, Selle Stream

Major General Arthur Solly-Flood's men took over from the New Zealanders on 13 October and Lieutenant Colonel MacLeod's 8th Lancashire Fusiliers immediately had to stop a counter-attack. The Lancashire men spent the next five days clearing the east bank of the Selle while the engineers prepared bridges.

37th Division, 8 to 12 October, Beaurevoir Line to the Selle stream

Major General Hugh Bruce-Williams' men faced the Beaurevoir Line where it curved around the Bel Aise salient. One tank was hit as the 10th Royal Fusiliers cleared the Beaurevoir Line but two others helped the 13th KRRC clear the Bel Aise salient. The 13th Royal Fusiliers and 1st Essex lost the barrage and were then delayed by machine-gun posts which had been missed. The 1st Hertfords were able to get through Briseux Wood but the 4th Middlesex could not capture Guillemin Farm. Brigadier General Oakley organised another attack by the 8th Somersets and the 8th Lincolns but they too failed. They eventually took Haucourt the following morning.

The 1/1st Hertfords cleared Ligny on 9 October but the 13th Royal Fusiliers were pinned down by the machine guns around Caudry. The 1st Essex and 13th Royal Fusiliers made a pincer attack early the following morning and they 'met with little resistance, except from the late barrage and our own tanks, which apparently did not expect British troops so far east'. The barrage on Caudry was stopped when it became clear that it was full of civilians and they unfurled their Tricolours and sang *La Marseillaise* as Major General Hugh Bruce-Williams' men passed through. The last time British soldiers had marched through the village was on 23 August 1914 during the battle of Le Cateau.

The 8th Somersets and 8th Lincolns passed through Béthencourt, only to come under fire from Neuvilly. The engineers made a footbridge out of barrels so the Somersets and the 8th Lincolns could cross early the following morning, but a more robust bridge followed. The 4th Middlesex advanced across the railway at 5 am on 12 October but were driven back and it required help from the 8th Somersets to retake it.

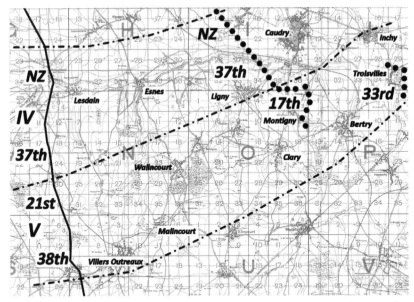

IV and V Corps advanced quickly on 8 October, reaching the 1914 Le Cateau battlefield the following day.

V Corps, 8 to 12 October

21st Division, 8 October, Beaurevoir Line to Walincourt

Two tanks led the 1st Wiltshires into the Beaurevoir Line and then the 6th and 7th Leicesters bombed north into 37th Division's sector, forcing an entire battalion to surrender. The 9th KOYLIs and 15th Durhams also cleared their sector of the Beaurevoir Line. Two tanks helped the 1st East Yorkshires capture 100 prisoners around Chateau des Angles but they had to pull back until engineers had disabled the booby traps. Six tanks then led the 1st Lincolns, 2nd Northumberland Fusiliers and 2nd Lincolns across the Sargrenon stream, finding that the Germans had withdrawn. The three battalions were able to push forward around Walincourt at dusk.

17th Division, 9 to 14 October, Walincourt to the Selle, north of Le Cateau

Major General Philip Robertson's men discovered that the Germans had abandoned Walincourt, Selvigny and Caullery early on 9 October, so there was 'the surprise of moving forward unopposed into peaceful country'. To begin with the villages were quiet and there was 'not a sign of life, a deserted eerie place', but soon 'hundreds of old men and old women, young women and children were flocking into the streets. Tricolours were hanging from

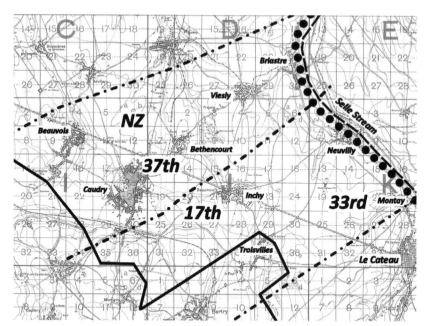

The Germans had withdrawn behind the Selle stream between Briastre and Le Cateau, ahead of IV Corps and V Corps, by 12 October.

the windows of nearly every house. Everyone was chattering, laughing, occasionally cheering and pressing around us, asking so many questions.' The 7th Lincolns and the 7th Borders reached Montigny and Tronquoy by dusk, having marched 5 miles.

The 6th Dorsets and the 10th West Yorkshires renewed the advance past Audencourt the following morning and were met by 'cheering crowds'. Brigadier General Hope's men came under artillery fire as they advanced down the open slope towards the Selle, so he called forward his own guns. Four enemy batteries had been silenced by the time the 7th East Yorkshires moved forward. Around Solesmes, to the north, 'columns of closed up troops and long lines of all kinds of transport' could be seen heading for the bridges while trains were pulling out of the station. Long range shots from the field guns caused havoc amongst the retreating enemy as the 2nd Argylls advanced towards Neuvilly.

Early on 11 October the 7th East Yorkshires waded, swam or scrambled across fallen trees along the Selle north of Neuvilly while some of the 10th West Yorkshires crossed a dam. But the rest of the Yorkshiremen were struggling because the Germans had made the village 'into an entanglement of barbed wire threaded through every fence and hedge and from tree to

tree. The gardens and houses behind them bristled with machine-guns.'
The 6th Dorsets failed to break the deadlock but outposts were established
on the far bank the following day.

The 12th Manchesters and 9th Duke's advanced either side of Neuvilly
early on 12 October but were driven back by counter-attacks. The
Manchesters held on but the Duke's had to withdraw across the Selle.
Meanwhile the 10th Lancashires were embroiled in a house-to-house battle
for Neuvilly. Corporal Frank Lester's section became trapped in a house by
falling rubble so he ran out and shot the sniper covering the street; he was
killed moments later. Lester's sacrifice allowed his men to escape and he was
posthumously awarded the Victoria Cross. By 14 October there were two
small footholds on the far bank of the Selle and the engineers were able to
build bridges ready to make another attempt.

38th Division, 8 October, Aubencheul to Troisvilles

The 13th and 16th Welsh Fusiliers advanced towards Mortho Wood at 1 am
but Lieutenant Colonel Beasley's 17th Welsh Fusiliers were pinned down in
front of Ville Farm. The 10th SWBs were also in difficulties until Sergeant
Jack Williams charged a strongpoint. He was disarming his prisoners when
they turned on him; he bayoneted five and the other ten surrendered.
Williams was awarded the Victoria Cross.

The two tanks were knocked out crawling through the Beaurevoir Line,
so the 10th Welsh Fusiliers and 10th SWBs were unable to surround Villers
Outreaux and the 2nd Welsh Fusiliers could not mop up the village. So
Lieutenant Colonel Norman organised a new barrage and Captain Kirkby's
men followed three more tanks through the ruins. Major General Cubitt
had planned to postpone 114 Brigade's attack but it was already engaged
alongside the 14th Welsh Fusiliers, so the 15th and 13th Welsh bypassed
Malincourt while the 14th Welsh mopped up the village.

33rd Division, 9 to 12 October, Clary to the Selle Stream

The 5th Scottish Rifles were stopped by crossfire from Montigny and
Gattigny Wood until the Canadian Cavalry Brigade passed through and they
then discovered that the South African Brigade had already cleared Bertry.
A rearguard abandoned Troisvilles and the 1st Scottish Rifles followed them
to the Selle stream north of Le Cateau, ending a 7 mile advance. But the
Canadian Cavalry Brigade had suffered many casualties and they withdrew
from Le Cateau 'leaving the countryside, and particularly the sunken roads,
filled with mangled horses'.

En route, a cavalry patrol of the 11th Hussars had encountered 'a bearded man attired in dishevelled gear. It turned out that he had been missing since the battle of Le Cateau in 1914 was a member of this officer's regiment.' After weeks hiding in the woods, Trooper Patrick Fowler had been taken in and looked after by Madame Belmont-Gobert and her daughter Angèle in Bertry, where he stayed for the next four years.

Machine-gun fire stopped the 4th King's and the 2nd Argylls getting to the Selle on 10 October while the King's had to withdraw the following day because the guns fired short. The 2nd Worcesters covered the engineers while they built their footbridges and the 1/9th HLI crossed the Selle early on 12 October. They also cleared the railway cutting on the right, so the 16th KRRC were able to roll up the German line north of Montay; they were soon driven back over the stream.

Third Army, 20 to 25 October

General Byng's men had to cross the Selle, either side of Solesmes, and then advance north-east towards Le Quesnoy. The German counter-barrages were usually fired around 4 am so zero hour was set for 2 am on 20 October. The moon was full and there would be no preliminary bombardment, so the infantry could get across the stream before the Germans realised they were under attack. Third Army would keep its twenty-four tanks in reserve while 6-inch mortars mounted on lorries would be deployed to knock out machine-gun posts.

XVII Corps, 20 to 25 October

19th Division, 20 October, Selle to the Harpies

'Vigorous patrolling' convinced the German outposts to withdraw from the east bank of the Selle between Saulzoir and Haussy. The engineers could then carry twenty footbridges forward on handcarts so the infantry could cross the stream before zero hour. The 9th Welsh Fusiliers, 2nd Wiltshires, 10th Worcesters and 8th Gloucesters advanced towards the Harpies stream but 'casualties were heavy from hostile machine-gun and artillery fire'. The engineers then built two pontoon bridges, so over one hundred field guns were able to cross and deploy ready for the next advance.

The same method was used to clear the Harpies stream late on 22 October, as the 5th SWBs helped the engineers set up four footbridges. The infantry advanced at 3.20 am and the 8th Gloucesters captured 350 prisoners en route to Sommaing and Vendegies. But the 10th Warwicks found the Germans

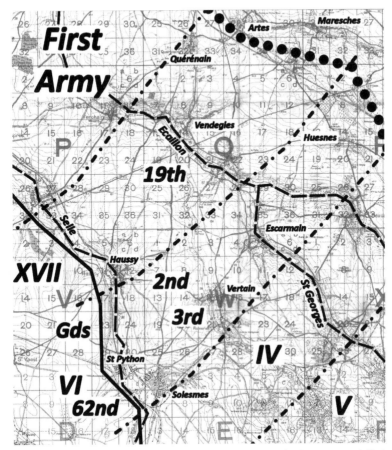

XVII and VI Corps crossed the Selle stream around Haussy and Solesmes on 20 October and then advanced quickly north-east across the Écaillon stream.

waiting for them around St Martin, behind yet another stream and it was impossible to cross the Écaillon in daylight.

61st Division, 24 October to 25 October, Écaillon Stream to the Rhonelle Stream

The engineers had placed twenty foot bridges across the Écaillon before 4 am on 23 October but the artillery missed the wire. Only a few of the 2/7th and 2/6th Warwicks got through and they could not hold on to Sommaing and Vendegies. The 11th Suffolks and 9th Northumberland Fusiliers suffered heavy casualties crossing the stream around St Martin and Bermerain and they too came under attack after the Warwicks were driven back. A second barrage was arranged and the Germans had abandoned Vendegies by the time the 2/8th Worcesters and 2/5th Gloucesters advanced.

VI Corps, 20 to 25 October

Guards Division, 20 October, crossing the Selle between Haussy and St Python

The engineers erected eight single-plank bridges during the evening so Major General Torquhil Matheson's men could advance at 2 am. The 1st Grenadier Guards crossed south of Haussy before handing over to the 2nd Scots Guards and the 1st Welsh Guards. Meanwhile the 2nd Coldstream Guards and 1st Irish Guards crossed north of St Python as they headed into the Harpies valley.

62nd Division, 20 October, crossing the Selle at Solesmes

The plan was to make a pincer attack on Solesmes and 62nd Division would form the north flank. Every company and platoon commander had been given an electric torch, every man would wear a white armband and the password Pelican (the division symbol) would be used for identification purposes.

The 5th Duke's covered the engineers as they installed footbridges in St Python while the 2/4th Duke's cleared the railway line in front of Solesmes. The 5th Duke's cleared St Python while the 2/4th Duke's advanced 'with a will and a dash beyond all praise'. The 2/4th Hampshires could then clear the north part of Solesmes.

Sergeant John Daykins silenced two machine-gun posts as the 2/4th York and Lancasters waded across the Selle south of Solesmes. It 'put the wind up' the rest, so his comrades could clear the south part of the town. Daykins was awarded the Victoria Cross. The next wave crossed the Selle to the north and south of Solesmes and Major Craddock's 2/20th London Regiment reached the ridge overlooking the Harpies stream. Meanwhile Lieutenant Colonel England's 8th West Yorkshires had to form a defensive flank until 42nd Division arrived on the right.

2nd Division, 21 October, Vertain towards Le Quesnoy

Part of the 24th Royal Fusiliers waded across the Harpies stream at 3.20 am, taking the 500-strong garrison in Vertain by surprise. The rest of the Royal Fusiliers and 2nd HLI followed an hour later and the HLI and 2nd Ox and

Bucks eventually reached the St Georges stream. On 24 October the 1st Berkshires and 23rd Royal Fusiliers reached Ruesnes where the inhabitants were 'all smiling and bowing', happy to be free 'after living cooped up in their cellars for a fortnight'. Some soldiers had changed into civilian clothing, worried that the British would shoot them, but the majority wanted to surrender, 'believing what is the good of going on, as we are beaten'. The rest of the Germans withdrew during the night, so the 23rd Royal Fusiliers and 1st Berkshires moved beyond the Valenciennes–Le Quesnoy railway. It was the last action of the war for 2nd Division.

3rd Division, 23 to 25 October, Romeries to the Rhonelle Stream

The 8th King's Own and 2nd Suffolk headed north-east at 3.20 am on 23 October, while the 1st Gordons entered the north end of the Romeries. The 2nd Royal Scots then waded and swam across a deeper section of the Harpies stream to take the Germans holding the rest of the village by surprise. Trench mortars silenced the machine guns in Escarmain so the King's Own and Suffolks could cross the St Georges, but the 1st Scots Fusiliers were pinned down along the stream. It needed help from the 7th Shropshires to break the deadlock in the afternoon. Major General Deverell sent a mobile force of the Oxfordshire Hussars and corps cyclists forward but they were unable to cross the Écaillon.

The stream was crossed at 4 am the following morning and Lewis gunners played havoc with the field guns protecting Ruesnes. The 1st Northumberland Fusiliers reached their objective but the 4th Royal Fusiliers halted on the wrong road and the barrage had moved on before they realised their mistake. It cost them many casualties to reach the objective.

Cavalry patrols located the German positions along the Valenciennes–Le Quesnoy railway on 25 October while Major General Deverell's men spent the day taking over all of VI Corps' front. The Germans withdrew from the railway during the night and patrols were able to investigate the Rhonelle the following afternoon. Again all the bridges around Villers Pol and Orsinval were down.

IV Corps, 20 to 25 October

42nd Division, 20 October, Crossing the Selle

Captain Neame's medics rescued over 150 ill and infirm civilians from Briastre before the attack began at 2 am. Mortars fired a bombardment as the 10th Manchesters and 5th East Lancashires crossed six bridges (each of them marked by a numbered lantern) in heavy rain. Two tanks struggled to crawl across their cribs and it would be some time before they caught the infantry up. In the meantime many would have heard the Lancashire bandsmen playing their regimental march as they climbed the 'bare glacis-like slope with two rows of double-apron wire and a cow fence'. Captain Taylor scattered the Germans facing the Manchesters with a captured machine gun while the East Lancashires took over 300 prisoners.

Captain Barker's 5th Manchesters advanced beyond the Béart stream during the afternoon but the 7th Manchesters were soon pinned down. Four runners had been killed by the time Private Alfred Wilkinson volunteered to go. He made it and a new barrage was organised, which helped Lieutenant Colonel Tickler's men capture their objective.

New Zealand Division, 23 October, St Georges Stream to Le Quesnoy

The 2nd Canterbury and the 1st Otago were crossing the Harpies stream at 8.40 am on 23 October around Vertigneul when there was an act of treachery. Several machine gunners wanted to surrender until they realised they only faced a patrol. 'Lieutenant Jenkins was wounded. The post was rushed and the Germans were one and all put to death.'

The 1st Canterbury waded across the St Georges stream and then the Écaillon stream around Beaudignies. The 2nd Otago 'used covering fire and rushing alternate sections down the slopes, plunged through the river and pressed up the eastern bank.' Patrols reported that Germans were falling back towards Le Quesnoy the following morning, so the 3rd and 4th Rifles moved up to the railway in front of the town. The 2nd Canterbury and 1st Otago moved closer on 25 October while the 4th and 2nd Rifles pushed north of it.

5th Division, 20 October, advancing to Beaurain

The engineers installed sixteen footbridges and two artillery bridges across the Selle before zero hour. The 16th Warwicks and 2nd KOSBs then found that 'enemy resistance was completely crippled by the accuracy of the machine-gun and artillery fire.' The 1st East Surreys then crossed the Béart stream but the 1st Devons were pinned down until a new barrage was arranged.

The Germans were expecting an early attack so they shelled 15 Brigade's assembly positions, causing many casualties; it also made two tanks late. The 1st Cheshires and 1st Bedfords faced fierce resistance until Lieutenant

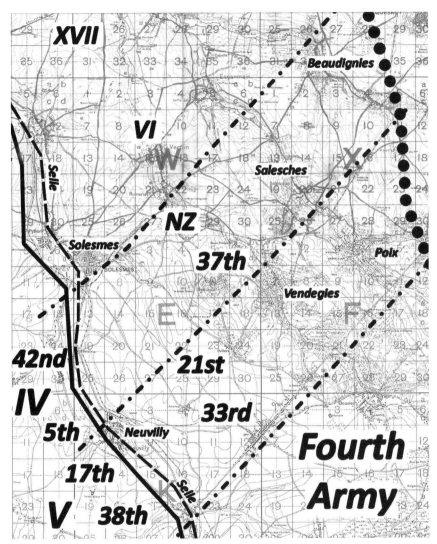

IV and V Corps crossed the Selle stream between Solesmes and Le Cateau on 20 October and then followed up the German withdrawal.

Sanson had manhandled his section of field guns forward. The remaining two tanks then broke down and the 1st Norfolks were unable clear Beaurain.

37th Division, 23 to 25 October, Beaurain to Ghissignies

It was late afternoon on 23 October before the 1st Essex and the 10th Royal Fusiliers secured Beaurain. Lorry-mounted mortars could not silence the machine guns on their right flank, where 21st Division was delayed, so the infantry had to wait for the artillery to catch up. A fresh attempt by the 13th KRRC failed to push the 10th Fusiliers further beyond the Harpies stream.

A special bombardment targeted the right flank during the night and then the 13th Royal Fusiliers advanced through Salesches, across the Écaillon stream and into Ghissignies. They remained under fire from the railway but the 1/1st Hertfords were unable to clear the Germans from the railway line south of Le Quesnoy.

V Corps, 20 to 25 October

17th Division, 20 October, Neuvilly

Two tanks led the 6th Dorsets and 7th East Yorkshires across the Selle at 2 am on 20 October. They then advanced to the railway while the 10th West Yorkshires rounded up a hundred prisoners in Neuvilly. The 10th Sherwood Foresters, 7th Lincolns and 7th Border Regiment passed through,but were pinned down by machine-gun fire from Ovillers and Amerval. One tank was knocked out while the other broke down and it required a new barrage with smoke before the Borders could take Amerval.

21st Division, 23 to 25 October, Ovillers to the Écaillon Stream

The early attack by Fourth Army alerted the German artillery and the assault troops were hit as they assembled along the Selle stream. The 6th Leicesters, 7th Leicesters and 1st Wiltshires then struggled to cross the Harpies stream around Vendegies-au-Bois. The 1st East Yorkshires, 9th KOYLIs and 15th Durhams saw two tanks knocked out around Ovillers while a third headed south into 33rd Division's area. Lieutenant Colonel Harry Greenwood silenced two machine-gun posts, reorganised his men and then led an attack which advanced beyond the village. The 1st and 2nd Lincolns also fought their way past Vendegies-au-Bois, only to be raked by machine-gun fire from across the St Georges stream; nearly 250 men were hit.

The artillery were banned from firing at Poix du Nord because it was full of civilians but the 1st Lincolns, 15th Durhams and 9th KOYLIs attacked the nearby Hermann II Line at 4 am. The 9th KOYLIs were held up until Lieutenant Colonel Greenwood led his men through a gap in the wire. They cleared Poix du Nord and crossed the St Georges stream, so the 2nd Lincolns and 1st East Yorkshire could advance to the Écaillon stream. Colonel Greenwood was awarded the Victoria Cross.

38th Division, 20 October, Montay

Major General Thomas Cubitt's men were crossing the Selle around Montay when some of the bridges collapsed, leaving the support companies having to wade through chest-deep water. The tank supporting the 14th and 13th Welsh ditched before zero hour so there was a fierce battle for the railway until Lieutenant Gundrey found a way through the wire. The 14th and 13th Welsh Fusiliers were also engaged in a desperate fight until Major Dale of the 15th Welsh Fusiliers gained a foothold across the railway with the help of a tank. The Germans then fell back.

33rd Division, 21 to 23 October, the Selle Stream to the Hermann Position II

At 2 am, Major General Reginald Pinney's men 'advanced by sections in easy rushes as if on the parade ground. Their advance was covered by well-directed fire from the batteries.' Two tanks broke down as the 1st Queen's and 1st Middlesex rounded up 200 prisoners around Forest. A third tank was knocked out as the 5th Scottish Rifles and 4th King's cleared Vendegies-au-Bois. The 1st Scottish Rifles and 2nd Argylls were then pinned down along the Harpies stream around Poix du Nord; they had come up against the Hermann Position II.

At 4 am on 24 October the artillery and machine guns fired rapidly for five minutes as platoons ran forward. The guns then slowed their rate of fire while the next line of men prepared to advance. The process was repeated all the way through the Hermann II Line: 'there were the artillery or machine guns ready to assist them with fire whenever the infantry was held up for a moment.'

Lieutenant General Cameron Shute was adamant that there were few Germans around Englefontaine but reconnaissance patrols proved otherwise. Major General Pinney organised a pincer attack involving all three brigades and the 1st Queen's and 4th King's moved around the village at 1 am on 25 October. The 1/9th HLI and 2nd Worcesters then mopped up and 'while the prisoners were being collected the 1,200 inhabitants came out of their cellars and literally fell around the necks of the British troops.' Pinney was able to report that his men had taken the objective and that they had rounded up 500 prisoners.

Chapter 12

A Magnificent Feat of Cool Resolution

Fourth Army

17 to 25 October

Rawlinson's troops faced the Selle between Le Cateau and the Andigny Forest. Bad weather had grounded the RAF but it was expected that the Germans would hold the railway east of Le Cateau and the high ground east of the stream. The preliminary bombardment started early on 15 October and zero was set for 5.20 am on the 17th.

XIII Corps, 17 to 19 October

The Selle either side of Le Cateau was 'from 15 to 20 feet wide, and usually about 4 feet deep, but with the recent heavy rains it was now rising fast.' The assault troops then had to breach the Hermann Line where 'wiring was everywhere elaborate, the machine-gun posts had been prepared on a lavish scale, and the buildings and cellars were admirably adapted for a prolonged resistance.'

66th Division, 17 and 18 October, Le Cateau

Second Lieutenant Hewat of the 2nd South African Regiment waded the stream on 15 October and his group held a bridgehead while the engineers spanned a ruined bridge. Lieutenants Gray and McMillan of the 1st South African Regiment then established a foothold on the far bank and cut holes in the wire while the engineers built four bridges around Baillon Farm. Brigadier General Hunter's men did the same for 198 Brigade in the northern outskirts of Le Cateau.

Major General Keppel Bethell's guns fired a barrage at 5.20 am but there was no attack, lulling the Germans around Le Cateau into a false sense of security. The assault troops crossed to the east bank during a second thirty-minute barrage, and then lay down in the mist until the 8.5 am zero hour.

The 4th South African Regiment faced a tough fight to clear a railway cutting, 'the sides of which were studded with machine-gun posts and rifle-pits.' Major Clerk led his men to a gap in the wire and they then 'slowly and patiently filtered through to the railway'. The 2nd South African Regiment continued the advance but Captain Jenkins' men were under fire from both flanks. The clearing of the railway cutting was 'a magnificent feat of cool resolution' described 'as one of the most astounding feats of the war'.

The 5th Inniskillings and the 6th Dublin Fusiliers used temporary bridges and fallen trees to cross the Selle. They spent all day clearing the houses and cellars before handing over to the 6th Lancashire Fusiliers during the night. 'Conditions were made worse by the dampness of the night, a thick mist and persistent high explosive and gas shelling.'

A 5.30 am advance was planned for 18 October towards an objective which was at an angle to the jumping off line. Major General Bethell had arranged for one artillery brigade to fire at zero with seven more joining in at three minutes intervals. The 6th Dublin Fusiliers and then the 5th Inniskillings failed to capture the Railway Triangle south-east of the town, so Brigadier General Hunter had to pull the 6th Lancashire Fusiliers out of the line. Lieutenant Colonel Gross moved south of the troublesome position and then waited until dusk, so his men 'were able to stalk many German posts in the darkness'.

50th Division, 17 to 19 October, from the Selle to Bazuel

The Germans had dammed the Selle, so it had flooded around St Benin, and had then dug in along the railway line on the far bank. Major General Henry Jackson had to take over the area north of St Souplet where his men could cross the stream. The artillery shelled the far bank for just three minutes before extending their range to the railway. It took the engineers only ten minutes to complete the bridges and the infantry then ran across without suffering a single casualty. Six tanks crossed the stream on cribs but the 1st KOYLIs and 4th KRRC were unable to see the machines in the fog, so they spread out on the far bank. The German machine gunners fired blindly but the 6th Inniskillings and 4th KRRC required help from the 13th Black Watch to clear the railway. The Inniskillings and Black Watch then captured the railway station but they could not clear the railway triangle south-east of the Le Cateau.

The 2nd Dublin Fusiliers and 1st KOYLIs were initially delayed crossing the Selle at St Benin and were then pinned down in the orchards along the Wassigny road. Three tanks helped the 3rd Royal Fusiliers reach Le Quennelet Farm on the right flank but the Germans counter-attacked as soon as the mist lifted. The KRRC, KOYLIs and the Royal Fusiliers were all driven back to the railway embankment; they would later re-establish themselves back on the Wassigny road.

Again the objective was at an angle to the jumping off line, so the artillery fired a ripple effect barrage at 5.30 am on 18 October, to cooperate with the different zero hours along the front. The 13th Black Watch took over 180

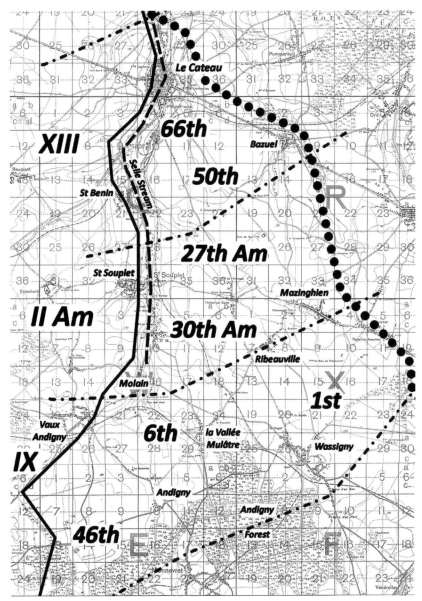

Fourth Army's left faced a tough battle around Le Cateau after crossing the Selle while the right had to fight its way past the Andigny Forest between 17 and 19 October.

prisoners in the railway triangle while the 2nd Dublin Fusiliers rounded up another 300 around the brickworks. Sergeant Horace Curtis silenced two machine-gun teams and another four surrendered, so the 2nd Dublin Fusiliers could advance towards the Landrecies railway. Curtis turned one of the German machine guns on a train which had just arrived with reinforcements and he was awarded the Victoria Cross for taking over one hundred prisoners.

The 4th KRRC were pinned down by fire from La Roue Farm where the Americans were delayed. Some 2nd Munsters entered Bazuel but they soon had to withdraw because they had advanced beyond their supporting barrage. Major General Jackson sent the 1/5th Gloucesters (attached from 25th Division) forward to secure the village and they found the Germans evacuating their artillery. The Lewis gun teams stopped the limbers and the 1/8th Worcesters captured many artillery pieces.

Sounds of evacuation were heard during the night so Major General Jackson told Brigadier General Frizell to advance beyond Bazuel early on 19 October. It turned out the Germans had no intention of retiring and 75 Brigade (attached) was stopped as soon as it came under fire.

II American Corps, 17 to 19 October

Zero hour was set for 27th and 30th Divisions at 5.20 am on 17 October between St Souplet and Molain. The nineteen Mark Vs of 301st American Tank Battalion struggled to negotiate the Selle and one slipped off its crib.

27th American Division, 17 to 19 October, St Souplet to the St Maurice stream

The 108th Regiment crossed the railway around at St Souplet before advancing to the Le Cateau road, where its left flank came under attack, because 50th Division was delayed. The 105th Regiment was also counter-attacked beyond the railway line but the support battalion reached the Le Cateau road. Nine tanks had been knocked out.

Major General John O'Ryan planned an advance at 5.30 am on 18 October but 107th Regiment was pinned down in front of La Roue Farm while 105th Regiment could not reach Jonc de Mer Farm. Colonels DeBevoise and Andrews regrouped their men and both regiments advanced towards the St Maurice stream when it was dark. They made a little more progress the following day.

30th American Division, 17 to 19 October, Molain to Mazinghien

The machine gunners in Molain stopped Colonel Spence's 117th Regiment advancing on the right before switching to Colonel McCully's 118th Regiment on the left. The barrage was lost and it was some time before Martin Rivière and Molain were taken.

The 120th Regiment encountered little opposition when it advanced at 5.30 am on 18 October but Colonel Minor's men had to call a halt in front of Mazinghien and wait for 119th Regiment to catch up. Colonel Metts' men renewed the advance when IX Corps advanced on its right flank, but the mist had cleared and the Germans were waiting for them. It was late afternoon before the British cleared Ribeauville and only then could the Americans enter Mazinghien. The sprawling village was cleared the following morning.

IX Corps, 17 to 19 October

Lieutenant General Sir Walter Braithwaite's men were to capture the ridge south-east of Vaux-Andigny. Both 6th and 46th Divisions would advance at 5.30 am and then 1st Division would pass through the left flank heading for Wassigny. The fighting was 'mostly of a confused character. The type of country was beginning to change and more hedges and wire were met with.'

6th Division, 17 October, Vaux-Andigny

Major General Thomas Marden's men advanced from the east side of Vaux-Andigny, spreading out in the mist as they approached the Andigny Forest. Major Morris's 1st Shropshires followed the Wassigny railway while the 2nd York and Lancasters and 1st Buffs continued the advance towards La Vallée Mulâtre. The five tanks took time to silence the machine guns around Vaux Andigny station and the 11th Essex lost the barrage. Some were pinned down in front of Angin Farm but the rest followed a trench to Belle Vue Farm. The rest of the tanks veered too far south, followed by the 2nd Durhams.

46th Division, 17 October, Riquerval Wood

Major General Boyd had deployed most of his troops on his left flank while 137 Brigade carried out a Chinese Attack in Riquerval Wood. Officers followed compass bearings through the mist but the 1/5th Lincolns and 4th Leicesters were soon drifting to the right. The Germans held onto Andigny les Fermes until 1st Division secured the Bellevue Ridge and the 8th Sherwoods became disorientated. However, three tanks helped the 5th South Staffords round up 150 prisoners around Regnicourt. The 6th North

Staffords eventually sent patrols into Riquerval Wood on the right, and the following morning the 5th Leicesters contacted the French.

1st Division, 17 to 19 October, Andigny Forest to the Sambre Canal

Major General Peter Strickland was supposed to send 2 and 1 Brigades through the north side of Andigny Forest but 6th Division had become disorientated. The German anti-tank guns opened fire as soon as the mist cleared, knocking out four of the Whippets supporting the 2nd KRRC. A heavy tank was also hit but three others followed the 1st Northants through the Andigny Forest. A counter-attack would drive Lieutenant Colonel Berkeley's men back towards La Vallée Mulâtre.

Two tanks helped the 1st Camerons clear the area south of La Vallée Mulâtre while the 1st Loyals captured 170 prisoners en route to Andigny-les-Fermes. The Camerons and Loyals made it into Andigny Forest but the 2nd Sussex were pinned down and both they and the 1st Northants had to withdraw. A gas bombardment later forced everyone out of the wood.

The 11.30 am advance towards Andigny Forest on 18 October was hidden by a smoke barrage created by bombs dropped by RAF planes. The Germans were caught by surprise and the 1st SWBs and 2nd Welch rounded up around 300 prisoners north of Wassigny. The 1st Black Watch took many more in the village cellars; over seventy were taken after a Lewis gunner 'fired a drum of ammunition down the steps of a dug-out'. 'All night long, loud explosions were heard' as the Germans withdrew across the Sambre, and the 1st SWBs, 2nd Welch and 1st Black Watch had occupied the low ridge overlooking the canal by nightfall on 19 October.

XIII Corps, 23 to 26 October

Lieutenant General Sir Thomas Morland had to advance to the Richemont stream at 1.20 am on 23 October to bring it in line with Third Army when it advanced forty minutes later. It would take advantage of the full moon and hopefully take the Germans by surprise.

18th Division, 23 to 26 October, L'Évêque Wood

The tanks could not cross the Selle on the division's front so they crossed at Montay in Third Army's area 'by a crib bridge and lay peacefully camouflaged' until zero hour. 'Scores of houses in Le Cateau flew the French colours' and Major General Lee's men were 'vastly interested to hear how the faithful citizens had kept them concealed' for so long.

Two tanks were hit early on but two others advanced parallel to the Roman road with the 2nd Bedfords and the 11th Royal Fusiliers. The creeping barrage was patchy while all four tanks were out of action, leaving the 10th Essex pinned down along the Richemont stream. Captain Macdonald's company of the 7th Queen's Own were isolated on the far side of the 'wide swamp' and the 8th Berkshires were also stopped. The Germans eventually withdrew after they had been outflanked by Third Army and 400 prisoners were captured along the north side of L'Évêque Wood.

Brigadier General Wood's men lost the barrage because 33rd Division drifted into his sector. Lieutenant Colonel Curtis's reply when he was asked why the 8th East Surreys were lagging behind the 7th Buffs was, 'we are knee-deep in water and Scotsmen.' Six tanks eventually helped them clear Épinette and Fayt Farms and reach Bousies. Major General Lee's men had advanced 4½ miles and had taken over 700 prisoners and 50 artillery pieces.

There were no tanks available for the attack at 4 am on 24 October and the infantry had to cut through hedges woven with wire by hand. The 6th Northants lost the barrage and were pinned down until Lieutenant Frederick Hedges' Lewis gun section silenced six machine-gun posts. Lieutenant Colonel Turner's men then breached the Hermann II Line but the 11th Royal Fusiliers and 2nd Bedfords could not get across the ridge beyond. Hedges would be awarded the Victoria Cross.

The 7th Queen's struggled to clear the Hermann II Line in front of Robersart but the 8th East Surreys cleared it during the evening. There was a new attack at 1 am on 26 October and the 7th Queen's Own, 8th Berkshires and 10th Essex struggled to get through the hedges and orchards to secure a 'better and more defensible line' on Mont Carmel.

25th Division, 23 and 24 October, L'Évêque Wood

Only two tanks turned up so it took time to clear Jacques Mill and Garde Mill beyond the Richemont. The 1/8th Worcesters advanced through the north end of Pommereuil before rounding up 400 prisoners along the edge of l'Évêque Wood. Private Francis Miles silenced two machine guns so the 1/5th Gloucesters could advance through the north side of the wood and he would be awarded the Victoria Cross. Captain Pridham led the 9th Devons across the St Maurice stream but the 21st Manchesters were pinned on the far bank until a tank turned up. The 20th Manchesters helped the Devons clear the south part of Pommereuil before advancing to the far side of L'Évêque Wood. The advance was renewed at 4 am on 24 October but six tanks could not help the 9th Green Howards break the Hermann Position II because 'nothing had been previously known of this line of trenches'.

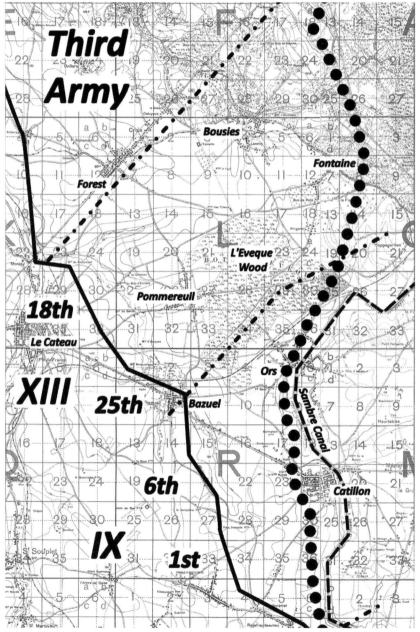

Fourth Army's left had to clear L'Évêque Forest between 23 and 25 October while its right drove the Germans back to the Sambre Canal.

IX Corps, 23 to 31 October

Lieutenant General Sir Walter Braithwaite's men faced a 2 mile advance to the Sambre Canal between Ors and Catillon. Zero hour was set for 2 am on 23 October to give XIII Corps forty minutes to come up on the left.

6th Division, 23 October, Bazuel to Ors on the Sambre Canal

Major General Marden's men struggled through hedges laced with wire while nine tanks mopped up behind them. Machine gunners on the far bank of the St Maurice valley meant that the 9th Norfolk and 1st Leicesters faced a long struggle to get into L'Évêque Wood. The Germans decided to withdraw during the afternoon, so the Norfolks made a flanking movement through 25th Division's area while the 2nd Sherwoods advanced along the forest rides to south end. Tanks helped the 1st West Yorkshires rip holes through the wired hedges around the St Maurice stream but the 2nd Durhams advanced faster beyond Le Plantin while the tanks mopped up behind them.

The Germans withdrew to the Sambre Canal late on 23 October and the 2nd York and Lancasters and 1st Shropshires followed a barrage through L'Évêque Wood. At the same time, the 1st West Yorkshires and 2nd Durhams moved up to the west bank of the canal around Ors and Catillon.

1st Division, 23 to 31 October, Catillon on the Sambre Canal

The 2nd Sussex fought the rearguard covering the engineers wiring up Catillon bridge on 23 October.

End of October Summary

The Allied commanders met at the Généralissime's headquarters in Senlis on 28 October. Foch thought the Germans were nearly defeated but warned, 'when one hunts a wild beast and finally comes upon him at bay, one faces greater danger. But it is not the time to stop; it is the time to redouble one's blows without paying attention to those received in return.' Pétain also wanted to keep the enemy on the run.

Haig reminded them that the BEF was short of men after nearly three months fighting. He was also concerned that the American Army needed more training and battle experience. Three days later, Haig met Generals Horne, Byng, Rawlinson and Birdwood at Cambrai. They all said the Germans were conducting organised withdrawals and that they were definitely not beaten.

Chapter 13

Practically a Route March

Second, Fifth and First Armies

1 to 11 November

Second Army

General Plumer knew the Germans were withdrawing from the River Schelde opposite the Fifth Army, so he told his corps commanders to prepare to follow up any retirement beyond the Schelde. There were signs that a withdrawal was imminent and the Germans' artillery slackened off, eventually stopping at dusk on 8 November. Second Army's engineers then launched bridges across the river in heavy rain.

XIX Corps, 8 to 11 November

41st Division, 9 to 11 November, Meersche

The 11th Queen's crossed the Schelde in canvas boats and cleared Meersche before moving east to Nukerke. The 10th Queen's had crossed at Kerkove but the Germans were dug in around Berchem, so they recrossed and waited for them to withdraw. The advance continued in earnest towards Nederbrakel on 10 November and Schendelbeke near the River Dendre. The men had seen no Germans during their long march.

35th Division, 8 to 11 November, Berchem

It took all day to find enough material to span the Berchem broken bridge. The 15th Sherwoods and 18th Highland Light Infantry eventually crossed early on 9 November. The 11th Lancashire Fusiliers continued the advance the following day, receiving 'an enthusiastic reception from the inhabitants. Bread, cigars and apples were handed out to the troops and Belgian flags made their appearance. The people appeared to be beside themselves with joy.' After hearing news of the armistice on the morning of the 11th, General Marindin drove to Grammont at the front. 'Excited crowds were

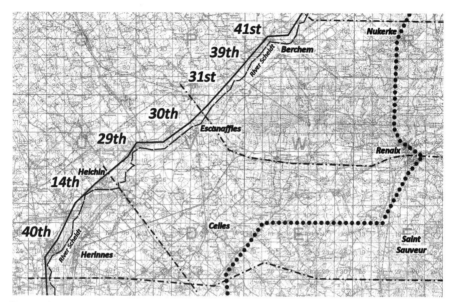

Second Army started crossing the Schelde Canal on 9 November and the Germans then fell back rapidly towards the River Dendre.

met here who threw flowers and climbed on the steps of the car in order to shake hands.' He made sure posts were established around the bridge and welcomed 200 British prisoners who had just been released.

31st Division, 9 to 11 November, Avelghem

Major General Campbell's men crossed the Schelde around Avelghem on 9 November and the 15/17th West Yorkshires were given 'a splendid reception' when they entered Renaix. They were again 'accompanied by the cheers of the populace' when they marched out the following morning en route to the River Dendre. They had reached Overboulaere by the time of the armistice and the end came 'quietly and without any of those manifestations of mad joy which convulsed the cities, towns and villages throughout Great Britain, France and Belgium'.

X Corps, 8 to 11 November

30th Division, 8 to 11 November, Renaix to Ghoy

The 2nd South Lancashires paddled across the Schelde in rafts and then cleared Escanaffles late on 8 November. The engineers installed footbridges so the 2/17th London could reinforce the bridgehead before dawn. Cyclists drove the German cavalry back to Ellezelles on 10 November but the 7th Dragoon Guards were unable to reach the River Dendre bridges east of Ghoy the following morning.

29th Division, 8 to 11 November, Bossuyt to Lessines

The 4th Worcesters crossed the Schelde at Bossuyt early on 8 November, only to find the Germans had left because the nearby Grand Courant stream had flooded. The 2nd Leinsters crossed using footbridges during the night, finding the same. The advance continued through Bois de Leuze on 10 November but the 7th Dragoon Guards came under fire from Lahamaide. One squadron was scouting ahead on 11 November when it came under fire from Ghoy just ten minutes before the armistice.

Major Chappell was determined to get across the Dendre so cantered forward at the head of one troop; they came under fire as they approached Lessines. He organised a pincer attack on the village, taking 130 prisoners and his men then took another forty on the far bank. Brigadier General Freyberg stopped the Germans blowing the bridges so the engineers could disarm the explosives. A few minutes later Chappell announced the armistice was in effect and his men escorted the released prisoners to their comrades to make sure the civilians did not attack them.

Elsewhere the final hour of the war was less thrilling. A staff officer cantered up to one battalion commander to announce, 'I am from headquarters to tell you the manoeuvres are over.' Along the column, 'no emotion was shown either of joy or thankfulness.' All except for one of the veterans. He 'found relief from his pent up feelings by taking off his pack, sitting on it and letting the tears flow'.

XV Corps, 5 to 11 November

14th Division, 26 October to 8 November, crossing the Schelde around Helcin

A bridgehead had already been established north of Warcoing and patrols discovered that the Germans were behind the flooded stream between Bossuyt and Helchin. Engineers bridged the Schelde at Lock 3, north of Warcoing, on 26 October, and south of it on the 28th, so the 23rd Cheshire could cross. Three more bridges were installed so the 33rd London could establish a third bridgehead early on 5 November. Then 14th Division was squeezed out of the line.

40th Division, 8 November, crossing the Schelde around Hérinnes

A patrol crossed the Schelde and engaged a small rearguard in Hérinnes late on 8 November. The engineers then built pontoon bridges so the 12th North Staffords and 13th East Lancashires could cross. Some the 12th Suffolk negotiated the canal sluice gates north of Hérinnes but wheeled transport could not cross. It meant XV Corps had to make forced crossings before advancing south-east, squeezing 40th Division out of the line.

Fifth Army

Fifth Army had reached the Schelde on its flanks but inundations made it impossible for XI Corps to cross north of Tournai. III Corps and I Corps faced Sixth Army's bridgehead around Tournai and Antoing but poor weather meant the RAF could not see the Germans pulling out and it was patrols that discovered that the Germans had left early on 8 November.

XI Corps, 9 to 11 November

59th Division, 9 to 11 November, Schelde to Velaines

Major General Nevill Smyth had a small bridgehead across the Schelde at Esquelmes and the 11th Scots Fusiliers eventually crossed early on 9 November. The King Edward's Horse then led them to Velaines while the 19th Hussars scouted as far ahead as Frasnes the following day. General Smyth then took over all of XI Corps' front, extending his right flank to Moustier. The final hours of the war were spent advancing to Papignies on the Dendre Canal north of Ath.

47th Division, 9 and 10 November, Pont-à-Chin

On 9 November the 1/22nd London Regiment and 1/17th London Regiment waded across the flooded fields around Pont-à-Chin to reach dry land. They found that the Germans had abandoned Mourcourt and Melles and the 19th Hussars reached Moustier by nightfall on 10 November. The 47th Division was then withdrawn into reserve.

III Corps, 7 to 11 November

74th Division, 7 to 10 November, Tournai

The Germans abandoned the west side of Tournai before dawn on 7 November and an aerial observer reported that all but one of the bridges had

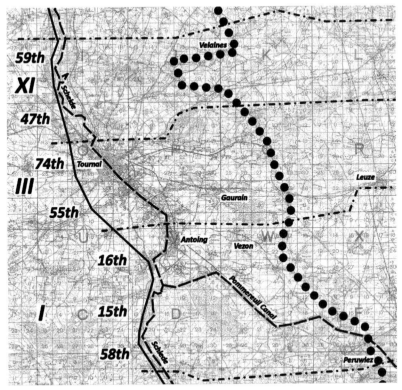

Fifth Army cleared the Tournai and Antoing bridgehead on 8 November and the Germans then fell back quickly towards the River Dendre.

been demolished. Machine-gun teams covered the Schelde in Tournai and artillery could not be used to dislodge them. The 10th Shropshires crossed at Pont des Trous on 7 November where the medieval city wall bridged the river, and the German guns fell silent as they advanced beyond the railway station to Faubourg de Morelle. Civilians reported the town had been abandoned and a single rearguard challenged the advance to the east on 9 November. The divisional sector narrowed during 10 November and it was squeezed out of the line between Frasnes and Leuze.

55th Division, 7 to 11 November, Tournai

The Germans withdrew across the Schelde early on 7 November and cheering crowds met the 1/6th King's when they entered Tournai. A rearguard stopped the 5th South Lancashires crossing the canal at Calonne until dusk. The two battalions then used boats to cross and protected the engineers as they spent the night building bridges. The King Edward's

Horse came under fire from Leuze, so 'Stockwell's Force', a mixed group of infantry, machine guns and field guns, was organised. The Germans had evacuated the village by the time it advanced while an RAF spotter plane reported Tricolours and people on the streets of Gaurain.

Major General Hugh Jeudwine took over III Corps' advance the following day and his cavalry and cyclist patrols came under fire from the rearguards covering the Dendre bridges in Ath. Lieutenant Colonel Brighten's 2/5th Lancashire Fusiliers caught up but they too were unable to capture the river crossings. The only good news Major Bodington had to report was that Captains Wheeler and Waterhouse had stopped the German engineers blowing up the railway bridge in the centre of the town.

Some of the King Edward's Horse and cyclists scouting ahead of 55th Division did not hear about the armistice until it was nearly too late and one patrol was preparing to attack Silly, four miles east of the River Dendre, when it finally received the message to cease fire.

I Corps, 8 to 11 November

16th Division, 8 November, Antoing

The 5th Irish Fusiliers discovered the Germans had withdrawn from Antoing, so the 18th Scottish Rifles crossed at Bruyelle after dusk. They covered the engineers while they launched two bridges so the 22nd Northumberland Fusiliers could advance beyond Fontenoy. The division was withdrawn into reserve later that night.

15th Division, 8 to 10 November, River Schelde to the River Dendre

The 4/5th Black Watch crossed the Schelde by a railway and road bridges while the 8th Seaforths paddled across on rafts. The Germans were falling back rapidly, so Major General Reed formed a combined arms group to take over the entire corps front, and it was 15 miles east of the Schelde by nightfall on 10 November. His men had formed a bridgehead at Nevergnies on the River Dendre south-east of Ath by the time of the armistice.

58th Division, 8 to 11 November, River Schelde towards the River Dendre

The 7th London had crossed the Schelde on a pontoon ferry as early as 30 October to secure Chateau de Montagne. The 6th and 7th London Regiments used rafts to cross at Bléharies on 8 November and they covered the engineers as they launched a pontoon bridge. The 2/2nd and 8th London Regiment then entered Laplaigne, only to discover that the Germans had left.

Major General Ramsay formed two combined arms groups but it took time to bridge the Antoing–Pommereuil and the Bladon canals. By the end of 10 November, they too were 15 miles east of the Schelde. The 1 Cavalry Brigade then covered the advance east of Neufmaison during the last hours of the war.

First Army

Haig believed the Germans would abandon the river line if First Army kept pushing, so General Horne discussed how to take Valenciennes with Lieutenant Generals Currie and Godley on 27 October. The artillery was banned from shelling the town centre but the gunners were allowed to target the houses which overlooked the flooded canal on the edge of the town. The plan was for the Canadian Corps to scale the ancient walls while XXII Corps pushed past the south side.

The key to liberating Valenciennes was the wooded hill to the south-east, called Mont Houy, where the Germans had spent several days fighting off 51st Division's attacks. There would be no preliminary bombardment but the Canadian gunners planned to fire a 'rather unique artillery barrage' of over 2,000 tons of shells at the hill. Fourteen field brigades would provide the creeping barrage while another three would cover the flanks; the heavy artillery would provide 'oblique, enfilade and even reverse fire'. Twelve batteries of machine guns would supplement the heaviest barrage fired in support for a single brigade attack during the war.

Canadian Corps, 1 and 2 November

4th Canadian Division, 1 November, Valenciennes

Major General Sir David Watson's men had to establish a line west of Valenciennes while pushing around the south side of town. The 72nd Battalion crossed the Schelde canal north-west of the town using 'collapsible boats and cork float bridges' while 38th Battalion did the same at the south-west corner. The attack on Mont Houy began well and 47th Battalion captured Le Poirier Station while 44th Battalion were met by Germans who 'surrendered in large numbers, stupefied by the overpowering barrage'.

Both 46th and 50th Battalions joined 47th Battalion in the fierce fighting around Marly and around the steelworks. Sergeant Hugh Cairns was wounded silencing three machine-gun posts in front of 46th Canadian Battalion but he still captured several field guns and dozens of prisoners. Sadly, he was treacherously injured as he disarmed one party. Cairns refused

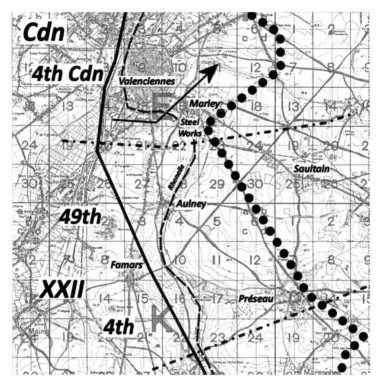

The Canadian Corps outflanked Valenciennes on 1 November while XXII Corps pushed forward south of the town.

to return to the aid post until he collapsed, and he died the following day; he was posthumously awarded the Victoria Cross.

The Germans eventually abandoned Marly after their counter-attacks failed. Over 1,800 prisoners had been taken while another 800 bodies were buried. Currie said it was 'one of the most successful operations the Corps has yet performed'. The 54th Battalion entered Marley the following morning and then 47th and 46th Battalions moved through and beyond Valenciennes. There was little fighting because the Germans were withdrawing as fast as they could toward Mons.

XXII Corps, 1 and 2 November

49th Division, 1 and 2 November, Aulnoy, south of Valenciennes
Lieutenant Colonel Oddie's 1/5th West Yorkshires joined the 6th Duke's as they crossed the Rhonelle steam on duckboards at 5.15 am on 1 November. They captured over 900 prisoners and 'great was the astonishment in Aulnoy

for the villagers had been told that all the English had been killed. They asked what American State they came from and were hardly believed when they said they were English.' A hurricane bombardment helped the 2/4th York and Lancasters capture 200 prisoners around the steelworks the following afternoon.

4th Division, 1 to 2 November, Préseau

The 1st Hampshires and 1st Rifle Brigade 'kept close up to an excellent barrage and made short work of crossing the Rhonelle'. The Hampshires advanced past the north side of Préseau and the Rifle Brigade had taken 750 prisoners around the village before a counter-attack drove them back. The 1st King's Own and 2nd Seaforths took another 680 prisoners on the ridge east of Préseau the following day.

VIII Corps, 8 to 11 November

After a week waiting along the Schelde Canal the sounds of evacuation were heard late on 8 November. Lieutenant General Aylmer Hunter-Weston warned his division commanders to be ready to move and issued a code word in case they had to reorganise for a pursuit. The Germans had left before the early morning bombardment began.

52nd Division, 8 to 11 November, Jard Canal to the Bois de Baudour

The Germans abandoned the Schelde and Jard Canals on 8 November and the 7th Scottish Rifles paddled over on rafts. The 7th Royal Scots crossed footbridges and entered Condé-sur-l'Escaut where they 'were not only greeted with tempestuous ovations but were loaded with gifts of flowers, cigars and coffee'. They filed across the lock gates in single file, avoiding the canal bridges in case they were booby trapped, en route to Ville Pommeroeul.

The 7th Scottish Rifles kept pushing but Major General Francis Marshall had to throw back his left flank because Fifth Army was 5 miles behind. The 4th and 7th Royal Scots were ordered up to drive a rearguard from Herchies but the 'men naturally had no desire to run into unnecessary danger with the knowledge that fighting was to end on the following day.' The advance stopped when they came under fire in Bois de Baudour.

8th Division, 10 and 11 November, Ville Pommeroeul to Mons

There were rumours that an armistice was about to be announced but the 2nd West Yorkshires and 2nd Middlesex wanted to engage their enemy one last time 'before the whistle blew'.

Canadian Corps, 3 to 11 November

3rd Canadian Division, 3 to 11 November, River Schelde to Mons

Brigadier General Draper's men established bridgeheads across the Schelde around Thiers, so the engineers could built bridges. The 5th Mounted Rifles were involved in 'vicious fighting' for Vicq on 4 November and the Germans only withdrew after 4th Canadian Division advanced to the south. The 8 Brigade took 200 prisoners around Quiévrechain on 6 November but the bridges across the Grand Honnelle around Crespin were down. The Germans were still holding Condé and the Mons canal to the north, so 8 Brigade formed a flank around Hensies while 7 Brigade advanced along the Mons railway, crossed the Mons canal and headed for Boussu.

The Germans had abandoned the mining villages and Major General Frederick Loomis noted 'that German animosity had been less pronounced. Buildings were relatively undamaged, the shop windows offered a wider range of commodities and more men were seen in the streets. Amid scenes of gaiety and holiday making they were hailed as liberators and greeted with cheers, handshakes and kisses and offerings of coffee, wine and beer.'

Late on 8 November, the 5th Mounted Rifles crossed the Condé Canal and advanced north to contact 52nd Division. At the same time, 49th Battalion

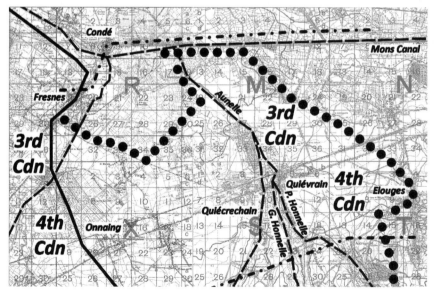

First Army's advance through the mining region, south of the Condé–Mons canal.

moved along the north side of the canal while the PPCLI advanced between the canal and the Mons road to Boussu. The Royal Canadian Regiment tried to enter Mons on 10 November but 'heavy mist, poor communications and strong enemy fire' meant that more troops were required. The 42nd Battalion took over the line south of the Condé Canal but it could not get into the town either.

Mons became quiet after dusk on the night of 10 November so Lieutenant General Currie decided to clear the town. The 42nd Battalion crossed the Canal du Centre, moved through Nimy and crossed a filled-in section of the town moat late on 10 November. They outflanked the German outposts and the Royal Canadian Regiment advanced as the firing died down. The two battalions would argue over who reached the Grand Place first but the burgomaster supported the Royal Canadian Regiment's claim. At dawn the 42nd Battalion's pipe band 'created tremendous enthusiasm' as it played through the streets. Patrols of the 5th Lancers had reached Bossuit, 6 miles east of Mons, by the time the cease-fire sounded.

4th Canadian Division, 3 to 6 November, Valenciennes to Quiévrechain and Marchipont

Patrols reached the ridge between Onnaing and Estreux on 3 November and the Germans pulled back behind the Aunelle stream. Two days later, 78th Battalion cleared Quarouble on the left and 87th Battalion took Rombies on the right but 85th Battalion could not capture a large slag heap in the centre. On 6 November, the 2nd Mounted Rifles and 78th Battalion worked together to clear Quiévrechain while 85th Battalion cleared the slag heap. On the right, 102nd Battalion took Marchipont and crossed both the Petite and Grande Honnelle streams around Baisieux.

2nd Canadian Division, 7 to 11 November, Baisieux to the South of Mons

Major General Burstall organised a mobile force with orders 'to act with the utmost boldness' but Brigadier General Tremblay had to wait until the engineers repaired the bridge over the Honnelle. Eventually 25th Battalion passed through Baisieux on 7 November and it then encountered 'a mixture of street fighting against enemy die-hards and a warm welcome from the civilian inhabitants' in Elouges the following day.

The Canadians struggled to get through the maze of collieries and mining villages but 24th Battalion still reached Dour. The 4 Brigade took over on 9 November and made 'practically a route march' to Mount Erebus, south of Mons.

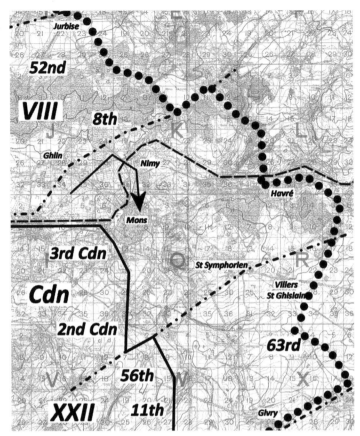

The advance into and beyond Mons on 11 November.

Lieutenant General Currie planned 'an encircling manoeuvre, so Mons was as far as possible to be spared damage'. On 10 November, the 4 Brigade encountered strong resistance south-east of Mons but both Bois la Haut and Hyon were captured during the night. Patrols of the 5th Lancers reached Villers-St-Ghislain while Brigadier General McCuiag's men entered St Symphorien before the cease-fire. They had suffered one casualty and Private George Ellison would be buried in the nearby military cemetery.

XXII Corps, 3 to 11 November

56th Division, 3 to 11 November, Saultain to Harmignies

At 5.15 am on 3 November, 169 and 168 Brigades advanced into Saultain, 'which was full of civilians'. The following day, the 1/4th London Regiment took Sebourquiaux and the 1/6th London Regiment occupied Sebourg while the Australian Light Horse and New Zealand cyclists found the Germans waiting beyond the Aunelle. On 5 November, the 1/13th and 1/14th London Regiments were unable to clear Honnelles but the 1/5th London Regiment secured Angreau in a tough battle along the Grande Honnelle. Neither the 1/13th London nor the 2nd London were able to cross the stream the following day but the 1/14th London outflanked the garrison of Angres in the centre.

Early on 7 November, the 7th and 8th Middlesex advanced though Onnezies, across the Petit Honnelle stream and into Montigny. 'Explosions and fires were more numerous at night' because the withdrawal had begun in earnest, and the two Middlesex battalions marched through Athis and Fayt-le-France the following day. Artillery units used churches as report centres while logistics units were given 'meeting points' to assemble at but there were many problems. The roads were cratered, bridges were down, railheads were far behind, supplies were late and the rain never stopped.

The Londoners reached the Mons–Maubeuge road on 9 November and the final act of resistance was fought around Harveng the following day. The infantry had to help the 16th Lancers cross the Nouvelles stream before 63rd Division took over the final advance. Major General Amyatt Hull would have had memories of Harmignies as he passed through; he fought there as a battalion commander back in August 1914.

11th Division, 3 to 11 November, Curgies to Givry

The 9th Sherwoods and the 9th West Yorkshires crossed the Valenciennes–Jenlain railway around Curgies on 3 November. The following morning the 9th Sherwoods crossed the Aunelle stream at Sebourg, but the 6th Lincolns were unable to get any further. The West Yorkshires were unlucky to be caught by machine-gun and artillery fire as they approached Le Triez and over one hundred men were hit. The four battalions advanced through Roisin the following day and the German artillery shelled it, 'despite the fact that the village was crowded with civilians'.

The 6th York and Lancasters and 2nd Green Howards took over the advance on 6 November but 'conditions were awful. The weather was very bad, rain was falling all day and night while the ground was a morass.' It meant they were unable to cross the Grande Honnelle until the following day, giving the Germans time to withdraw beyond the Mons–Maubeuge road.

Major General Henry Davies' men were struggling to keep up and 'no rations arrived, for the advance had been so rapid that there had been no time to get them up. Most of the roads had been blown up by the enemy and transport was impossible but aeroplanes dropped a certain amount of bully beef and biscuits which temporarily satisfied the hunger of the troops.' Despite the difficulties the enemy rear guards were driven out of Havay and onto the high ground beyond. The leading battalions were beyond Givry by the time news of the armistice came through and 'the officers and men took the news very calmly; it seemed too good to be true.'

63rd Division, 7 to 11 November, Grand Honnelle Stream to Villers-Saint-Ghislain

Brigadier General Curling's 189 Brigade crossed the Grande Honnelle stream north of Angreau at 9 am on 7 November. 'From then onward, the advance was continuous and almost unopposed by the enemy infantry. However, isolated machine-gun detachments and sporadic artillery exacted their toll in what was no longer a battle but a pursuit.' They passed through Honnelles, Audregnies and Wihéries as the advance swung to the east, eventually coming under fire from the huge wood beyond Offignies and Blaugies.

Brigadier General Lesslie's 190 Brigade had reached Sars-la Bruyère before handing over to 188 Brigade. Brigadier General Coleridge then swung north-east heading for Nouvelles. On the morning of 11 November, the 16th Lancers led 189 and 188 Brigades beyond Villers-St-Ghislain.

Summary

Foch had messaged Haig with the following words of encouragement on 9 November: 'The enemy, disorganised by our repeated attacks, is yielding ground on the whole front. Our advance should be kept going and hastened. I appeal to the energy and the initiative of the commanders-in-chief to make the results obtained decisive.' It came towards the end of an exhausting advance which had tested the men of the BEF to the limits of their endurance.

On 11 November, 'just before 11 am, all batteries opened fire. Each gunner was determined to be the last man to fire a shot at the Germans. And then in the midst of the rolling thunder of rapid fire, eleven o'clock struck, the first blast of bugles pierced the air and with the last note, silence reigned.' After the hardships of the final advance, 'the end left the men dumb, amazed almost, that there could be anything in the nature of peace after four long years of warfare.'

Chapter 14

Hammering the Hun had Broken Jerry's Heart

Third and Fourth Armies

1 to 11 November

General Byng had set zero hour on 4 November for 5.30 am but V Corps' right had to attack forty-five minutes later, in cooperation with Fourth Army. Everyone was cold, wet and tired and most battalions were below half strength. 'Indeed, the progress of our advance was governed mainly by the state of the roads and the difficulty of getting rations to the troops in the forward area.'

XVII Corps, 25 October to 11 November

61st Division, 25 October to 2 November, Maresches

The 2/4th Berkshires and 2/4th Ox and Bucks advanced across the Rhonelle stream under a smoke barrage on 25 October but were driven back by fire from Sepmeries. The 2/5th Gloucesters expanded the bridgehead early on 29 October but an attempt to cross at Maresches forty-eight hours later was thwarted when a burning cottage lit up the stream.

Major General John Duncan was to cover First Army's flank as it surrounded Valenciennes to the north. The engineers installed footbridges in Artres, so the 2/8th Worcesters and the 2/7th Warwicks could cross the Rhonelle stream before zero on 1 November. They took over 750 prisoners around Maresches only to be pinned down by fire from St Hubert Chateau when they crossed the next ridge. They were waiting for the 9th Northumberland Fusiliers to move up on their left flank when they saw four captured British tanks approaching; two were knocked out and the other two withdrew. The 2/5th Gloucesters failed to capture the chateau during the night but the 2/4th Ox and Bucks and the 2/5th Gloucesters advanced beyond St Hubert the following day, capturing two tanks and 620 prisoners.

19th Division, 3 to 10 November, Jenlain to Malplaquet

The 9th Cheshires cleared the north part of Jenlain during the afternoon of 3 November and the 8th North Staffords entered the south part when it was dark. They crossed the Petite Aunelle stream the following morning but 'the enemy abandoned their guns and ran away before the infantry could come to close quarters.' The 2nd Wiltshires and 9th Welch reached Eth but the 9th Cheshires encountered stiff resistance in Wargnies-le-Grand. A second attempt to cross the stream around Eth and Bry by the 2nd Wiltshires and 8th North Staffords also failed. The Aunelle was finally crossed the following morning but artillery fire stopped 58 and 56 Brigades catching the Germans as they withdrew across Hogneau stream.

On 6 November, 58 Brigade cleared Bettrechies but 56 Brigade could not enter St-Waast 'owing to the intense shelling and machine-gun fire'. The Germans abandoned the Hogneau stream during the night but 57 Brigade came under machine-gun fire as it advanced north of Bavai. Brigadier General Glasgow deployed 58 Brigade on the left flank because First Army was delayed, but Major General George Jeffreys wanted to keep pushing, 'in spite of the fatigue of the troops'. Taisnières had been evacuated but the 10th Warwicks had to fight their way through Bois de la Lanière while the 3rd Worcesters pushed past the south side. The division was withdrawn into reserve early on 10 November.

24th Division, 3 to 11 November, Villers Pol to Maubeuge

The 9th Sussex cleared Villers Pol on 3 November and then fought their way across the Petite Aunelle stream the following morning. The 13th Middlesex followed sunken roads into Wargnies-le-Grand while the 7th Northants cleared Wargnies-le-Petit. 'Now it was a case of taking up the hunt of a really retreating enemy… We felt we were now really entering into the open fighting we had hoped for all through the long years of the war.'

The 1st Royal Fusiliers advanced to the Hogneau stream on 5 November and then crossed it the following morning. They could not enter Bavai but the 3rd Rifle Brigade followed the Germans through the town on 7 November. The following day, the 6th Dragoon Guards scouted ahead while the 8th Queen's Own and 1st North Staffords passed through Bois de la Lanière, only to be pinned down in front of Feignies.

A rapid advance towards the Belgian border followed and Major General Arthur Daly took over XVII Corps' front north of Maubeuge on 10 November. The Germans had stripped the countryside of food, leaving the divisional column responsible for the many hungry civilians, so the Dragoon Guards had to wait for the infantry to catch up before crossing the Belgian border. The 12th Rifle Brigade and the 12th KRRC (from 20th Division) took over the front line north of Maubeuge on 11 November and advanced along the north bank of the River Sambre until 11 am.

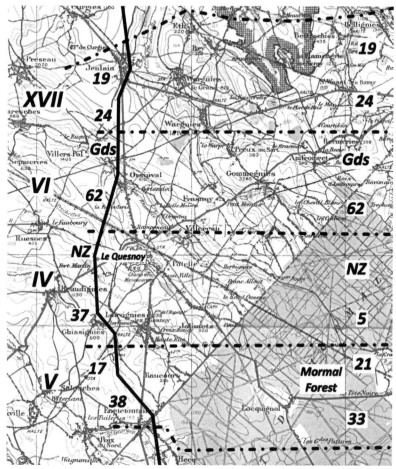

Third Army's advance north of and through the Mormal Forest started with the New Zealand Division's spectacular capture of Le Quesnoy on 4 November.

VI Corps, 4 to 11 November

Guards Division, 4 to 11 November, Villers Pol to Maubeuge

The 1st Coldstream Guards cleared Villers Pol during a dark, wet night while the rest of 2 Guards and 1 Guards Brigade reached the rest of the first objective before zero hour on 4 November. The 2nd Coldstream Guards then headed south-east along the north bank of the Rhonelle but the 2nd Grenadier Guards had a difficult fight in the woods south-west of Wargnies-le-Petit. They then crossed the Petit Aunelle stream while the 1st Irish Guards passed through Preux au Sart. The 1st Coldstream Guards waded across the Rhonelle stream and then the 3rd Grenadier Guards advanced through Frasnoy before coming under fire from Gommegnies.

Whippets supported the 2nd Scots Guards and 1st Grenadier Guards during their 3 mile advance on 5 November but they were unable to capture Bermeries on their left flank. 'The main difficulty against which the troops had to contend was the enclosed nature of the country. The maintenance of direction and connection was no easy matter. Once a company or platoon had been sent off, it could not be found again.' Many prisoners were taken and there were few casualties but one was 3 Guards Brigade's commander, Brigadier General Heywood.

The 1st Scots Guards and 1st Grenadier Guards followed hedges and ditches to outflank the Germans holding Mecquignies the following day. The 1st Welsh Guards sent patrols into Bavai early on 7 November; they discovered that the Germans had just left. Brigadier Sergison-Brooke was told to pursue them but a rearguard in La Longueville was waiting for the 3rd Grenadier Guards. The 1st Scots Guards were trying to outflank the village when their prisoners told them their comrades were leaving. The 1st Coldstream Guards and 1st Scots Guards found the next group of rearguards around Feignies and Fort Gravaux (one of Maubeuge's outlying forts) the following day.

A captured order stated that the Germans were withdrawing beyond Maubeuge, so Major General Matheson asked Brigadier General Sergison-Brooke to push into the town while it was still dark. The 3rd Grenadier Guards took less than forty prisoners but hundreds of townspeople emerged from their hiding places to greet them. Cavalry and cyclist patrols located the new German line late on 10 November. At 11 am the following day, 'there was no exuberant outburst of enthusiasm, no wild scenes of rejoicing. Officers and men went about their ordinary duties, scarcely realising at first that the end had really come.'

62nd Division, 4 to 11 November, Le Quesnoy to Maubeuge

The 5th KOYLIs and the 2/4th Hampshires advanced through a mist made thicker by the smoke from Le Quesnoy. The 2/4th Duke's and the 2/4th KOYLIs then crossed the Rhonelle stream and headed for Frasnoy. Finally, the 5th Duke's and the 2/4th York and Lancasters found the Germans waiting beyond the Petite Aunelle stream.

The 2/20th London Regiment and the 1/5th Devons entered Gommegnies on 5 November behind a barrage which created 'a wonderful display of fireworks with red, green, yellow, white and golden rain'. Whippets then accompanied the 5th KOYLIs and the 8th West Yorkshires towards Bermeries as the locals waved them on singing the Marseillaise.

The 2/20th London and the 8th West Yorkshires made the morning advance and then the 2/4th Hampshires and 2/4th Duke's continued along the road south of Bavai. The weather was miserable but 'through the dark night of war men began to see the light; a brighter dawn was near.' The 8th West Yorkshires, 1/5th Devons and the 5th Duke's came under fire as they emerged from Bois Delhaye, so Major General Whigham called a halt while the divisions on the flank caught up.

The 2/4th York and Lancasters and the 2/4th KOYLIs advanced through Hoyaux Wood on 8 November, but when the mist cleared they came under artillery fire. It then took the 5th KOYLIs until the early hours of 9 November to capture Fort Gravaux (another of Maubeuge's outlying forts). The rearguard had given their comrades time to evacuate Maubeuge, as the 1/4th York and Lancasters and 2/4th KOYLIs found out when they entered Sous-Bois and then Faubourg St Lazare. Patrols entered the south side of the town as the Guards moved in from the north. They received a great welcome and 'large quantities of booty of every description were captured'. The cavalry and cyclist patrols moved along the south bank of the Sambre but the only sound of battle came from Mons, where the Canadians were still fighting.

IV Corps, 4 to 11 November

New Zealand Division, 4 and 5 November, Le Quesnoy

Le Quesnoy was another of Vauban's fortified towns, surrounded by earthworks, bastions and a dry moat. It was also full of civilians. Two orange flares at 5.20 am signalled the New Zealander outposts had withdrawn and a barrage of shells and barrels of burning oil exploded along the ancient ramparts ten minutes later. The batteries ceased firing at the west wall after fifteen minutes and the 4th Rifles' patrols checked the German response. Meanwhile the other batteries smothered the rest of the walls with smoke, screening the 2nd and 1st Rifles as they moved to the north and south.

Lieutenant Colonel Cockcroft led the 3rd Rifles through the 1st Rifles, rounding up dozens of prisoners who were escaping 37th Division's attack to the south. The 1st Auckland Battalion covered the gates through Le Quesnoy's walls while the 2nd and 1st Wellington Battalions surrounded the town. Firing had all but stopped because most of the garrison wanted to surrender but there were no white flags because some officers wanted to fight on.

The New Zealanders now faced the most difficult task because the moat was 'divided into an inner and outer moat by a line of disconnected fortifications which act as an outlying rampart. Their sides are faced with brick or sandstone, supported by thick banks of earth, and the trees and thick undergrowth which crown their summits and cover the earth banks make the whole of this outer rampart a bewildering labyrinth.'

Smoke covered the walls as Lieutenant Colonel Barraclough's 4th Rifles scaled the outer wall and Lieutenant Colonel Jardine's 2nd Rifles scrambled across a destroyed bridge. Three prisoners were then sent to the German headquarters with the following note: 'Le Quesnoy is now completely closed and our troops are east of the city. You are challenged to surrender and your garrison will be treated as honest prisoners of war.' A contact plane flew over the town and dropped a similar message.

Brigadier General Hart organised a trench mortar barrage at 4 pm to drive the Germans into their shelters. At the same time, Lieutenant Averill and Second Lieutenant Kerr crossed the moat, led their men up a ladder and entered the town. 'The Germans recognising the fait accompli threw up the sponge, and some fifteen minutes later the 2nd Rifles marched in through the Valenciennes Gate. In no time at all the streets were filled with a tumultuous mass of indescribably excited townsfolk.' An English speaking prisoner led the New Zealanders to the underground tunnels where 800 Germans were hiding. They were put to work putting out fires and disarming booby-traps.

The capture of Le Quesnoy had been 'an outstanding day' for the New Zealanders but there was still work to be done because they now faced the north side of the Mormal Forest. It was a vast area with many clearings where Allied prisoners had cut down trees for the German Army. The 1st Canterbury Battalion and the 2nd Otago Battalion entered early on 5 November; they found the Germans had abandoned the west half. A few machine gun teams covered the roads and rides but the New Zealanders were along the far edge, 4 miles to the east, by nightfall.

42nd Division, 6 to 9 November, Mormal Forest to Hautmont

Early on 6 November, Major General Solly-Flood's men advanced out of the Mormal Forest and into a maze of hedgerows. Rearguards in Hargnies and Vieux Mesnil pinned down the 8th Manchesters but the 5th East Lancashires reached the Sambre Canal. The rearguards withdrew into Bois Hautmont overnight.

On 8 November, the 10th Manchesters and 5th East Lancashires advanced to the Sambre south of Hautmont while the 8th Manchesters cleared the wood only to find the bridges were down. But the explosions 'had partially demolished houses, so there was ample material on the spot'. The civilians dragged 'doors, beds and mattresses to the river bank' so the soldiers could bridge the lock. As they marched through the streets, 'women threw their arms around the necks of soldiers, old men embraced them and girls ran up with cakes, flowers and wine.' The town was cleared by nightfall.

Pontoons failed to arrive, so Brigadier General Fargus crossed the Sambre at Pont-sur-Sambre in 5th Division's sector. The 8th Lancashire

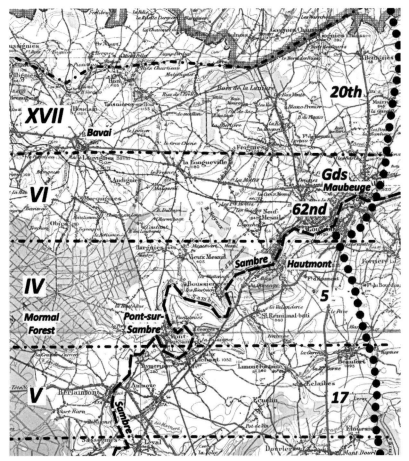

Third Army's right had to fight its way across the Sambre Canal between 6 and 8 November but had reached a north-south line either side of Maubeuge by dawn on 11 November.

Fusiliers then covered the south side of Hautmont while the 7th Lancashire Fusiliers drove the rearguard out of Fort d'Hautmont and the 8th Lancashire Fusiliers cleared the nearby high ground. 'Hammering the Hun had broken Jerry's heart and he was really on the run.' On 9 November, the 7th Lancashire Fusiliers took over the divisional front and advanced 2 miles without seeing the enemy. They did, however, find three trains loaded with ammunition abandoned on a railway siding south of Maubeuge before they were withdrawn into reserve.

37th Division, 4 November, Mormal Forest

Burning oil drums were fired at Louvignies early on 4 November and then a tank helped the 13th KRRC round up 240 prisoners. A second tank drove along the railway east of Ghissignies with the 10th Royal Fusiliers, while a third helped the 2nd Essex clear Jolimetz. The 8th Somersets and 13th Royal Fusiliers came under 'spasmodic machine-gun fire down the railway and the rides' as they moved through Mormal Forest.

5th Division, 5 to 11 November, Pont-sur-Sambre to the Belgian Border

The 1st Bedfords, 1st East Surreys and 1st DCLI passed through the Mormal Forest on 5 November, finding the Aymeries bridge over the Sambre was down. The DCLI reached Pont-du-Sambre by dusk and the East Surreys caught up with them the following morning. Major Brett Cloutman ran down to the river after men of 59th Field Company reported that the bridge north of Pont-sur-Sambre was prepared for demolition. He 'rolled across the tow path, swam the bullet-splattered river and cut the leads' before swimming back. The bridge was later damaged by shell fire but Cloutman's act had saved the abutments, making it far easier to build a replacement during the night. His act of bravery was the last one to be awarded the Victoria Cross during the war.

The 1st DCLI, 1st Norfolks and 1st Cheshires crossed the Sambre on pontoons early on 7 November but there was plenty of fire from Boussières, where 42nd Division had been held up. The 1st Devons came next and they advanced towards the south edge of Hautmont. Cyclists then accompanied the 3rd Hussars as they led the 1st East Surreys and the 1st DCLI past the town. The 1st Queen's Own and the 2nd KOSBs took over after dusk and continued marching through the night 'because it was obvious the enemy was retiring helter-skelter'.

The 1st East Surreys and the 1st DCLI entered St Remy early on 8 November while the cavalry and cyclists crossed the Solre stream, but all 'the troops were now thoroughly exhausted. Rain had fallen continuously, the ground was sodden and movement across cultivated land became a matter of great difficulty.' No Germans were seen on 9 November and the cavalry seized three trains loaded with machine guns and munitions beyond Ferrière-le-Grande the following day. Major General Ponsonby then took over responsibility for the whole of IV Corps front as the cavalry advanced to the Belgian border.

V Corps, 4 to 11 November

17th Division, 4 November, Mormal Forest

Oil drums exploded in flames around the road junction north-east of Englefontaine but the 10th Lancashire Fusiliers, the 9th Duke's and the 12th Manchesters suffered heavy casualties struggling through the many orchards. The 10th Sherwoods, 7th Lincolns and 7th Borders had an easier passage through the forest because 'there was little undergrowth, there were several large clearings and the trees had been thinned.' The artillery fired shrapnel shells only along the rides because high explosive shells often exploded prematurely in the tree-tops causing friendly casualties. Next came the 7th East Yorkshires, 6th Dorsets and 10th West Yorkshires, and they crossing the Locquignol clearing as soon as the artillery had moved up.

21st Division, 5 to 7 November, crossing the Sambre at Berlaimont

The 12th/13th Northumberland Fusiliers and 1st Lincolns left the Mormal Forest and advanced to the Sambre around Aymeries and Berlaimont. It was possible to cross the lock gates but the bridges were down and the river was 'a strong current, carrying down a considerable volume of water rising with the deluge of rain that had been pouring down all day'. A Royal Engineer major found a bridge at Berlaimont during the evening and two companies of the 1st Lincolns crossed as the Germans prepared to blow it up. The 6th Leicesters and 1st Wiltshire formed a bridgehead early the following morning and advanced to the Bavai road while the engineers bridged the raging torrent for the artillery. The 9th KOYLIs and 15th Durhams faced a stiff fight with the rearguard covering Limont Fontaine on 7 November.

17th Division, 8 and 9 November

Early on 8 November, the 10th Sherwoods, the 7th Lincolns and 7th Border Regiment found the Germans waiting from them on the Maubeuge–Avesnes road. During the night they withdrew to the Thure stream near the Belgian border.

38th Division, 4 and 5 November, Mormal Forest

The Welsh men followed the handful of tanks as they crashed through hedges laced with barbed wire and 'each column was led by an officer marching by compass bearing'. Brigadier General de Pree's 115 Brigade led through the forest and then 113 Brigade captured ten field guns. Finally, Captains Morgan and Wilcoxon led the 13th Welsh through the dark, wet woods while Captain Butler's company of the 2nd Welsh Fusiliers faced a struggle on the right flank. The 13th Welsh Fusiliers reached the far side of the Mormal Forest early on 5 November. The division had advanced nearly 10 miles in two days and it had taken over 500 men and 23 field guns.

33rd Division, 5 to 7 November, Mormal Forest and the Sambre

Major General Pinney took over the advance in the middle of the Mormal Forest and Brigadier General Baird's men had reached the Sambre by dusk on 5 November. 'Despite the congestion of traffic on the road and in the drives, the enormous craters which had been blown and the obstacles formed by fallen trees, rapid progress was made.'

Lieutenant Colonel Owen's 1st Middlesex carried timber down to the canal bank and Major Anderson's engineers floated a bridge on cork rafts. Lieutenant Colonel Hutchinson's Argylls crossed on a makeshift bridge made of limbers and ropes and entered Aulnoye before dawn. The 2nd Worcesters reached Leval but the 1st Queen's had to swim across with ammunition when they started to run out. The 1st Queen's and the 1st and 5th Scots Rifles reached the Bavai road late on 6 November but they were pinned down in front of Écuélin the following day.

38th Division, 8 November, Through the Bois le Roy

The advance 'kept pushing on with gradually increasing speed and it looked as if the campaign would end in a running fight, finishing in Berlin'. The 13th and 16th Welsh Fusiliers advanced through Bois le Roy on 8 November, crossing the Braquenière stream when it was dark. The Oxfordshire Hussars eventually found the Germans along the Thure stream.

Fourth Army Crosses the Sambre Canal

Poor weather meant the RAF could do little flying, so the infantry were kept busy checking the enemy positions in the Mormal Forest and along the Sambre–Oise Canal. Fourth Army engineers had also spent ten days bridging the waterway around Catillon. Rawlinson's order to attack was finally issued on 29 October and it called for a staggered attack on the morning of 4 November. On the right, IX Corps would cross the canal at 5.45 am followed by a battalion of tanks and a battalion of armoured cars. Thirty minutes later two battalions of tanks would accompany XIII Corps as it entered the forest on the left. A battalion of Whippets waited with the cavalry in reserve.

XIII Corps, 4 to 6 November

Lieutenant General Sir Thomas Morland faced the Mormal Forest, a huge expanse of woods, clearings and rides. Patrols searched for the German positions between 1 to 3 November but poor weather meant the RAF observers struggled to get into the air most of the time. Morland received his order to attack on 29 October and zero hour was set for 6.15 am on 4 November.

18th Division, 4 November, Mormal Forest to the Sambre Canal

Major General Richard Lee had to organise a complicated three stage attack to get into the Mormal Forest. Two tanks were disabled making the first attempt but another four helped the 7th Queen's Own and the 6th Northants enter Hecq. The 11th Royal Fusiliers held the line in front of Preux-aux-Bois while three tanks led Captain Doake's 2nd Bedfords into the town. Over 1,400 civilians cheered the troops on before stripping socks and boots from the German dead. Two more tanks were put out of action fighting alongside the 10th Essex and 8th Berkshires but four others reached the edge of Mormal Forest. Lieutenant Powell's company of the Berkshires were cut off for three hours until his flanks caught up and then Lieutenant Colonel Forbes exploited a gap in the German line, trapping many in Preux.

German resistance collapsed once the west edge of the forest had been cleared, so Lieutenant Colonel Irwin could lead the 8th East Surreys and 7th Buffs through the Mormal Forest. They moved, where possible, 'along the edges of the uncut portions of the Forest, large patches of which had been felled by the Boche and special arrangements were made to picket the sides'. The Germans fell back across the Sambre Canal around Sassegnies the following day and patrols from the Northumberland Hussars found that all the bridges were down.

50th Division, 4 to 6 November, across the Sambre north-east of Landrecies

Some of the German machine-gun teams along the west edge of the trees let the 7th Wiltshires and 2nd Northumberland Fusiliers pass through their lines, hoping to cut them off. But their plan was thwarted because Captain Livingston and Lieutenant Rathbone led the 2nd Munsters and three tanks along the edge of the forest, taking them by surprise. The Germans were withdrawing to the Sambre, so Major General Jackson sent the 6th Inniskillings along the forest rides to reinforce the division's left flank.

Tanks helped the 13th Black Watch and 3rd Royal Fusiliers advance along the south edge of the forest where 'the machine-gun defence was very elaborate'. But the Germans soon fell back, uneasy because the Sambre was close behind them. The 2nd Dublin Fusiliers reached a loop in the river north-east of Landrecies and sent patrols across the river during the night. The shelling continued into the night but the people around Landrecies were free and 'the women and children crept from their lairs to stare and exclaim at the Scots in their kilts.'

Three footbridges had been left around Hachette Farm so the 6th Inniskillings, 1st KOYLIs and 4th KRRC formed a bridgehead while the engineers spanned the broken road crossing. The rest of the division crossed and followed 25th Division as far as Les Basses Noyelles. Two armoured cars led the 20th Hussars across the Petite Helpe stream at Maroilles on 6 November while the 10th Argylls paddled over in boats. The 2nd KOYLIs and 5th Border Regiment dumped carts in the stream around Grand Fayt so they could scramble over.

25th Division, 4 and 5 November, crossing the Sambre at Landrecies

A competition as to who would get their timber walkways onto the petrol tin rafts prepared by the engineers had been declared. The 1/8th Warwicks came under fire from Faubourg Soyères and then saw a mounted officer gallop into Landrecies to blow up the road bridge. Meanwhile the 1/5th Gloucesters had a piece of luck which allowed them to win the race. An engineer sergeant had swum across La Vielle Sambre stream to disarm the explosives on the only bridge; it meant they could get to the canal quickly.

The 1/8th Warwicks found a temporary bridge the Germans had forgotten to destroy, so Lance Corporal William Amey led his section across and captured seventy prisoners; he was awarded the Victoria Cross. Some of the 1/8th Worcesters captured three field batteries, others cleared the town and the rest were ferried across the Sambre on petrol tin rafts. One tank was knocked out but two others silenced forty machine guns south-east of the village. Around 800 prisoners had been rounded up around Landrecies, with the help of the 11th Sherwoods, and some had even surrendered to two unarmed supply tanks.

Major General Roland Charles had to form a defensive flank because 32nd Division was struggling to advance south of Landrecies. The 9th Green Howards and 13th Durhams switched to the left flank, crossed the Sambre by 'bridges made of petrol tins' and then advanced to the Petite Helpe stream. The 11th Sherwoods advanced to Maroilles on 5 November and stopped the Germans blowing up the bridge across the Petite Helpe stream. The 21st Manchesters waded across the same stream, on the division's left flank, and reached Basse Noyelles.

Two armoured cars followed the roads while the 12th Lancers moved across country ahead of 7 and 74 Brigades on 6 November. The Germans blew up the bridge in Taisnières as the infantry approached but they were still able to wade across and reach Dompierre. The engineers then faced a race against time to erect a pontoon bridge before the rainwaters rose. On the right, Captain Blow led the 9th Green Howards to Marbaix, 'in a running fight with the enemy'.

IX Corps, 1 to 6 November

Lieutenant General Braithwaite wanted to cross the Sambre Canal around Ors and Catillon as soon as possible and he planned to clear the west bank before XIII Corps advanced on 4 November. But Catillon was still in enemy hands while his right flank faced reservoirs and streams, making it necessary to form two bridgeheads.

32nd Division, 1 to 6 November, crossing the Sambre at Landrecies

Three tanks helped the 15th Lancashire Fusiliers get closer to Landrecies and Company Sergeant Major James Clarke silenced seven machine-gun teams before guiding a tank towards the rest. The 16th Lancashire Fusiliers helped stop a large counter-attack later on, meaning that 32nd Division would be ready to bridge the Sambre early on 4 November.

Major Arnold Waters' plan to float a temporary span on a pontoon to the demolished bridge at Ors failed due to heavy fire from the far bank. It was impossible to cross on boats north of the bridge, so Waters set 218th Field Company, Royal Engineers, to work building a bridge of kerosene tins south

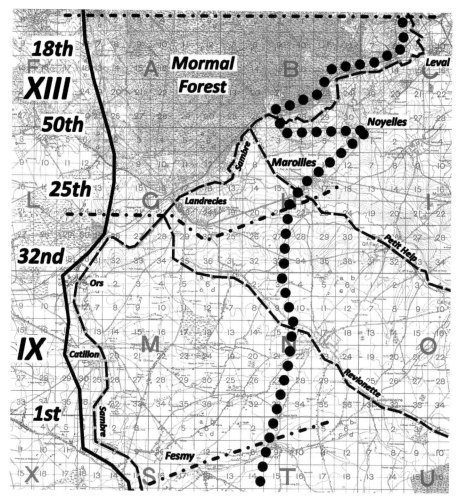

Fourth Army's left faced a long march through the Mormal Forest while its centre and right crossed the Sambre Canal between Landrecies and Catillon on 4 and 5 November.

of the village. He and Sapper Adam Archibald supervised the installation of the bridge. Archibald eventually collapsed due to gas poisoning but he survived; both men would be awarded the Victoria Cross.

Company Sergeant Major Clarke again saved the day for the 15th Lancashire Fusiliers as they cleared the west bank of the canal around Landrecies, with the help of two 2nd KOYLIs companies. He used his Lewis gun to give covering fire, allowing his comrades to reach their objective; he too would be awarded the Victoria Cross.

Machine-gun fire covered the bridge north of Ors, so Second Lieutenant James Kirk paddled a raft across, taking his Lewis gun with him. Kirk was killed covering the 2nd Manchesters' bridging party and the bridge was soon destroyed but a foothold had been established on the far bank. He would be posthumously awarded the Victoria Cross. The rest of the Manchesters had to follow the 1st Dorsets across the canal south of the village, and the celebrated war poet Lieutenant Wilfred Owen was one of the two hundred casualties suffered around Ors. Lieutenant Colonel James Marshall supervised the repair of another smashed bridge but he was killed leading the 16th Lancashire Fusiliers east of the canal; he was posthumously awarded the Victoria Cross.

The 1st Dorsets crossed the canal at the south end of Ors, taking 150 prisoners on the east bank, but the 5th/6th Royal Scots were pinned down in front of Le Donjon (the Keep) on the west bank. Brigadier General Evans VC (awarded in October 1917 for actions near Ypres) sent the rest of the Royal Scots and the 15th HLI across to expand the Dorsets' bridgehead and the fortification surrendered. The 5th Border Regiment and 10th Argylls advanced past the north side of Toaillon Wood and crossed the Revienette stream around Favril on 5 November.

1st Division, 4 November, crossing the Sambre Canal south of Catillon

Three tanks crawled through Catillon while the 1st Gloucesters rounded up 450 Germans sheltering in the cellars. The 1st SWBs took another 120 prisoners south of the village while the 2nd Welch helped expand the bridgehead. Meanwhile the 1st Loyals and 1st Camerons were across the Sambre by 6.10 am and took many prisoners in Bois de l'Abbaye before the 1st Black Watch advanced to Mezières.

The engineers discovered that most of their footbridges were too short to cross the Sambre and the lakes either side of the canal bend east of Rejet de Beaulieu. But one bridge was completed and a few of the 2nd Sussex held a bridgehead while the engineers bridged a nearby lock. Lieutenant Colonel Dudley Johnson would be awarded the Victoria Cross for leading the 2nd Sussex during their 2 mile advance beyond the river.

Artillery fire smashed the footbridges while machine-gun fire ripped through the collapsible boats used by the 2nd KRRC. But Major George Findlay made sure 409th Field Company, Royal Engineers, kept one bridge open. The 1st Northants followed and the two battalions took many prisoners around Fesmy. Findlay was wounded but he would be awarded the Victoria Cross.

46th Division, 4 and 5 November, advancing beyond the Sambre, east of Catillon

The 5th Leicesters crossed the Sambre at Rejet de Beaulieu during the afternoon of 4 November at the head of 46th Division. The 1/5th Lincolns advanced half a mile but the Sherwoods and the Staffords found the Germans waiting for them between Prisches and Barzy. A barrage was organised for the morning of 6 November but the Germans had already fallen back. The 1/8th Sherwoods found them waiting along the Petit Helpe stream around Cartignies.

Fourth Army's Pursuit to the Belgian Border

XIII Corps, 6 to 11 November

50th Division, 6 to 8 November, Solre-le-Château

The 7th Wiltshires were supposed to move down the far bank of the Grande Helpe stream but the 2nd Munsters made an early frontal attack on Noyelles and the German engineers blew up the bridge in Captain Livingston's face. His men still scrambled over the rubble and the two battalions then pushed across the Leval–Avesnes-sur-Helpe railway. The 13th Black Watch had crossed at Hachette Farm and then marched to Haute Noyelles and crossed the Grande Helpe stream. The rest of the brigade followed but it took until the early hours to clear the Dompierre–Leval railway.

Brigadier General Sugden's men advanced to St Aubin and Dourlers as the Germans fell back and 'weariness was the chief handicap of the time. The transport animals were in poor condition owing to overwork and still there was not enough transport. The roads were very heavy and much damaged by mines.' The 6th Inniskillings and 1st KOYLI were pinned down in front of Floursies, Mont Douriers and Semeries, so the 2nd Dublin Fusiliers and 3rd Royal Fusiliers took over the front. It took well into the night to enter Beugnies Wood while 'the sounds of exploding mines told their tale of continued retirement.'

25th Division, 7 November, St Hilaire

Both 7 and 75 Brigades pushed east, astride the Grand Helpe stream as far as St Hilaire.

IX Corps, 7 to 11 November

32nd Division, 7 and 8 November, Avesnes

The 2nd KOYLIs were unable to capture Avesnes on 7 November, so they had to wait until the engineers had built a trestle bridge over the Petit Helpe stream near Cartignies. Heavier batteries moved forward during the night and they shelled the village while the 10th Argylls and 2nd KOYLIs edged forward in small groups.

46th Division, 7 and 8 November, advancing beyond the Sambre, east of Catillon

All arms were able to ford the Chevreuil stream on 7 November but the Petite Helpe stream was a serious obstacle. The floodwater washed away the footbridge so the Leicesters and civilians piled branches and carts into the water until the soldiers could cross. Lieutenant Colonel Wilson led the 1/5th Lincolns across a plank walkway in single file and they 'were surrounded by civilians who insisted on shaking hands with everyone'. The 1/5th Leicesters chopped down trees and scrambled across so they could deploy on their right. They found the Germans waiting on the high ground south of Avesnes the following day.

66th Division, 8 to 11 November, Avesnes to Solre-le-Château

Major General Bethell took over responsibility for the whole of Fourth Army's front on 8 November. The 5th Connaught Rangers, 6th Lancashire Fusiliers, 5th Inniskillings and 18th King's found rearguards waiting for them on the high ground north of Avesnes. There was news the following day 'that troops farther north had advanced a considerable distance without meeting any opposition.' The three battalions found the same as they advanced towards the Belgian border. The division took over the entire corps front on 10 November as the South African Brigade continued the advance around Solre-le-Château'. One by one the guns fell silent as the minutes ticked by and then opposite the 1st South African Regiment, 'at two minutes to 11 am a machine gun opened about 200 yards from our leading troops at Grandrieu, and fired off a whole belt without a pause. A German machine gunner was then seen to stand up beside his weapon, take off his helmet, bow, and turning about, walk slowly to the rear.'

The Armistice

The headquarters of the five armies of the BEF knew within thirty minutes of the Armistice being signed, which left little time to get the news to the front line units. This is a summary of the instructions:

1. Troops could not go beyond the designated line while planes had to keep 1 mile to the west.
2. No unauthorised intercourse or fraternization with the Germans.
3. Enemy parties approaching with a white flag were to be taken prisoner.
4. Enemy parties approaching without a white flag to be stopped, and shot at if they would not.
5. Enemy aircraft would be attacked or shot at if they crossed the designated line.
6. Discipline and smartness had to be maintained.
7. Troops had to be allowed time to address their discipline, smartness and well-being.
8. No civilians to cross the line until instructions had been issued.

It was a cold and misty morning and while the fighting continued right up to the last minute in a few areas it died down in most as the news sank in. All fell silent at 11 am. But 'there was no cheering and very little outward excitement, only a great and wonderful calm.' The 'news was received with apathy and perhaps a tinge of disappointment that the pursuit of a routed and disorganised foe was not to be continued.'

Many a German gunner had 'signalised its arrival by increasing his bombardment, as if he had resolved to have no surplus ammunition left when the hour of truce arrived.' Then 'there came a moment of dramatic silence, and then a sound as of a light wind blowing down the lines: the echo of men cheering on the long battle front.' But it soon died away; 'the men seemed too tired and no one seemed able to realise that it was all over.' They put on a show of celebration if there was a cameraman about but otherwise they went about their work or went to sleep as the news sank in.

'For some hours the intelligence was barely credible; it seemed part of a pleasant dream and men were afraid of waking up to the bitter reality of continued war. All parades were cancelled, men gathered together in groups and in the streets to discuss the great event.' That night a host of celebrations took place and searchlights lit up the sky as rockets and flares of all colours exploded amongst the stars. Bonfires were also lit but men had to be careful in case there was any discarded ammunition lying around.

'The lifting of the ever-present cloud of death, which had been with them for four and a half years, was not at first apparent to the muddy, rain-soaked, and exhausted troops, and though the dramatic events of the past few days had prepared us for it, it took some time before its tremendous import could be realised.' The Allied armies had been on the offensive since 18 July. They had captured 330,000 prisoners and 6,600 guns during the 117 day advance; the BEF had taken 190,000 of them.

The German engineers handed over their demolition plans but they did not detail the location and type of mines and delay-action charges that had recently been laid. They would help the British engineers but it would take a long time to find and disarm over 900 tons of explosive. Only eight men were killed. Some of the final casualties of the war.

Chapter 15

Completely Used Up and Burnt to Cinders

The Armistice Negotiations

A s the fighting intensified at the end of September 1918, so did the discussions between the Supreme Army Command and Germany's politicians. Over the next six weeks, ideas and assessments changed according to the fortunes at the front. There were also changes in personnel, as differences in opinions came to a head and tempers rose. What follows is a summary of the political crisis which Germany faced during October and the early days of November 1918.

The successful attacks between 26 and 29 September left the OHL (*Oberste Heeresleitung* – Supreme Army Command) in crisis. It appeared the Allies had enough reserves to pursue all their breakthroughs, while there were insufficient German divisions to check them all. Matters came to a head during a Council of War at OHL's headquarters in Spa on 30 September. Kaiser Wilhelm II and the Imperial Chancellor, Count Georg von Hertling, heard Ludendorff report, 'the situation of the Army demands an immediate armistice', and Hindenburg agreed.

Foreign Minister Admiral Paul von Hintze suggested making an appeal to American President, Woodrow Wilson, based on his Fourteen Points, the list of demands calling for peace which had been outlined in January 1918. They called for an end to private international agreements, for freedom on the seas, a resumption of equal trade conditions, a reduction in arms and a revision of colonial claims. Germany and Austria-Hungary also had to withdraw their troops from occupied territories.

Ludendorff's aim was to save the German army from a humiliating defeat while placing the blame for the lost war on the politicians. He also wanted to start a revolution, because it would make the people of Germany think the country was united and ready to fight. The Kaiser even agreed that Hindenburg, Ludendorff and Hintze could establish a government. Vice Chancellor Friedrich von Payer agreed but Chancellor Hertling resigned over the suggestion; Prince Maximilian of Baden took his place.

Hindenburg and Ludendorff sent a message to the new Chancellor on 1 October: 'If Prince Max of Baden will form a government, we agree to the postponement of the publication of the demand for an armistice until tomorrow morning. Should, on the other hand, the formation of the government be in any way doubtful, we want a declaration to the foreign governments tonight.'

The German politicians wanted to push the Allied casualty count up, to improve Germany's bargaining situation. But the Beaurevoir Line had been broken on 1 October and the Hermann Position was incomplete. There were too few reserves to either stem the BEF's advance or finish the fortifications.

Hindenburg agreed with Ludendorff when he said he could 'accept no responsibility if a catastrophe, or at least the gravest consequences, ensue' after the next Allied attack. Chancellor Prince Max objected to their suggestion of making a peace deal and instead posed three questions to them:

1. How long could the German Army hold the enemy beyond the nation's frontier?
2. Did he think a military collapse was imminent?
3. Would such a collapse bring an end to military resistance?

Ludendorff refused to answer, so a request for an armistice was sent to Washington DC on 4 October. It said:

> The German Government requests the President of the United States of America to take steps for the restoration of peace, to notify all belligerents of this request and to invite them to delegate plenipotentiaries for the purpose of taking up negotiations. The German Government accepts, as a basis for the peace negotiations, the programme laid down by the President of the United States in his message to Congress of 8 January 1918... In order to avoid further bloodshed, the German Government requests the President to bring about the immediate conclusion of a general armistice on land, on water and in the air.

The Kaiser then issued a special order to the people of Germany, stating that he had made a peace offer to the Allies. He blamed the situation on the armistice on the Macedonian front and the abdication of Tsar Ferdinand of Bulgaria, not on the deteriorating situation on the Western Front.

OHL wanted to stall the British advance long enough to complete the Hermann Line, so their armies could regroup and inflict heavy casualties on the BEF. The 5 October Order of the Day called on the soldiers to keep fighting and so give the politicians the chance to secure the best peace terms for Germany.

> For months past the enemy has been striving against your lines with powerful efforts, almost without a pause. You have had to resist by fighting for weeks on end, frequently without rest, and to show a front to a foe vastly superior in numbers. Therein lies the immensity of the task which has been given you and you are fulfilling it... Your front is unbroken and will remain so. In agreement with my Allies, I have decided to offer peace once more to our enemies; but we will only stretch out our hands for an honourable peace.

But the soldiers knew that Ludendorff's order bore little relation to the desperate situation at the front line. Many battalions were down to company strength, while some companies only had a few dozen soldiers. There were never enough men to hold the line, leaving everyone 'completely used up and burnt to cinders'.

The soldiers' concerns over the military situation were reinforced when OHL issued the order to withdraw to the Hermann Line on 8 October. A second order split Boehn's army group while Boehn was on leave; he would be demoted soon afterwards. Control of General Adolph von Carlowitz's Second Army was handed over to Crown Prince Rupprecht while General Oskar Hutier's Eighteenth Army joined the Crown Prince's group.

President Wilson's reply to the armistice offer was received on 9 October and it demanded a number of preconditions before negotiations could begin. Germany had to agree to stop wanton destruction of civilian property and 'other illegal and inhuman practices'. The armies also had to withdraw from Belgium and France. The new Minister of War, Lieutenant General Heinrich Scheuch, refused to sanction such a long withdrawal. He believed it amounted to an unconditional surrender which would leave Germany open to attack if the talks failed.

The German War Cabinet summoned Ludendorff to discuss the reply but his answer was ambiguous: 'War is not like an arithmetical sum... In war there are many probabilities and improbabilities and you need soldier's luck... Perhaps Germany will still enjoy soldier's luck once more.' Ludendorff reported a shortage of men but he believed the German Army could hold on over the winter if the War Ministry sent the promised replacements. He also believed the Allies were tiring and told the politicians that 'we shall then no longer be obliged to accept any terms.'

It would be a gamble if OHL did not press for steps towards peace. It may be that we can hold out until the spring; but events may take a different turn any day... Steps towards peace, still more towards an armistice, are absolutely necessary. It was only by a hair's breadth that a breakthrough was avoided yesterday.

Scheuch offered to find another 600,000 men by combing industry for conscripts or by calling up the class of 1900 early. The problem was that both methods would take several weeks to organise and so Ludendorff refused the offer.

Chancellor Prince Max von Baden asked Ludendorff to send a selection of generals to Berlin so the War Cabinet could question them about the situation at the front. Ludendorff refused because he thought OHL's staff were the only ones capable of making an objective assessment.

Ludendorff assured the politicians that his soldiers would fight to the end, as long as unrestricted U-boat warfare continued, but Chancellor Prince Max von Baden threatened to stand down if it did not stop. So Ludendorff issued the following message and took a step back: 'OHL does not regard itself as a factor of political power. It therefore bears no political responsibility. Its political consent to the Note is not necessary.' The reply sent to President Wilson agreed to suspend U-Boat warfare.

Crown Prince Rupprecht had believed the war had been lost for some time but he now let the Chancellor hear his thoughts. The soldiers were exhausted; all units were short of officers; divisions were at a quarter of their strength. The support arms lacked trained men and transport units were short of horses, lorries and fuel. The rapid retirement meant that huge quantities of ammunition had been abandoned or destroyed and it was all bad for morale. Rupprecht summarised the Army Group's situation with the following words:

Our situation is already exceedingly dangerous, and a catastrophe can occur overnight under certain circumstances. Ludendorff does not realize the whole seriousness of the situation. Whatever happens, we must obtain peace before the enemy breaks through into Germany; if he does, woe on us.

But as the days passed, Ludendorff changed his mind about an armistice, believing that the Allies' conditions were unacceptable. He now wanted to fight to the end and issued a defiant Order of the Day on 25 October:

President Wilson's answer means military capitulation. It is therefore unacceptable to us soldiers… Wilson's answer can be for us soldiers only a challenge to continue resistance to the utmost of our power. When the enemy realises that the German front is not to be broken through in spite of every sacrifice, he will be ready for a peace which ensures Germany's future.

Hindenburg and Ludendorff then asked the Kaiser to reject Wilson's terms, prompting Chancellor Prince Max von Baden to ask for Ludendorff's dismissal. An angry Kaiser then blamed OHL's failure to stop the Allied attacks for Germany's difficult political situation so both Hindenburg and Ludendorff offered their resignation. The Kaiser rejected Hindenburg's offer but he accepted Ludendorff's.

As the generals and politicians argued, the troops took matters into their own hands. Admiral Franz von Hipper wanted one last pitched battle with the Royal Navy. Some of his sailors disagreed and they refused to sail from Wilhelmshaven when they received the order on 29 October. They were arrested but news of the rebellion spread quickly and sailors and soldiers were soon refusing to take orders.

Germany's allies were also facing their own difficulties. The Ottoman Empire signed the Armistice of Mudros on 30 October and hostilities in the Eastern Mediterranean ended the following day. The Austro–Hungarian armies had been driven back from the River Piave and the Empire came to an end when Hungary withdrew from the union on 31 October. The Armistice of Villa Giusti was signed and it came into effect on 4 November.

The initial draft by State Minister for Foreign Affairs Wilhelm Solf to President Wilson stated that Germany wanted an armistice rather than a surrender. Now Ludendorff had gone, the politicians were able to interview the generals about the front. Most gave ambiguous answers to loaded questions so as not to jeopardise their careers. Despite being engaged in the 'heaviest fighting since the great defeat of 8 August with its direful results', the flawed conclusion was that the armies were in a better condition than they actually were. There was talk of suspending the armistice negotiations but Ludendorff's replacement, General Wilhelm Groener, convinced the politicians to keep talking.

The Allies finally agreed to start truce negotiations on 5 November and Matthias Erzberger headed the German delegation which was escorted across no man's land the following night. Five cars took the delegation deep into the Compiègne Forest where Maréchal Foch's private train was parked on a siding. They arrived early on 8 November and Foch turned up to ask what the German delegation wanted. It made no difference because they were then handed the Allied demand for German demilitarisation. There was no opportunity to negotiate and, while their protests were noted, they could change little.

The German delegates asked the Allies to lift the naval blockade to alleviate the starvation across their nation but Foch refused. He believed 'my responsibility ends at the Rhine. I have no concern with the rest of Germany. It is your affair. I would remind you that this is a military armistice, that the war is ended thereby and that it is directed at preventing your nation from continuing the war.' He then reminded them of German Chancellor Otto von Bismarck's words after the French defeat during the Franco-Prussian War in 1871: '*Krieg ist Krieg* and I say to you *la guerre est la guerre*' – war is war. Foch eventually said, 'we will see, I will help you'; and the period allowed for evacuation was extended from two weeks to eight weeks.

The German armies were in a state of confusion during the final days of the war, as they headed east for the Antwerp–Meuse Line. The machine gunners fired all their ammunition before retiring; the gunners exhausted their stocks of shells before limbering up; the engineers still kept blowing up bridges and cratering the roads. But in general, it was every man for himself as some refused to take orders, others looted and some deserted.

On 9 November there were strikes; workers' and soldiers' councils were organised while key buildings were taken over. A Republic was proclaimed in Berlin and Prince Max of Baden resigned as Chancellor. He was replaced by the leader of the Socialist Democrat Party, Friedrich Ebert, who called for calm.

At the same time, First Quartermaster General Wilhelm Groener assembled a group of thirty senior officers at his headquarters in Spa. The consensus was that the army was in no position to stop the revolution spreading. Pessimistic reports of rebels stopping troops crossing the Rhine bridges and looting supply depots made the situation sound worse than it was. But enough was enough. The following day, the Kaiser and the Crown Prince headed for Holland while the Chancellor announced their dual abdication.

The armistice terms were sent to Berlin for approval and the first reply arrived during the evening of 10 November. Hindenburg reported that OHL was in a difficult situation because the American Expeditionary Force had reached Sedan, cutting the last railway south of the Ardennes. It meant that a large part of the Crown Prince's Army Group was in danger of being cut off. Hindenburg had been unable to contact the Reich Chancellor, so he had accepted the armistice terms because OHL was 'not only justified but bound to approve on its own initiative'. A second message from Reich Chancellor Friedrich Ebert authorized Matthias Erzberger to sign the Armistice. He did so at 5 am on 11 November and the papers were signed twenty minutes later.

Foch had returned to his carriage for the first time since the discussions began and he signed as the Allied Supreme commander while First Sea Lord, Admiral Rosslyn Wemyss, signed on behalf of the British. Four men signed on behalf of Germany: Secretary of State (without portfolio) Matthias Erzberger and Count Alfred von Oberndorff of the Foreign Ministry signed for the government, Major General Detlof von Winterfeldt signed on behalf of the army, and Captain Ernst Vanselow for the navy. Foch's Chief of Staff, General Maxime Weygand, was the French representative while Deputy First Sea Lord, Rear Admiral George Hope, and Captain Jack Marriott, Naval Assistant to the First Sea Lord, acted for Great Britain.

The following message was wired to all armies at 6.50 am:

> Hostilities will cease at 11.00 hours to-day, 11 November. Troops will stand fast on the line reached at that hour, which will be reported by wire to Advanced GHQ. Defensive precautions will be maintained. There will be no intercourse of any description with the enemy until the receipt of instructions from GHQ. Further instructions follow.

The war was over but men would keep dying, some from their wounds and others while clearing up the battlefields. Many others would be affected by the scars, both physical and mental, for life. The people of Belgium and France could return home, to discover if anything was left of their properties; in many cases there was not. But families would be reunited and work could begin on rebuilding their communities. The soldiers would have to wait many months before they could return home, as the armed services worked their way through the men with essential skills to turn industries once more back to peacetime working.

It could be said one of the last casualties of the war was Matthias Erzberger. He was seen as a traitor because he had pushed for the armistice and then signed it. He was murdered by the right-wing terrorist group *Organisation Consul* in October 1919.

Conclusions

The grinding battle through the old British trenches between 12 and 26 September gave the Germans time to repair the Hindenburg Line. It also gave their Supreme Army Command high hopes that the British could be held at bay long enough for replacements to be sent to the front. They hoped that a costly offensive battle for the Hindenburg Line would lower the morale of the Allied soldiers and undermine the confidence of the generals. It would also reduce the expectations of their political leaders and even make them reconsider the situation. Indeed, the War Cabinet had warned that Britain was running out of men and Haig had been advised to keep casualties to a minimum.

However, the four successive offensives along the entire front shocked Hindenburg, Ludendorff and their subordinates. Starting on 26 September, the Fourth French Army and the First US Army made good progress in the Argonne. The following morning, the First British Army and Third British Army forced their way into the Hindenburg Line west of Cambrai, 135 miles to the north-west. An attack by the Flanders Army Group (which included Second British Army) on the third day drove the Germans from large parts of Flanders, including the infamous Ypres salient. The Fourth British Army made the final attack on 29 September, denting the Hindenburg Line around the St Quentin Canal.

In each of the four attacks, the Allies were at least partially successful, and while casualties had often been high, many prisoners and guns had been taken. Over the next few days the British fought their way through several fortified lines. Eventually they were where the generals had wanted to be for the past three years: the green fields beyond.

The Germans had insufficient reserves to drive back the Allies, so all OHL could do was to order a withdrawal. But the only defensive position was the far-from-complete Hermann Line, and that would involve a withdrawal of up to 25 miles in places with the enemy in hot pursuit. So after being driven from good fortified positions, the German soldier faced a rapid retirement to half-prepared defences. They consisted of nothing more than a few shallow trenches and plenty of wire. The only advantage of the new line was that most of it was behind a stream which would impede the British infantry and hopefully stop their tanks.

A second problem with ordering a prolonged withdrawal was that troops often had to abandon perfectly good defensive positions because the British had advanced behind their flanks. At the end of a long march the best they could hope for was that the engineers would blow up all the bridges in time, leaving the pursuing enemy facing flooded watercourses and fields.

A third problem was that the constant withdrawals was stressful on man and animal alike, especially in adverse weather conditions. It took a great deal of skill to coordinate a retirement during dark, wet nights. As they marched to their new positions they would have seen the lines of limbers and wagons crowding the roads. They would have also seen the piles of abandoned stores burning and surplus ammunition exploding against the night sky. Repeated withdrawals were both disheartening and tiring, while the chosen few left to act as rearguards knew they had little chance of survival.

It has to be said, the Germans did not reckon with the bravery and ingenuity of the British soldier who used every means possible to cross the icy-cold waters. Some swam across, some paddled on makeshift rafts, others scrambled over the wreckage of demolished structures. Often at night, sometimes under cover of smoke and usually under fire, engineers used what materials they could lay their hands on to bridge the floods. They built everything from single plank walkways for the infantry up to huge trestle bridges capable of supporting twenty-nine ton Mark V tanks. Many engineers were hit because the enemy artillery targeted the congested crossing points, but time and again they returned to repair any damage.

The late autumn weather often grounded the RAF's observer planes, so the planners had to rely on prisoner reports until contact with the enemy was made. But it was often a combination of bad weather, blown up bridges and poor or damaged roads which delayed the British advance more than the rearguards. The fiercest resistance came from the German rearguards which were covering the bridgeheads until their comrades had crossed. The machine gunners kept the British at bay until their engineers had blown the bridges and they then made their escape across the river on boats.

The welcome given by the Belgians and French lifted the Tommies' spirits as they marched through their towns and villages. Tricolours flew from the windows as the crowds cheered, gave hugs and handed out gifts. The end of hunger and fear was in sight for them and they could look forward to seeing their loved ones who had been fighting far away.

The daily routine of fighting rearguards followed by the welcome of the local population would have been surreal and it must have been difficult to stay focused after such welcomes. Many dilemmas must have been faced as men confronted danger, knowing that the end of the war could only be a matter of days away.

The tactics used in the final offensives were ones which had been tried and tested over the past twelve months. The infantry now had a range of reliable weapons, including light machine guns, mortars, hand grenades and rifle grenades, giving them firepower at all ranges. Sections instinctively knew how to reconnoitre bunkers before laying down suppressive fire and smoke to blind the garrison. They then moved in for the kill and most garrisons surrendered as soon as they saw their escape route had been cut.

Attacks were nearly always made under cover of darkness, when it was often misty, or with the aid of smoke screens. The areas targeted by the German artillery were observed so that units could avoid the places they chose to shell. The timing of enemy bombardments were also noted so that, where possible, attacks were launched before the early morning interdiction shoots began.

Tanks had been completely integrated into tactics by this stage of the war and the infantry knew how to get the best support from the improved Mark V. They were often used to engage a strongpoint while the infantry looked for weak spots in the enemy line to exploit with the help of the faster moving Whippets. The main problem with tanks was the lack of them. There had been 580 available for Fourth Army's offensive on 8 August 1918 but nearly half had been knocked out or disabled in just one day.By now each army only had a few tanks to deploy and a chance encounter with an anti-tank position or 'tank fort' could result in several losses in a matter of minutes. The cratering of roads and the destruction of bridges often meant the infantry had to fight on alone until the engineers had opened the roads. Even so the Tank Corps had cooperated in over twenty-five engagements.By the end of the war and it 'had almost been fought to a standstill', with only one tank brigade left in action.

Once they were fighting in open country, the Germans faced the dilemma of where to defend. Villages had shelter but the British gunners could easily range in on them, hammering the buildings with high explosives while smoke hid the outflanking manoeuvres. Again it was all about using fire and movement tactics which were suited to warfare in open terrain. Woods were to be avoided at all costs because a deluge of gas shells would turn them into unhealthy places.

There was never enough time to build a new defensive position, beyond a shallow trench and a few strands of barbed wire, so natural positions were often selected. These included canals and streams, which were difficult to cross, and sunken roads, which provided cover. Railways were often used because the embankments and cuttings created natural defensive lines. They were, however, easy to locate and could then be subjected to a bombardment while the infantry penetrated the position.

The main lines of defences were created behind rivers and canals. Many of the final battles involved establishing bridgeheads across watercourses. The Germans used every trick they could to make it harder to cross: opening sluices, building dams, or breaching dykes to flood expanses of land. The Tommies spent many of the last days of the war wading across flooded fields while the rain poured down.

Haig had warned his army commanders to be prepared to form combined arms groups if it appeared the enemy were withdrawing. Many times cavalry, cyclists and motorcycle combinations were grouped together to scout ahead. A force of infantry and artillery equipped to operate independently were on hand to tackle any rearguards.

The Germans had learnt the art of withdrawing during the spring of 1917 when they fell back to the Hindenburg Line, and they used similar tactics during the October and November withdrawals. Wagons and limbers would remove as much ammunition and stores as possible. The artillery would fire off all their surplus shells before withdrawing, while the infantry took everything they could carry. The engineers then blew up or burnt what was left.

The British troops soon came to recognise the sounds of withdrawal. It started with a crescendo of artillery fire followed by explosions and fires behind the enemy lines. Ground and air patrols then probed the enemy positions, looking to take prisoners who could confirm there was a withdrawal.

The German engineers were also busy booby-trapping buildings, cratering road junctions and demolishing bridges. Little concern was shown for the loss of civilian lives until President Wilson's call to stop 'destruction and other illegal and inhuman practices' in mid-October. Despite the request, bridges and roads were continually damaged, leaving the Allies always one step behind. But some, including Lieutenant General Currie of the Canadian Corps, believed that poor logistics had also contributed to the slow advance: 'Our higher authorities do not seem well enough organised to push their railheads forward fast enough.' But such criticism is harsh when we consider the difficulties faced by the British and Empire soldiers:

> Long forced marches and many hours of lost sleep had taken their toll of physical energy. Getting supplies forward continued to be a major problem despite the sustained efforts of the engineers, aided by squads of already weary infantry toiling to repair roads

and bridges. A considerable amount of transport was tied up in distributing army rations to the hungry population. Particularly hard pressed were the medical services, who now had to care for large numbers of civilian sick and wounded.

The influenza pandemic, which had started in January 1918, would infect 500 million people as it spread around the world. Soldiers were vulnerable to it because they usually fought in cold and wet clothes. They often had to sleep in the open and rations were sometimes in short supply. The pandemic was the worst of its kind in history and by the time it died out at the end of 1920 it had claimed more lives than the war.

Often in the diaries and histories, battalions are noted as being at a fraction of their full strength due to casualties, illness and a shortage of replacements. Britain and France were running out of men to send to the front, while Ireland and Australian had refused to introduce conscription. Such policies led to the withdrawal of the Australian Corps from the front line at the beginning of October. The Canadian Corps, however, was able to fight right up to the last hour of the war.

The Germans were also running short of replacements. Their armies had suffered over one million casualties during their spring offensives. They had lost many more men, including over 300,000 prisoners, by the time the late September attacks were made; they had also lost over 3,000 guns. The total number of prisoners and guns taken during the Allied offensives (18 July to 11 November) would top a third of a million and 6,600 respectively.

End Note

The Canadian attack on Mons during the final hours before the armistice was called a 'deliberate and useless waste of human life' in a newspaper article in 1927. An infuriated Lieutenant General Currie paid for the incident to be researched and it proved that only one man had been killed and fifteen wounded. It also confirmed that the armistice message had arrived after the firing had stopped in the town. Currie successfully sued the newspaper but the story kept doing the rounds, and still does today. Private George Price was the last Canadian soldier killed in action during the Great War. He was buried at St Symphorien Military Cemetery. Only a few yards away is the grave of Private John Parr, the first British soldier killed on the Western Front on 21 August 1914. Hundreds of thousands of lives had been lost or changed forever in the months between, in the 'war to end all wars'.

Index

Abancourt, 24, 28
Acheville, 22, 113
Aisne, River, 1
Albert, 1, 45
Albert, King of the Belgians, 119
American Expeditionary Force, 196
First American Army, 3, 199
   II Corps, 59–62, 86, 91–3, 150–1
   27th Division, 58–62, 150–1
   30th Division, 60, 62, 88–9, 91–3, 150–1
Amerval, 144
Andigny Forest, 147, 149, 151–2
Angres, 169
Anneux, 32–3, 39, 120
Annoeulin, 80
Antoing, 79–81, 160–2
Antwerp–Meuse Line, 196
Argonne Forest, 3–4, 199
Arleux, 24, 116, 124
Armentières, 56, 104
Armin, Gen Friedrich Sixt von, 46, 50
Armistice negotiations, 188–9, 191–7
Arras, 1
Ath, 160, 162
Aubencheul-au-Bac, 24, 28, 43–4, 137
Aubencheul-au-Bois, 43
Aubers, 73–4
Aubers–Fromelles Line, 74
Aubigny-au-Bac, 116
Auby, 115
Auchy-la-Bassée, 76
Aulnoy, 164, 180
Autryve, 110–11
Australian Imperial Force
Corps, 15–17, 58–9, 62–5, 68–70, 85–7,
   88, 203
   1st Division, 16
   2nd Division, 85–7
   3rd Division, 60, 62–4, 68
   4th Division, 16–17, 19
   5th Division, 60

Battalions
2nd, 16
3rd, 16
4th, 16
10th, 16
11th, 16
12th, 16
13th, 16
15th, 16
16th, 16
17th, 86
18th, 86
20th, 86
21st, 86
22nd, 86
23rd, 86
24th, 86
25th, 85
26th, 86
27th, 85
28th, 86
29th, 64, 68
30th, 69
31st, 69
32nd, 64, 68–9
34th, 68
37th, 68
38th, 62, 64, 68–9
39th, 64, 69
40th, 62, 64
41st, 63–4
44th, 63–4
45th, 17
46th, 17
50th, 16
51st, 16
53rd, 68
54th, 69
55th, 68, 69
57th, 64, 68–9
58th, 64, 69

59th, 63–4
Austria-Hungary, 191
Avelghem, 108, 110–11, 158
Avesnes, 187
Avesnes-le-Sec, 118–19, 124
Awoingt, 130

Baisieux, 79, 167
Banteux, 37, 42–3
Bantigny, 28, 117
Barnes, Maj Gen Reginald, 33, 129
Bavai, 172, 174, 175, 179, 180
Baudour, Bois de, 165
Bazuel, 148, 150, 155
Beaucamp, 36–8, 42, 74
Beaurain, 142–3
Beauregard, 96
Beaurevoir, 83–6, 89
Beaurevoir Line, 43–4, 57, 66, 69–71, 83–9,
    129, 134–5, 137, 192
Beauvais, 133
Beauvin, 76
Becelaere, 46, 51
Beekstraat, 110
Belgian Army, 3, 45–6, 51
Belgian-French border, 172, 178–9, 186–7
Bellicourt, 12, 17, 19, 57–8, 62–4
Bellicourt tunnel, 58, 60
Bellenglise, 17, 58, 65–8
Berlaimont, 179
Bermerain, 139
Bermeries, 174–5
Berthelot, Gen Henri, 3
Bertry, 90, 95, 137–8
Bethell, Maj Gen Keppel, 89, 91,
    147–8, 187
Béthencourt, 134
Biache St Vaast, 22
Blécourt, 28–30
Bléharies, 81, 162
Boehn, Gen Max von, 1, 193
Bois Grenier, 73
Bony, 60, 68–9
Bossuyt, 111, 159
Bossuyt Canal, 109–11
Bourlon, 25–6
Bourlon Wood, 26, 33

Bousies, 153
Boussières, 133, 178
Boyd, Maj Gen Gerald, 19, 65, 87–8, 96,
    151
Braithwaite, Lt Gen Sir Walter, 151, 155,
    183
Brancourt, 93–4, 96
Branscourt-le-Grand, 87
Briastre, 133–4, 136, 141
BRITISH EXPEDITIONARY FORCE
Armies
    First, 3, 21–30, 89, 113–27, 163–72
    Second, 3, 45–56, 97–112, 120, 157–60
    Third, 1–3, 7–11, 31–44, 89, 120, 126–7,
        129–45, 152–3, 171–80
    Fourth, 1, 7, 11–19, 44, 57–71, 83–96,
        120, 129, 144, 147–55, 171, 180–7, 201
    Fifth, 73–81, 105, 120, 157, 160–3, 165
Corps
    I, 75–6, 77, 80–1, 113, 120, 160, 162–3
    II, 46–8, 51–3, 97–101, 105–10
    II American, 58–62, 86, 91, 93, 150–1
    III, 12–15, 57–8, 78–80, 160–2
    IV, 8–9, 31, 34, 36–8, 41–2, 133–6,
        141–4, 175–9
    V, 9, 37–8, 42–4, 135–8, 143–5, 171,
        179–80
    VI, 7, 31–2, 33–6, 39–41, 130–3, 139–41,
        173–5
    VIII, 21–3, 113–15, 120–3, 125, 165
    IX, 17–19, 58, 65–8, 70–1, 83, 85, 87–8,
        95–6, 151–2, 155, 181, 183–6, 187
    X, 48–50, 54–5, 101–103, 105, 111,
        158–9
    XI, 73–4, 76–8, 160
    XIII, 83–5, 89–91, 147–50, 152–5,
        181–3, 186
    XV, 49–50, 54–5, 103–105, 112, 159–60
    XVII, 31–3, 39–40, 129–32, 138–40,
        171–3
    XIX, 47–8, 52–4, 100–102, 105, 109–11,
        157–8
    XXII, 21, 23, 115–16, 120, 124–7,
        163–5, 168–70
    Cavalry, 4, 71, 83, 93–5
Divisions
    1st Division, 17–19, 66–7, 70, 88, 123,

151–2, 155, 185
1st Cavalry Division, 93–5
2nd Division, 34, 36, 39, 131–2, 140–1
2nd Cavalry Division, 93–5
3rd Division, 7, 34–5, 41, 131–2, 141
3rd Cavalry Division, 95
4th Division, 126–7, 165
5th Division, 9, 37–8, 41–3, 142–3,
    178–9
6th Division, 18–19, 67, 95–6, 151–2,
    155
8th Division, 22, 115–16, 121–3, 165
9th Division, 46–7, 51, 97–8, 108
11th Division, 24, 27–8, 116–18, 169–70
12th Division, 12–13, 58–9, 113–15,
    120–1
14th Division, 48, 50, 54, 103, 112,
    159–60
15th Division, 76, 80, 162
16th Division, 76, 80, 162
17th Division, 10–11, 135–7, 144, 179
18th Division, 13–15, 59, 152–3, 181
19th Division, 74, 138–9, 171–2
20th Division, 22, 172
21st Division, 11, 38, 43, 135, 143–4, 179
24th Division, 130–1, 172
25th Division, 84, 91, 150, 153–4, 182–3,
    186
29th Division, 47–8, 53–4, 98, 109–10,
    159
30th Division, 50, 54–5, 102–103, 111,
    158–9
31st Division, 50, 56, 103, 108, 112, 158
32nd Division, 67, 71–2, 87–8, 183,
    183–5, 187
33rd Division, 11, 38, 43, 137–8, 145,
    153, 180
34th Division, 48–50, 54, 102, 107–108,
    111
35th Division, 48, 53, 100, 110, 157–8
36th Division, 51–2, 91–2, 100, 106–108,
37th Division, 9, 43, 134, 143–4, 178
38th Division, 10, 89, 137, 145, 180
40th Division, 56, 104–105, 160
41st Division, 48, 53–4, 101–102,
    110–11, 157
42nd Division, 134, 140–2, 176–8

46th Division, 19, 65–8, 87–8, 95–6, 141,
    186–7
47th Division, 73–4, 78, 160
49th Division, 118–20, 126, 164–5
50th Division, 83–4, 89, 148–50, 182,
    186
51st Division, 23, 119, 124–6
52nd Division, 7, 31, 165–6
55th Division, 75, 80, 161–2
56th Division, 24, 116, 168
57th Division, 30, 32–3, 39, 78–9, 129
58th Division, 11–12, 21–2, 81, 113,
    162–3
59th Division, 73, 76–8, 160
61st Division, 73, 139–40, 171
62nd Division, 8–9, 34–6, 39–41, 133,
    140, 174–5
63rd Division, 31–3, 39, 129, 170
66th Division, 89–91, 147–8, 187
74th Division, 15, 74, 78–80, 160–1

Infantry Regiments
Bedfords
    1st, 38, 42, 142, 178
    2nd, 14, 153, 181
    4th, 31
Berkshires
    1st, 36, 39, 131, 141
    2nd, 22, 115
    2/4th, 73, 171
    5th, 12–13, 115, 121
    8th, 153, 181
Black Watch
    1st, 67, 70, 152, 185
    2nd, 18
    4/5th, 76, 162
    1/6th, 126
    1/7th, 125–6
    8th, 46, 51, 97, 108
    9th, 80
    13th, 83–4, 148–9, 182, 186
    14th, 78, 80
Border Regiment
    1st, 47, 98
    1/5th, 71, 182, 185
    7th, 11, 136, 144, 179
Buffs
    1st, 19, 96, 151

6th, 13, 58, 113, 121
7th, 14, 59, 153, 181
10th, 15, 74
Cambridgeshire
1st, 113–15
Camerons
1st, 18, 70, 152, 185
5th, 46, 51, 97, 108
Cheshires
1st, 38, 43, 142, 178
1/4th, 102, 111
6th, 111
7th, 54, 102, 111
9th, 171–2
15th, 53, 100, 110
Coldstream Guards
1st, 33, 132–3, 173–4
2nd, 132, 140, 173
Connaughts
5th, 89, 91, 187
Devons
1st, 38, 142, 178
2nd, 22, 115, 123
5th, 35, 41, 174–5
9th, 84, 91, 153
16th, 15, 78
Dorsets
1st, 67, 71, 88, 185
5th, 27–8
6th, 10–11, 136–7, 144, 179
Dublin Fusiliers
1st, 47, 53, 98, 109
2nd, 83–4, 89, 148, 150, 182, 186
6th, 89, 148
Duke of Cornwall's
42, 178
7th, 22
Duke of Wellington's
2nd, 126–7
1/4th, 120
2/4th, 9, 39, 140, 174–5
5th, 9, 35–6, 140, 174–5
6th, 120, 164
7th, 119
9th, 10, 137, 179
13th, 73
Durhams

2nd, 19, 151, 155
2/6th, 73
9th, 9
13th, 84, 91, 183
15th, 135, 144, 179
18th, 56
19th, 48, 53, 100, 110
20th, 101, 110–11
29th, 103
East Lancashires
2nd, 22, 115, 122–3
5th, 142, 176, 177
11th, 50, 103, 108
13th, 160
East Surreys,
1st, 142, 178
8th, 59, 153, 181
9th, 130–1
12th, 101, 110–11
East Yorkshires
1st, 11, 135, 144
7th, 10, 136, 144, 179
10th, 50, 103
11th, 56, 103, 108
Essex
1st, 134, 143
2nd, 137, 178
9th, 12, 115, 121
10th, 14, 153, 181
11th, 18, 151
15th, 73
Gloucesters
1st, 18, 67, 88, 185
1/5th, 84, 91, 140, 150, 153, 171, 182
8th, 138
12th, 42
Gordons
1st, 35, 41, 132, 141
4th, 125–6
6/7th, 124, 126
Green Howards
1st, 108
2nd, 24, 27, 117, 169
9th, 84, 91, 154, 183
Grenadier Guards
1st, 34, 133, 140, 174
2nd, 33, 132

3rd, 33, 132, 173–4
Hampshires
  1st, 126–7, 165
  2nd, 98, 109
  2/4th, 9, 35, 40, 140
  15th, 54, 101, 110–11
Herefords
  1st, 111
Hertfords
  1/1st, 9, 134, 144
Highland Light Infantry
  2nd, 39, 140
  1/5th, 7, 148
  6th, 148
  7th, 31
  9th, 11, 38, 138, 145
  10th, 103
  12th, 48, 53, 110
  15th, 67, 71, 88, 185
  18th, 48, 53, 100, 157
Inniskilling Fusiliers
  1st, 52, 99, 106
  2nd, 52, 99, 106
  5th, 89, 148, 186–7
  6th, 83, 148, 182, 186
  9th, 52, 99, 106
Irish Fusiliers
  1st, 106
  5th, 162
  9th, 52
Irish Guards
  1st, 33, 133, 140, 173
Irish Regiment
  2nd, 32, 39
  7th, 102
Irish Rifles
  1st, 52, 99, 106
  2nd, 106, 129
  12th, 52, 100, 106
  15th, 99, 106
King's
  1st, 34, 36
  4th, 11, 38, 138, 145
  5th, 80
  1/6th, 75, 80, 91, 161
  2/6th, 33, 78, 129
  2/7th, 33, 39, 78, 80

8th, 33, 39, 78, 129
9th, 33, 78
10th, 75
12th, 22
13th, 34, 131
18th, 89, 90–1, 187
25th, 73
King's Own
  1st, 127, 165
  4th, 75, 80
  2/5th, 39, 78, 129
  8th, 35, 41, 132, 141
KOSBs
  1st, 9, 98, 109
  2nd, 9, 142, 178
  1/4th, 7
  1/5th, 48, 102, 108
  6th, 51, 98, 108
  8th, 81
KOYLIs
  1st, 83–4, 148, 182, 186
  2nd, 67, 71, 88, 182, 184, 187
  4th, 120
  2/4th, 35, 40, 174–5
  5th, 9, 35, 40, 174–5
  9th, 11, 135, 144, 179
King's Royal Rifle Corps
  1st, 39, 131
  2nd, 8, 152, 185
  4th, 83, 89, 148, 150, 182
  11th, 22
  12th, 22, 101, 172
  13th, 9, 43, 134, 144, 178
  16th, 138
  18th, 110–11
Lancashire Fusiliers
  1st, 47, 53, 98
  2nd, 127
  5th, 37, 75, 80
  2/5th, 162
  6th, 89, 91, 148, 187
  7th, 36, 178
  8th, 37, 134, 178
  10th, 10, 179
  11th, 157
  15th, 70–1, 183–4
  16th, 71, 183, 185

17th, 48, 100, 110
18th, 48, 53, 100, 110
23rd, 104
Leicesters
  1st, 19, 96, 155
  1/4th, 66, 151
  5th, 19, 66, 151, 186–7
  6th, 11, 43, 144, 179
  7th, 43, 135, 144
Leinsters
  2nd, 53, 98, 109, 159
Lincolns
  1st, 11, 38, 43, 135, 144, 179
  2nd, 11, 43, 135, 144
  5th, 19, 66, 96, 151, 186–7
  6th, 28, 116, 169
  7th, 10, 136, 144, 179
  8th, 134
London
  2nd, 24, 116, 169
  2/2nd, 12, 22, 81, 113, 162
  3rd, 12, 113
  1/4th, 168
  2/4th, 22
  1/5th, 24, 169
  1/6th, 162, 168
  7th, 22, 81, 113, 162
  8th, 22, 81, 162
  9th, 12, 81, 113
  10th, 81
  2/10th, 113
  12th, 12, 113
  1/13th, 116, 169
  14th, 54, 169
  2/14th, 102, 111
  15th, 54
  2/15th, 102
  16th, 24
  17th, 50, 54, 160
  2/17th, 158
  18th, 73
  19th, 73
  1/20th, 35, 174–5
  2/20th, 40, 140
  22nd, 73, 160
  2/22th, 113
  2/23rd, 102

2/24th, 12, 81, 113
28th, 32, 39
33rd, 103, 159
Loyals
  1st, 18, 67, 70, 88, 152, 185
  2nd, 50, 54, 102
  4th, 75, 80
  2/4th, 78
  1/5th, 39, 129
Manchesters
  2nd, 71, 185
  5th, 36, 142
  6th, 36
  7th, 36, 142
  8th, 37, 176
  9th, 89
  10th, 37, 142, 176
  11th, 23, 28
  12th, 137, 179
  16th, 112
  20th, 84, 91, 153
  21st, 84, 91, 153, 183
Middlesex
  1st, 38, 145, 180
  2nd, 22, 115, 165
  4th, 134
  7th, 116
  8th, 24, 169
  13th, 130, 172
  20th, 48, 103
  23rd, 48, 53, 102, 111
Monmouths
  1st, 96
Munsters
  1st, 39
  2nd, 83, 84, 150, 182, 186
Norfolks
  1st, 38, 42, 143, 178
  7th, 12, 113–14, 121
  9th, 19, 96, 155
  12th, 56
Northants
  1st, 18, 123, 152, 185
  2nd, 22
  5th, 12
  6th, 14, 59, 153, 181
  7th, 130, 172

North Staffords
1st, 131, 172
4th, 48, 53, 100
1/6th, 65, 87, 96
8th, 74, 171
12th, 160
Northumberland Fusiliers
1st, 34, 131, 141
2nd, 83–4, 135, 182
8th, 24, 28
9th, 139, 171
12/13th, 11, 38, 179
22nd, 162
36th, 76
Ox and Bucks
2nd, 29, 140
2/4th, 171
Queen's
1st, 11, 145, 180
4th, 102, 108
6th, 13, 113–14, 121
7th, 14, 59, 153
8th, 131
10th, 53, 110–11, 157
11th, 54, 102, 157
Queen's Own
1st, 38, 178
6th, 13, 58, 114, 121
7th, 14, 153, 181
8th, 131, 172
10th, 53
11th, 110
Rifle Brigade
1st, 9, 126–7, 165
2nd, 9, 22, 121
3rd, 130, 172
4th, 9
12th, 172
13th, 9, 43
Royal Fusiliers
1st, 130, 172
2nd, 47, 98, 109
3rd, 83, 148, 182, 186
4th, 34–5, 131, 141
7th, 31, 39
9th, 12–13, 113–15, 121
10th, 9, 134, 143, 178

11th, 14, 59, 153, 181
13th, 134, 143, 178
17th, 36, 39, 131
23rd, 39, 131, 140–1
24th, 39, 140
26th, 48, 53, 110–11
Royal Scots
2nd, 7, 34, 141
1/4th, 7, 31
5/6th, 71, 185
1/7th, 7, 165
9th, 80–1
11th, 46, 51, 97–8, 108
12th, 46, 51, 97–8
13th, 76, 81
17th, 53, 100
Scots Fusiliers
1st, 34, 141
2nd, 46, 97, 108
5th, 31
11th, 76–7, 160
12th, 109
Scots Guards
1st, 33, 132–3, 174
2nd, 133, 140, 174
Scottish Rifles
1st, 11, 137
2nd, 22
5th, 11, 137, 145
6th, 11
7th, 165
8th, 102, 108
9th, 51, 108
18th, 162
Seaforths
2nd, 126, 165
4th, 119, 125–6
5th, 119, 124
6th, 124, 126
7th, 46, 51, 108
8th, 76, 162
Sherwood Foresters
1st, 22, 115, 122–3
2nd, 19, 96, 155
5th, 19, 67, 87, 186
6th, 19, 67, 87, 186
8th, 67, 87, 151, 186

9th, 169
10th, 11, 144, 179
11th, 84, 91, 183
15th, 48, 53, 100, 110, 157
Shropshires
1st, 19, 96, 151, 155
6th, 22
7th, 34, 41, 141
10th, 15, 161
Somersets
1st, 127
8th, 134, 178
11th, 73
12th, 15
South Lancashires
2nd, 111, 158
1/5th, 80, 161
South Staffords
2nd, 34, 36
4th, 110
1/5th, 65, 87, 151, 186
1/6th, 65, 87–8, 186
7th, 116
South Wales Borderers
1st, 17, 67, 70, 152, 185
2nd, 47, 53, 98
5th, 138
10th, 137
Suffolks
2nd, 41, 131–2, 141
11th, 139
12th, 48, 112, 160
1/4th, 12
15th, 15, 79
Sussex
2nd, 18, 152, 155, 185
1/4th, 102
7th, 12–13, 113, 120–1
9th, 130, 172
16th, 15
17th, 73
Warwicks
1st, 127
2/6th, 139
2/7th, 171
8th, 84, 91, 182
10th, 138, 172

14th, 38
15th, 38, 42
16th, 42, 142
Welsh
1st, 133
2nd, 17–18
13th, 10, 145, 180
14th, 145
15th, 14
24th, 14, 15
Welsh Fusiliers
2nd, 137, 180
9th, 74
10th, 137
13th, 10, 137, 145
15th, 145
14th, 10, 137, 145
16th, 10, 137
17th, 137
25th, 15
26th, 73
Welsh Guards
1st, 34, 140, 174
West Yorkshires
1st, 18–19, 96, 155
2nd, 22, 27, 165
1/5th, 120, 164
6th, 119
8th, 35, 41, 140, 175
9th, 24, 28, 116, 169
10th, 10–11, 136, 144, 179
15th, 50, 56
17th, 158
Wiltshires
1st, 11, 135, 144, 179, 182, 186
2nd, 138, 172
6th, 48
7th, 83–4
Worcesters
1st, 22, 115
2nd, 11, 38, 115, 138, 145, 180
3rd, 172
4th, 47, 53, 98, 159
1/8th, 91, 84, 150, 153, 182
2/8th, 73, 140, 171
10th, 138
York and Lancasters

2nd, 19, 96, 151, 155
2/4th, 9, 35, 120, 140, 165, 174–5
5th, 120
6th, 28, 117, 169
Cavalry Regiments
  17th Armoured Car Battalion, 95
  2nd Dragoons, 94
  1st Dragoon Guards, 95
  3rd Dragoon Guards, 95
  6th Dragoon Guards, 172
  7th Dragoon Guards, 159
  3rd Hussars, 37, 133, 178
  4th Hussars, 121
  11th Hussars, 138
  19th Hussars, 93, 160
  20th Hussars, 71, 94, 182
  5th Lancers, 167–8
  12th Lancers, 95, 183
  16th Lancers, 169–70
  Fort Garry Horse, 95
  Lord Strathcona's Horse, 95
  Northumberland Hussars, 181
  Oxfordshire Hussars, 133, 141, 180
  Royal Canadian Dragoons, 95
Broodseinde, 46, 51
Bruce-Williams, Maj Gen Hugh, 134
Budworth, Maj Gen Charles, 57
Butler, Lt Gen Richard, 58
Burstall, Maj General Sir Henry, 117–18, 167
Buzancy Line, 3
Byng, Gen Julian, 3, 21, 31, 44, 88–9, 129, 138, 155, 171

Cambrai, 2–3, 8, 25, 27, 29–30, 39, 41, 91, 117–19, 129–30, 132–3, 155, 199
Cameron, Maj Gen Neville, 120
Campbell, Maj Gen David, 43, 158
Campbell, Maj Gen John, 50
Camphin, 79–80
Canadian Expeditionary Force
  Corps, 21–7, 29, 113, 116–20, 122–4, 163–4, 166–8, 202–203
  1st Division, 21, 24–6, 28, 115–16, 124
  2nd Division, 117–18, 124, 167–8
  3rd Division, 21, 27, 30, 118, 123, 166–7
  4th Division, 21, 25–7, 28–9, 116, 124,

    163–4, 166–7
Battalions
  1st, 25, 28
  1st Mounted Rifles, 30
  2nd, 25
  2nd Mounted Rifles, 30, 167
  3rd, 25
  4th, 24–5, 28
  5th, 25
  5th Mounted Rifles, 166
  7th, 116
  8th, 25, 28
  10th, 25
  13th, 25, 28, 115
  14th, 25, 28
  15th, 25, 116
  16th, 28, 116
  18th, 124
  19th, 118
  20th, 118
  21st, 118
  22nd, 118
  23rd, 118
  24th, 167
  25th, 118
  26th, 118
  27th, 118
  28th, 118
  29th, 118, 124
  31st, 117–18
  38th, 26, 28, 163
  42nd, 30, 167
  43rd, 27, 30
  44th, 27
  45th, 26
  46th, 27, 163–4
  47th, 26–7, 163–4
  49th, 27, 30, 166
  50th, 26, 27, 163
  52nd, 30
  54th, 26, 29–30, 164
  58th, 27, 30
  72nd, 25–6, 28, 163
  75th, 26, 29
  78th, 26, 28, 124, 167
  85th, 26, 124, 167
  87th, 26, 29, 124, 167

102nd, 26–7, 29, 167
116th, 27, 30
Princess Patricia's, 30, 167
Royal Canadian Regiment, 167
Canal du Nord, 7–8, 21, 24–6, 32–4, 93, 116
Cantaing Line, 33–4, 36
Canteleu, 78
Carlowitz, Gen Adolph von, 193
Cartignies, 186–7
Carvin, 81
Catillon, 155, 181, 183–7
Caudry, 134
Cayley, Maj Gen Douglas, 53
Charles, Maj Gen Ronald, 183
Chemin des Dames, 1
Cité Bruno, 115
Clemenceau, PM Georges, 112
Coffin, Maj Gen Clifford, 51, 106
Comines, 55, 103
Comines Canal, 48, 53–4
Compiègne Forest, 195
Condé Canal, 166
Condé-sur-l'Escaut, 165, 167
Courcelles, 115
Courrières, 81, 113–15
Courtrai, 97–101, 111–13
Courtrai Switch, 110–12
Coyghem, 111
Crèvecoeur, 41–3, 133
Crown Prince, 4, 196
Crown Prince's Army Group, 196
Crown Prince Rupprecht, 50, 193–4
Cubitt, Maj Gen Thomas, 44, 137, 145
Curgies, 169
Currie, Lt Gen Sir Arthur, 21, 27, 126, 163–4, 167–8, 202–203
Cuvillers, 28, 118

Dadizeele, 51–2
Daly, Maj Gen Arthur, 172
Davies, Maj Gen Henry, 24, 116, 170
De Lisle, Lt Gen Beauvoir, 50
Debeney, Gen Marie-Eugène, 3, 71
Deerlyck, 106, 108
Degoutte, Gen Jean, 3, 45
Denain, 124–5

Dendre, River, 157–62
Deverell, Maj Gen Cyril, 34, 141
Dottignies, 103, 112
Douai, 27, 114–15, 120–3
Douai railway, 28, 30, 79, 81
Dourges, 81, 115, 121
Douvrin, 76
Dover Patrol, 45
Dries, 106
Drocourt-Quéant Line, 1, 21, 27, 114–16
Duncan, Maj Gen John, 171

Ebert, Friedrich, 196, 197
Écaillon stream, 123, 126–7, 139, 141–2, 144
Elouges, 167
Ennetières, 73
Epéhy, 12
Épinoy, 24, 27
Ereclin stream, 118, 130
Erquinghem-le-Sec, 73
Erzberger, Matthias, 195, 197
Escarmain, 141
Espierres Canal, 112
Esquelmes, 78, 160
Estrées, 69, 86, 116

Famars, 126
Fayet, 19, 67
Feignies, 172, 174
Feilding, Maj Gen Geoffrey, 7
Ferdinand of Bulgaria Tsar, 192
Férin, 116
Flanders I Line, 51–2, 97, 102
Flanders II Line, 51–2, 97–9, 102
Flanders Group of Armies, 3, 45, 97, 199
Flesquières, 33–6
Fleurbaix, 73
Foch, Généralissime Ferdinand, xi, 1, 3–4, 45, 71, 88, 112, 155, 170, 195–7
Fontaine-Notre-Dame, 26–7, 33
Forenville, 131
Fouquières, 114
Fourteen Points, 191
Frasnes, 160–1
Frasnoy, 174
French Armies
    First, 1

Third, 2–3
Fourth, 3–4, 199
Fifth, 3, 73, 76, 79, 105, 120, 157, 160–1, 165
Tenth, 2–3
French-Belgian border, 172, 178–9, 186–7
Fresnoy, 18, 22
Fresnoy-le-Grand, 96
Fresnoy-le-Petit, 18–19
Fressies, 116, 124
Friedensturm, Operation *see* Operation Peace Storm
Froidmont, 80
Froyennes, 78

Gallwitz, Gen von Max, 4
Gauche Wood, 10, 11
Gellibrand, Maj Gen John, 64, 68
Gheluvelt, 47–8
Gheluwe Switch, 52–4, 99–100
Ghissignies, 143–4, 178
Ghoy, 158–9
Girdwood, Maj Gen Eric, 15
Givry, 169–70
Gommegnies, 174
Gonnelieu, 42–3
Gouraud, Gen Henri, 3, 4
Gouzeaucourt, 9–10, 38
Gouzeaucourt Wood, 9
Gouy, 83
Graincourt, 31–3
Grand Honnelle stream, 166, 170
Gricourt, 18–19, 67
Groener, Gen Wilhelm, 195–6

Haig, FM Sir Douglas, 2–3, 45, 71, 87–9, 112, 120, 133, 165, 170, 199, 202
Haking, Lt Gen Richard, 78
Haldane, Lt Gen Sir Aylmer, 31, 33
Hantay, 75
Hargicourt, 16, 62
Harlebeke, 98, 106, 108
Harmignies, 168–9
Harman, Maj Gen Anthony, 95
Harpies stream, 138, 140–2, 144–5
Haspres, 120, 126
Haubourdin, 78–9

Haucourt, 134
Haute Deule Canal, 73–81, 113–15, 120–1
Haute Noyelles, 186
Haussy, 131–2, 138–40
Hautmont, 176–8
Haussy, 131–2, 138–40
Havrincourt, 7–9, 33–4
Havrincourt Wood, 9
Haynecourt, 24, 26, 28
Heinweg, 106
Helchin, 111, 159
Hem-Lenglet, 116
Heneker, Maj Gen William, 121
Hérinnes, 160
Hermann I Line, 89, 120, 147, 192–3, 199
Hermann II Line, 145, 154
Herseaux, 103
Herstert, 111
Hertling, Count Georg von, 191
Hesbécourt, 12
Higginson, Maj Gen Harold, 58, 113, 121
Hindenburg Line, 1, 3, 8, 11, 13–14, 17, 19, 31, 33–5, 37, 43, 57–8, 60, 62, 65–6, 68–9, 199, 202
Hindenburg Outpost Line, 14, 17, 58, 68
Hindenburg Reserve Line *see* Beaurevoir Line
Hindenburg Support Line, 31, 43, 62, 65, 67–8
Hintze, Adml Paul von, 191
Hipper, Adml Franz von, 195
Hogneau stream, 172
Holland, 196
Hollebeke, 48, 53, 54
Holnon, 12
Honnechy, 95
Honnecourt, 38, 43
Honnelles, 169–70
Hope, R/Adml George, 197
Horne, Gen Henry, 3, 88–9, 155, 163
Houthem, 53–4
Houthulst Forest, 46
Hull, Maj Gen Amyatt, 169
Hulluch, 76
Hunter-Weston, Lt Gen Aylmer, 165
Hutier, Gen Oskar, 193

Illies, 74
Inchy, 21, 24, 26
Iwuy, 117–18

Jackson, Maj Gen Henry, 83, 148, 150, 182
Jacob, Lt Gen Claud, 51, 100, 106
Jard, Canal du, 123, 165
Jeffreys, Maj Gen George, 172
Jenlain, 169, 171
Jeudwine, Maj Gen Hugh, 162
Joncourt, 69–71

Kavanagh, Lt Gen Charles, 93, 95
Keyes, V/Adml Sir Roger, 45
Kezelberg, 100
Knokke, 110
Kortewilde, 48
Kruiseecke, 54

La Bassée, 75
La Bassée canal, 73, 75
La Bassée-Vendin Line, 75
Lambert, Maj Gen Thomas, 67
Landrecies, 182–4
Lannoy, 105
Laplaigne, 162
Lawford, Maj Gen Sydney, 48, 54, 110
l'Escaut Canal, 30, 34–6, 39, 41, 43
L'Évêque Wood, 152–3, 155
Le Cateau, 89, 91, 94–5, 134, 136–8, 143,
    147–9, 152
Le Catelet, 83
Le Poirier, 126, 163
Le Quesnoy, 138, 140–2, 144, 173–6
Le Tronquoy, 67, 70–1
Le Verguier, 16–17
Lecelles, 121
Ledeghem, 51, 97–8
Lee, Maj Gen Richard, 13, 152, 153, 181
Lehaucourt, 67
Lempire, 13–15
Lens, 21, 23, 113
Les Basses Noyelles, 182
Lesdins, 71
Lessines, 159
Leuze, 159, 161–2
Levergies, 67, 70–1

Lewis, Maj Gen Edward, 58, 62, 91
Lieu St Amand, 119, 124
Lille, 76–81, 105
Locquignol, 179
Loison, 113
Loomis, Maj Gen Frederick, 166
Lucas, Maj Gen Cuthbert, 126
Ludendorff, Gen Erich, 1, 58, 191–5, 199
Lys River, 51–3, 55–6, 97–109

Macdonell, Maj Gen Archibald, 115
Magny-la-Fosse, 66, 68
Maing, 126–7
Malincourt, 137
Malplaquet, 171
Mangin, Gen Charles, 3
Marindin, Maj Gen Arthur, 48, 110
Marne River, 1
Marquillies, 75
Marquion, 21, 24, 26
Marwitz, Gen Georg von der, 12, 58
Maubeuge, 3, 169, 172–5, 177–9
Maulde, 81, 121
Mannequin Hill, 87–8, 96
Marchipont, 167
Marcoing, 35, 36
Marcoing Line, 26–8, 30, 36, 39–40, 42
Marden, Maj Gen Thomas, 67, 95, 151,
    155
Maresches, 171
Maretz, 90–1, 95
Marly, 163–4
Maroilles, 182–3
Marshall, Maj Gen Francis, 31, 165
Masnières, 35, 40–1
Matheson, Maj Gen Torquhil, 7, 33,
    132–3, 140, 174
Maurois, 90
Maximilian of Baden, Prince, 191
Mazinghien, 151
Meersche, 157
Menin, 51, 102
Méricourt, 22, 95–6, 113
Messines, 50
Messines ridge, 45, 49–50, 54
Meuse River, 2–3
Meuse-Argonne attack, 4

Mezières, 2–3, 185
Moeuvres, 7, 26, 31, 33
Molain, 150–1
Monash, Lt Gen Sir John, 15, 58, 60, 88
Monchaux, 126–7
Mons, 164–9, 175, 203
Mons Canal, 166
Mont Douriers, 186
Mont Houy, 124, 126, 163
Mont sur l'Oeuvre, 36, 39–41
Montague, Lt Gen Sir Harper, 31
Montay, 91, 95, 138, 145, 152
Montbréhain, 83, 86–8, 91, 93–4
Montigny, 136–7, 169
Montrécourt, 131
Moorslede, 99
Morenchies, 30
Morland, Lt Gen Sir Thomas, 152, 181
Mormal Forest, 173, 176, 178–81, 184
Mount Erebus, 167
Moustier, 160
Mudros, Armistice of, 195
Mullens, Maj Gen Richard, 93

Nauroy, 64, 69
Naves, 118
Neuville, 30, 95
Neuville-Saint-Rémy, 30
Neuvilly, 95, 134, 136–7, 144
New Zealand Battalions
    1st Auckland, 41–2, 175
    2nd Auckland, 41–2, 134
    1st Canterbury, 41, 133, 142, 176
    2nd Canterbury, 43, 133, 142
    1st Otago, 41, 133, 142
    2nd Otago, 41, 133, 142, 176
    1st Rifle Brigade, 133, 175
    2nd Rifle Brigade, 142, 176
    3rd Rifle Brigade, 133, 175
    4th Rifle Brigade, 133, 142, 175–6
    1st Wellington, 134, 175
    2nd Wellington, 41–2
Nicholson, Maj Gen Lothian, 107
Niergnies, 129
Nimy, 167
Noyelles, 36, 113, 114, 115, 125
Noyelles Godault, 115

OHL *see* German Supreme Army
    Command
Oberndorff, Count Alfred von, 197
Oberste Heeresleitung see German Supreme
    Army Command
Odomez, 123
Oignies, 81, 121
Oosttaverne, 54
Ooteghem, 108, 111
O'Ryan, Maj Gen John, 58, 60, 150
Orchies, 121
Organisation Consul, 197
Ors, 155, 183, 185
Orsinval, 141
Ottoman Empire, 195
Ovillers, 144

Paillencourt, 116, 124
Palluel, 24, 116, 124
Passchendaele, 45–6
Payer, Vice Chancellor Fredrich von, 191
Peace Storm, Operation, 1
Peizières, 11–12
Pereira, Maj Gen Cecil, 34, 36
Peronne, 80
Pershing, Gen John, 2–4, 89
Pétain, Gen Philippe, 1–3, 155
Petit Aunelle stream, 173
Petit Honnelle stream, 169
Petite Helpe stream, 182–3, 187
Peyton, Maj Gen William, 56
Picantin, 73
Pinney, Maj Gen Sir Reginald, 43, 145, 180
Ploegsteert Wood, 49–50, 56
Poix du Nord, 144–5
Polderhoek, 47
Pommereuil, 153
Ponchaux, 84, 86, 91, 93
Ponsonby, Maj Gen John, 37–8, 179
Pont-à-Chin, 77, 160
Pont-à-Vendin, 80, 120
Pont-sur-Sambre, 177–8
Pontruet, 17–19, 67
Préseau, 165
Preux, 181

Quarouble, 167

Quast, Gen Ferdinand von, 73
Quiévrechain, 166–7

Radinghem, 73
Raillencourt, 27–8
Raismes Forest, 123, 125
Ramicourt, 71, 87
Ramillies, 30, 118
Ramsay, Maj Gen Frank, 12, 21, 81, 163
Rawlinson, Gen Henry, 3, 12, 57–8, 60–1,
    71, 88–90, 93, 95, 129, 155, 181
Read, Maj Gen George, 58, 60
Reed VC, Maj Gen Hamilton, 80, 162
Reims, 3
Renaix, 158
Rethel-Vouziers Line, 3
Reumont, 91
Rhine River, 62, 88, 196
Rhonelle Stream, 126–7, 139, 164–5, 171,
    173–4
Ribécourt, 34–5
Richemont stream, 152–3
Riqueval bridge, 65–7
Riquerval Wood, 96, 151–2
Ritchie, Maj Gen Archibald, 76, 80
Robertson, Maj Gen Philip, 135
Romeries, 141
Ronssoy, 13–15
Rosenthal, Maj Gen Charles, 85–6
Roubaix, 104–105
Rouvroy, 114
Rouvroy-Fresnes Line, 22–3, 114–15
Ruesnes, 141
Rugge, 110
Russell, Maj Gen Andrew, 9, 41

Sailly-en-Ostrevent, 115
Sainghin, 74
Sains-lez-Marquion, 21, 24–5
St Benin, 91, 93, 148
St Georges Stream, 141–2, 144
St Hilaire, 133, 186
St Hubert, 171
St Martin, 139
St Maurice stream, 150, 153, 155
St Mihiel, 2
St Pieter, 51

St Python, 132–3, 140
St Quentin, 2–3
St Quentin Canal, 13, 16–17, 19, 31, 38,
    43, 57–9, 63, 65–7, 70–1, 87, 199
St Quentin tunnel, 12, 63
St Souplet, 91, 93–4, 148, 150
Sainte Olle, 27
Sàllaumines, 113
Sambre Canal, 152, 154–5, 176–7, 180–1,
    183–5
Sambre River, 172
Saméon, 121
Sancourt, 28
Sauchy-Lestrée, 26
Saultain, 168
Saulzoir, 120, 126, 138
Schelde Canal, 76–7, 80–1, 110–12,
    116–18, 121, 123–5, 158, 163, 165
Schelde River, 78, 80, 103, 109–10, 112,
    157, 162, 166
Scheuch, Lt Gen Heinrich, 193–4
Sebourg, 169
Selle stream, 89–95, 113, 119–20, 125–6,
    130, 132, 134–45, 147–50, 152
Semeries, 186
Senlis, 155
Sensée Canal, 27–8, 114, 116–17, 122–4
Sequehart, 71, 87–8, 95–6
Serain, 89
Séranvillers, 131–2
Shute, Lt Gen Cameron, 145
Skinner, Maj Gen Percy, 54
Smyth VC, Maj Gen Nevill, 73, 160
Soissons, 2–3
Solesmes, 132–4, 136, 138–40, 143
Solf, Wilhelm, 195
Solly-Flood, Maj Gen Arthur, 36, 134, 176
Solre stream, 178
Solre-le-Château, 186–7
Sommaing, 138–9
Somme River, 1, 65
South African Regiments
    1st, 90, 187
    2nd, 89–90, 147
    4th, 89–90, 147
Spa, 191, 196
Stanley, Earl of Derby Edward, 112

Stephens, Lt Gen Reginald, 102
Stopford, Maj Gen Sydney, 111
Strickland, Maj Gen Peter, 67, 70–1, 152
Supreme Army Command, German,
    191–4, 196–7, 199
Sweveghem, 110

Taintignies, 80
Taisnières, 172, 183
Targelle Ravine, 11, 38
Templeux-le-Guérard, 15
Ten-Brielen, 53
Terhand, 51–2
Terhand Line, 98, 101–102
Thorigny, 70
Thun, l'Évêque, 117–18
Thun Saint Martin, 117
Tilloy, 30
Toufflers, 103
Tournai, 79–80, 160–1
Tourcoing, 103
Trescault, 9, 36
Troisville, 95, 137
Tronquoy, 136
Tudor, Maj Gen Hugh, 46, 98, 108

Valenciennes, 124–5, 163–4, 167, 171
Vaucelles, 41, 43
Vaux-Andigny, 91, 93, 151
Velaines, 160
Vendhuille, 12, 14, 57–9, 83
Vendegies, 138–40, 144–5
Verchain, 126
Verdun, 2–3
Vertain, 140
Vichte, 108
Vicoigne, 123
Villa Giusti, Armistice of, 195

Ville Pommeroeul, 165
Villeret, 16
Villers-en-Cauchies, 119
Villers Guislain, 10–11, 38, 43
Villers Outreaux, 89, 129, 137
Villers Pol, 141, 172, 173
Villers-St-Ghislain, 168, 170
Vitry-en-Artois, 22, 115–16

Walincourt, 135
Wambrechies, 104
Warcoing, 112, 159
Wargnies-le-Grand, 172
Warneton, 54, 56, 103
Wassigny, 148, 151–2
Watson, Maj Gen Sir David, 26, 124, 163
Wattrelos, 103
Watts, Lt Gen Herbert, 54, 106
Wemyss, Adml Rosslyn, 197
Wervicq, 53, 102–103
Westhoek, 46
Wevelghem, 100–102
Wez Macquart, 73, 76
Whigham, Maj Gen Robert, 8, 35, 39, 175
Wiancourt, 87
Wilhelm II, Kaiser, 191
Wilhelmshaven, 195
Wilson, President Woodrow, 191, 193–5,
    202
Winterfeldt, Maj Gen Detlof von, 197
Weygand, Gen Maxime, 197
Wytschaete, 48, 50, 54

Ypres, 3, 45–6, 199

Zandvoorde, 48, 53
Zillebeke, 47–8
Zonnebeke, 48, 51